VINCENT CRONIN

The Wise Man from the West

D1396454

Collins
FOUNT PAPERBACKS

First published by Rupert Hart-Davis 1955
First issued in Fontana Books 1961
This edition first published
by Fount Paperbacks, London, 1984

© Vincent Cronin, 1955 and 1984

Printed in Great Britain
at the University Press, Oxford

For Chantal

CONTENTS

ILLUSTRATIONS AND MAPS

NOTE

The chief sources of this biography are Ricci's own history of the Chinese mission, his letters and those of his companions, reports made by his superiors and a short life by his contemporary, Sabatino De Ursis. The history has been edited, with a multitude of identifications and copious extracts from contemporary Chinese documents, by Pasquale D'Elia, s. j., as part of a work bearing the general title *Fonti Ricciane*. Perusal of his volumes will reveal the extent to which the present book is dependent upon Father D'Elia's scholarship and research. To this great sinologue and pioneer of Ricci studies I am very deeply indebted. I am no less grateful to Mr. Herbert Agar for invaluable advice regarding the form of the biography. I also wish to thank the founders and trustees of the Richard Millary Trust, Father Basil FitzGibbon, who first mentioned Ricci's name to me, Mr. H. McAleavy of the School of Oriental Studies, Father Philip Caraman, Doctor Werner Eichhorn and the Very Rev. Columba Cary-Elwes, who has written a history of the Catholic Church in the Middle Kingdom, shortly to be published under the title *China and the Cross*.

AUTHOR'S INTRODUCTION

Four hundred years ago, when the first Queen Elizabeth ruled England and Spanish conquistadors were despoiling South America of its gold, a young Italian priest named Matteo Ricci left the safety of the Portuguese colony of Macao and entered the Kingdom of China. He was to spend his whole working life there, the first European ever to do so. He learned to speak Chinese and wrote books in Chinese. He discovered a hitherto unsuspected world, with greater implications even than Galileo's moons of Jupiter.

Unlike some missionaries of his day, Ricci did not adopt a superior attitude to the Chinese people. Nor did he seek to gain a political advantage over them; on the contrary, he made a clear distinction between politics and religion. And in the interests of a people he had come to admire and love, he sought to adapt Christianity, save in essentials, to Chinese values and traditional practices.

Ricci's twenty-eight years in distant China passed almost unnoticed in the West. But shortly before his death, on the orders of his superiors, he wrote in Italian a history of his mission. It is a quarter of a million words long and was published, with Ricci's surviving letters, in a three-volume scholarly edition between 1942 and 1949, edited by an eminent Sinologist, Pasquale D'Elia. Ricci's history and letters form the basis of the biography which follows. It is a true account of Ricci's life. Events happened as described, the dialogue was spoken.

After his death, for reasons explained in the Epilogue, Ricci's name became a bad word in the Catholic Church. In adapting Christianity he was considered to have jeopardized some of its essential truths. Only in the pontificate of Pius XII (1939-58) did Sinologists and historians of the missions begin to realize that this was not so, and that Ricci had correctly interpreted Chinese ancestor veneration as well as Chinese appellations for God.

In the period after World War II the West, and with it the Catholic Church, dropped its superior attitude to other world cultures. Missionaries no longer sought to Westernize their converts, but rather to present Christianity in terms which other groups, be they Chinese, African or South American, could understand. 'Inculturation' was the order of the day.

In these changed circumstances Matteo Ricci came at last to be seen by many in his true colours, as a pioneer and a model. His life at the end of the sixteenth century had attracted more attention in China than in the West, but now the reverse happened. Ricci was, so to speak, reborn symbolically.

During the fourth centenary year of Ricci entering China, the bishops of China in Taiwan requested Pope John Paul II to put in hand Ricci's cause of beatification: that is, to set up a commission to examine Ricci's life and writings to discover whether they evince the Christian virtues to a heroic degree. The Pope acceded to the bishops' request and that commission is now at work. It is possible that before long Matteo Ricci will be declared a saint.

On 25 October 1982, speaking in Rome to the International Ricci Studies Congress, the Pope made clear his personal feelings for Ricci and stated the Church's attitude to his methods:

'It is a great joy for me to meet with you . . . and to express by my visit the deep appreciation I have for the figure of the great Jesuit humanist and missionary, Father Matteo Ricci. . . . He intended to demonstrate that religious faith does not lead to a flight from society, but to involvement with the world as a way of perfecting social life, so opening it to redemption in Christ and to a life of grace in the Church. . . . Father Ricci was rightly convinced that faith in Christ would have brought no harm to Chinese culture, but would have enriched and perfected it. . . . He succeeded in establishing between the Church and Chinese culture a bridge which still appears solid and safe. . . . I am convinced that the Church, without fear and with eyes fixed on the future, can follow that route.'

PROLOGUE

The Sealed Empire

ASIA, endowed with the first fruits of the sun, participating in
the daily rite of creation, in the very origin of light, and, as the
colours of dawn seemed to betoken, resplendently rich, was
held by early Western peoples to be the world's perfect and
more marvellous part : a belief endorsed for Christendom
when its nearer shores became the Holy Land. On medieval
maps, those alchemic mixtures of legend, classical books and
the Bible, which created the world as men wanted it to be, Asia
was given, without question, pride of place. The central
framework of these atlases, linking the East to northern Africa
and Europe—its wavering coastline, in contrast to the bold
sweeps elsewhere, a sign of certain knowledge—were the four
rivers of Paradise, identified with the Indus, Nile, Tigris and
Euphrates, their distance explained by subterranean water-
courses. East of the Nile lay Palestine, the only part of Asia
familiar to Christians. Pilgrims had travelled there to see the
Sepulchre and new-found Cross, to wonder at hermits who,
on pillar and in cave, chose extravagantly Oriental forms even
for their sanctity; and in later centuries the pilgrim's staff had
become the mailed crusader's lance. South-west of the Black
Sea and Caspian was located with less assurance the land
whence priests of Zoroaster, versed in astrology, had brought
to Bethlehem gold, frankincense and myrrh—scriptural testimony to Asia's wisdom no less than to her wealth. Further east
lay Bactria, which Alexander had conquered, and the
mountains whose tops touched the sky. Beyond, where no
European traveller had ever ventured, lay furthest Asia, marked
on the maps like chunks of unchiselled marble. Here the
geographer became poet and prophet. He located precisely
the beginning and end of time : the garden of Eden, surrounded by its fiery wall, and the quarter where Christ would

9

finally appear, in recognition of which maps, like the churches of Europe, were oriented.

Just as the severe lines of a Gothic cathedral were broken at the extreme points by gargoyles, so in distant Asia the neat categories of genera and species were burst asunder by a riot of grotesques. The unexplored continent was peopled with pygmies who fought storks, Arimaspians—men with one eye, manticores and unicorns, with headless men having eyes in their stomachs, others who lived on the smell of spices, loup-garoux and the Sciapodoi, who would lie on their backs during periods of extreme heat and protect themselves from the sun by the shade of their feat. Although its hills abounded in gold and gems, gryphons tore to pieces any intruder. Beyond the mysterious Ophir, whence came the jewels of Solomon, lay a great island, where Adam's tomb was surrounded by a lake of tears which Eve and he had wept during a hundred years. In the north-east corner of Asia were located the tribes of Gog and Magog, whom Alexander the Great was supposed to have barricaded with an immense wall. Civilisation, like light itself, was held to have flowed from the East, from Eden, Assyria and Greece to Rome, and when it reached the Atlantic shore, these cannibal tribes would burst out and destroy the human race. At the eastern confines, following the Roman geographers, lived the Seres, who combed silk from the trees—terminus of the caravan trail to the Far East. The sea route ended at what was believed to be another country, the land of Thin, or as Ptolemy put it, Sinae.

Since perfection implied the true religion, there was a strong tendency to christen these unknown spaces. While the Atlantic was dotted with such Christian domains as the Isle of the Seven Cities and St. Brandan's Isle, the apocryphal acts of St. Thomas sent the apostle to evangelise India, and his disciples into central Asia. When in 1141 a Buddhist chief founded an empire in Chinese Turkestan, Europe, harassed by Islam, gave substance to her hopes by construing from the vague reports that a certain John, Christian priest and king, had won a great victory over the Persians. Soon a forged letter was circulating, addressed to the Emperor of Byzantium by

Prester John, ruler of the three Indias, with seventy kings as his tributaries, a potentate surrounded by all the well-known Oriental properties. In his palace, the letter claimed, the windows of which were crystal, the tables of gold and amethyst, thirty thousand men, besides occasional visitors, were daily entertained. His capital city lay on one of the four rivers of Paradise. In one direction his territory extended four months' journey to the tower of Babel, in the other it was measureless to man. The letter was accepted as authentic, and Prester John's country added to the maps of Asia.

In the next century that continent, from Hungary to its eastern limits, was united by Genghis Khan and his successors, discipline imposed on the marauding tribes, and direct travel between Europe and Asia became feasible. Louis IX of France first conceived the idea of communicating with the Mongol emperors, and, if possible, with Prester John, in the hope of procuring allies for the crusade against Islam. At his instigation Innocent IV sent Franciscan legates across the longitude of Asia. They did not find Prester John but their reports, supplemented by those of Marco Polo, described a no less marvellous kingdom far east of Persia and south of Tartary, on the confines of Asia, called Great Cathay, of immense extent, with the largest cities, widest rivers and greatest plains ever seen, where gunpowder, coal, paper-money and printing were in general use. Its huge population were idolaters, but in the capital city, Cambaluc, at the court of the Great Khan, lived a community of Christians.

From these reports, neglecting all that was disappointingly normal, Europe shaped the idea of a Christian Cathay ruled by Prester John. Mandeville wonderfully particularised. Beyond the mountains of India, where diamonds grow " as it were hazel-nuts, and they are all square and pointed of their own kind, and they grow both together, male and female, and are nourished with the dew of heaven, and then engender commonly and bring forth small children that multiply and grow all the year," lay the land of Prester John, characterised by " trees that at the rising of the sun each day begin to grow, and so grow they to midday, and bear fruit, but no man dare eat of that fruit, for it is a manner of iron, and after midday it turneth again to the earth, so that when the sun goeth down it is nothing seen, and so doeth it every day." Such wonders were believed, and when in the middle of the fourteenth century the collapse of the Mongol Empire once again made travel impossible, Europe, sea-bound on every other quarter, still further idealised the princess Asia, imprisoned in her walled castle.

Islam, the duenna, amassed a fortune by passing gifts between the two separated lovers. Europe shipped crude essentials, timber and iron, receiving in return turquoises from Nishapur, rubies from Yemen and pearls from the Persian Gulf, glass ware from the Syrian coast and marble from Azerbaijan. The gardens of Irak and Persia were plundered to provide violet and rose water; melons were carried from Turkestan and sturgeon from the Lake of Van to be served in halls fragrant with ambergris and sarcocol. The very incense burnt on Christian altars originally exuded in infidel Arabia. By way of Aleppo or Alexandria aloes, cedar wood and cinnamon flowed from Ceylon, pepper, tin and sugar from India and, changing hands at Calicut, whither they were carried by Kwangtung junks, cloves and nutmegs grown in the Moluccas, rhubarb and ginseng, fine porcelain and twenty-three types of raw silk from the land of the Sinae.

Such goods, all that made life sweet, soft and spiced, were tangible proof that Asia combined luxury with beauty, refinement with wealth. They also provided yet another incitement to action. It became imperative to circumvent the duenna, to find another way to Asia in all her fullness, daring, since it was necessary, a route across uncharted Southern seas.

Rigging was improved to permit closer sailing to the wind, main topsails added for greater speed on the first tentative coasting of West Africa. But it was a Chinese invention, the compass, perhaps transmitted by Arab sailors, which made possible the age of discovery and the eventual unveiling of China herself. By the end of the fifteenth century modes of travel had altered but the final cause remained the same as in the days of the Franciscan legates. Cathay, Asia at her most idealised, lured Columbus across the Atlantic. When he reached Cuba the Genoese explorer believed the island part of the mainland described by Polo, and Haiti he identified with Chipangu. Vasco da Gama, likewise, sailed from Portugal with letters for Prester John, whom a few imaginative geographers had transferred to the more accessible continent of Africa, in particular to Abyssinia.

An array of cumulus suddenly massed across the blue; the earth was magnified ten times as North and South America, the full extent of Africa, India and Ceylon, the Philippines, Malacca and the Moluccas, fountainhead of spices, were wrested from the sea by a single generation of navigators. Furthest east of all, the Portuguese in 1513 discovered the coast of China, a land which from its position and silk products was identified with the Roman Thin or Sinae. New outlines were added to the maps, but the interior of every distant country still remained a repository of myth.

In the explorers' wake Christian priests sailed to baptise the new-born worlds. From Prince Henry, who first planned Guinea as a Christian dependency of Portugal, to Albuquerque, who sailed for India not only to capture the spice trade but to wrest the Holy Places from Islam, a twin desire—slaves and salvation, gain and grace—had driven men eastwards. As the new islands and continents were slowly differentiated, so too were the roles of merchant and missionary.

The mendicant orders had already been at work in India for several decades when Francis Xavier left Rome in 1540 to evangelise the East Indies. Not even the apocryphal acts of St. Thomas had envisaged such travels which, within seven years, brought the gospel to Malabar, Ceylon, Malacca, the Molucca Islands and, shortly after its discovery by the Portuguese, to Japan. There he soon learned that her language, literature, fine arts, cult of the dead, Buddhism, all these and much else remained Chinese under a Japanese lacquer, that the island was intellectually dependent upon the mainland. He did not shrink from the formidable conclusion. "When the Japanese know," he wrote to Ignatius de Loyola in the last year of his life, "that the Chinese have accepted the law of God, they will more readily abandon their idols." He sailed

from Japan in November 1551 and nine months later had succeeded in reaching the island of Shangchwan, seven miles from
the China coast. For four months he tried in vain to arrange a
landing in a country which refused entrance to foreigners. On
December 3rd, 1552, attended by a Chinese servant, gazing
from a bamboo hut across at the inaccessible coast, he died.

Neither Xavier nor the other great Iberian travellers had
attained Cathay, tentatively marked on maps as lying north-
west of China. England now began to direct her efforts to this
country, with its supposedly cold climate, hoping to barter her
broadcloth for silks and silver. First Sir Hugh Willoughby
attempted a north-east passage, only to be frozen to death with
his crews in Russian Lapland. Jenkinson, Chief Factor of
the Muscovy Company, whose articles bound him to " use all
ways and means possible to learn how men may pass from
Russia to Cathaia," attempted a land route with as little success.
Following another line, Sir Humphrey Gilbert wrote a learned
work to prove that north of America, which he identified
with the lost Atlantis of medieval geographers, a passage must
exist to Cathay and the Spice Islands corresponding, in a
symmetrical world, to the Straits of Magellan. Frobisher put
this theory to the test in three voyages, but again Arctic ice
proved a barrier more forbidding than the steppes and mountains of continental Asia.

Had the Franciscans, at the end of their desert trek, been
deceived by a mirage? Was Polo's story as fictitious as that of
Mandeville? The world had been circumnavigated, un-
imagined continents discovered, yet two marvellous countries of
the remote East refused to yield their secret. Cathay, Europe's
fondest fancy, had been lost for two hundred years, while silken
China remained a sealed empire, unknown as though her coast
had never been descried.

Francis Xavier's last design was realised soon after his death
by an Italian, who solved the mystery of Cathay, first explored
China and revealed to Europe, in fullest detail, the marvels
towards which she had been groping with unmistaken insight.
While other merchants sailed east for spices and silk, for
silver and sandalwood, he sought the pearl of great price and

became a worthy apostle to the highest civilisation outside Europe. The discoverer emerges with the country he discovered, surviving in reports by his superiors and his colleagues' correspondence, in almost fifty of his own letters and above all in his description of China and his mission there, a manuscript which was recovered at the beginning of the present century after being lost for almost three hundred years. The word-of-mouth reports and garbled romances of Oriental travellers are here superseded by a hundred and thirty-one folio pages containing a quarter of a million words, the neat script, instinct with life just as it left its author's hand at Peking, with the occasional misspellings and faulty grammar of one more at home in Chinese than in his mother tongue : the answer to Europe's age-old questions, the discovery worthy of so long a search. With the other documents it makes known the travels, actions and sometimes the very words of the first and greatest mediator between China and the West. It is an authentic record, tallying with the dynastic annals, of events which really happened. Invention was unnecessary. The wonders, immensity and extravagance Europe expected of the East, the wealth and beauty associated with dawn, the legends and dreams of centuries were finally surpassed by the simple truth.

CHAPTER ONE

Call to the East

ON a high hill, its slopes restless with wind-swept cypress trees, a boy was born in 1552, on the eighth of October, feast of St. Bridget, midway under the sign of the Balance, with Saturn in the ascendant; an excellent augury, so the astrologers claimed, foretelling an equable and just nature.

Macerata was a town of some thirteen thousand inhabitants built high in the Marches between two torrential streams, looking across to the Adriatic, eastwards beyond the crescent moon of the threatening Ottoman Empire, to the rising sun. The town stood midway in the peninsula between north and south, and its people prided themselves on a similar balance of vigour and good humour. Lying in the papal domains, Macerata was linked intimately with Rome, but its particular spirituality, for which it was known far and wide, resulted from another physical circumstance. Twenty miles north-east lay Loreto, whither, it was devoutly believed, the house of the holy family had been miraculously transported through the air, like a magic carpet out of the East, from Nazareth. Loreto was a holy, chosen place, a centre of pilgrimage, and all the surrounding countryside participated in that miracle, to the reality of which four stone walls afforded lasting proof.

The provincial town of Macerata boasted a handful of patrician families, among them the Riccis, ennobled three centuries before, their coat of arms, a blue hedgehog on a red background, being an illustration of the meaning of their name. Ser Giovan Battista Ricci made his living as a pharmacist but much of his time was given to civic affairs. He held a papal magistracy and for a period acted as governor of the town, where his prudence was respected. He had married Giovanna Angiolelli, a gentlewoman distinguished for her virtue, and by her had thirteen children, nine sons and four daughters.

Matteo, as the boy born in 1552 had been christened, was the eldest child. Because his mother was occupied with so large a family and his father with local politics, he was entrusted at an early age first to his grandmother, Laria, then to a Siennese priest who lived in Macerata, Nicolò Bencivegni. Even before he reached the age of reason, God and the spiritual world had come to possess as much reality as the streets of his native town, while prayers, in the church which faced the Ricci *palazzo*, were the most important act of the day. The young boy loved his tutor and wanted to grow up like him.

Until the age of seven he was instructed by Father Bencivegni in reading, writing and Latin. In 1559 his tutor joined the Society of Jesus and when two years later thirteen Jesuits arrived to found a school his mother enrolled Matthew as one of their first pupils. The college gained a reputation and in 1565 moved from its original house outside the walls to a new building and church in the centre of the town. Here Matthew perfected his Latin and learned Greek, not by rote but according to the imaginative methods his masters took such pains to devise.

As he grew up he looked beyond the walls of Macerata and learned something of the age he lived in. Two series of changes dominated Europe. The first derived from the fact that the Church, having failed in large measure to remain holy, had continued to demand the privileges accorded to sanctity. The vigorous north had rebelled and Christendom was now divided against itself. This earthquake in the old world coincided with the second important process, intervention from the depths of new and greater continents. Their chief colonisers, the peoples of the Iberian peninsula, had provided what they hoped was an answer to this dual challenge. The flower of Europe and all the resources of the new humanism had been mobilised by the Society of Jesus in an intellectual and spiritual crusade. Distinguished men of every nation had enlisted, at home to renew fervour, to teach and form a well-educated laity, abroad to circle the globe with missionaries. The Council of Trent and the triumphs of Francis Xavier already stood as the measure of their zeal.

As leaders of this enterprise, Italy partnered Portugal and Spain, whose troops occupied her northern provinces. Just as Columbus the Genoese had led a Spanish expedition, Italian philosophers and preachers now added glory to the Order founded by a Spaniard. The highest civilisation of Europe consolidated and refined the gains of the greatest military powers.

Revival was rendered doubly urgent by the aggressive hordes of the Ottoman Empire across the Adriatic. Athens had been repeatedly assailed by the Persians; the Roman Empire by their successors; now a militant religion and accumulated treasure greatly increased an age-old danger. On his accession as Pope in 1566, Pius V called for help against the Turk. Macerata, loyal and gallant, provided thirty-seven oarsmen for the pontifical galleys and a contingent of two hundred and fifty soldiers, two for every hundred of the population. Europe, unless she rallied to all that was best in her heritage, might suffer worse than religious schism.

In such a world Matthew grew up and sought his place. The early imitative wish to become a priest was ripening into a desire to serve his Creator. His father took it for granted that he would follow in his footsteps, but the boy felt drawn to meet the essential challenge of an age when God, it seemed, had such need of dedicated men. He asked that he might unmistakably be called, and his petition was not refused. After the first weeks of mingled joy and trepidation he was faced with a dilemma which prayer alone could not resolve. In what Order could he render most service? Instinctively he thought of the Franciscans. St. Francis had been born nearby, over the hills; the brown-cowled, sandalled friars whom he had seen in Macerata drew him by their humility and total abnegation. On the other hand, his first teacher, whom he loved and admired as a second father, had joined the Jesuits; several of his friends intended to enter the Society, he himself admired his present masters, so learned but always in an interesting way. He had listened to stories of their brethren abroad, in the wilds of America, Africa and India—stories which brought to life those rare alluring substances, alligator, spotted lizard, mercury and guiac, electuaries and syrups of hellebore and *radix chinae* in the two-handled jars of the apothecary shop, possessing more powerful properties the remoter their origin.

Very intelligent but also very affectionate : so he appeared to his masters at Macerata. First in his class yet favourite, too, with the other boys. At the age of sixteen a strongly-built youth, his well-proportioned, finely moulded head crowned by thick black hair and distinguished by searching blue eyes, he completed his course at the Jesuit college. Macerata possessed its own small university, with a law faculty, but his father decided that Matthew should study at Rome. He dismissed all talk of the priesthood. As the eldest son, it was Matthew's duty to succeed to the family honours and a magistracy at Macerata. His Jesuit masters counselled the boy to obey : he was young and had still to make choice of an Order.

The journey across the Apennines to Rome—a mere hundred miles in space and two days in time—produced the effect of reincarnation : from a provincial town to the centre of Christendom, the capital city of the world, the Rome of Virgil and Horace, of the early martyrs and first churches. He stepped from a small closed society to the pontifical court, where men of all nations congregated, where their spiritual destinies were decided. His father had many influential friends in the Cardinals' retinue, and his masters supplied him with introductions to their brethren, so that he entered at once the cosmopolitan city. He visited the Jesuit college and joined the sodality of Mary attached to it, a congregation whose lay members received frequent communion and attended discourses. While his studies were secular, he remained true to his vocation.

At the great university, in the faculty of law which had originated and reached its culminating point in the city, he became aware of how little he knew and of the fields of learning still to be conquered. He bought the *Mirabilia Urbis Romae*, a guide-book compiled in the Middle Ages which placed the monuments of Rome in the framework of Livy and Tacitus, adding many quaint legends. This in hand he visited the ruined arches and splintered shafts, among which new

churches in a restrained classical style were everywhere rising.
St. Peter's was well advanced, but no one had yet dared to
vault the dome, so that its uncrowned Greek columns in the
form of a cross stood now as the symbol of those Tridentine
reforms which Pius V was putting into execution with such
zeal.

Florus, the second-century panegyrist of the Roman people,
was Matthew's other cicerone. He relived Rome's ancient
shame and glory and found in every sentence a prophecy for the
Christian capital. "Wealth spoiled the morals of the age and
ruined the State, which was engulfed in its own vices as in a
common sewer," while in another sense it was true now as then
that "Not a single place in the whole world was left unassailed
by the arms of Rome." The book happened to contain a rare
reference to those merchants who, by camel and yak, once
shuttled silk across half the world to the imperial city, where it
commanded its weight in gold: "Among the numerous
missions from remote lands that sought the footstool of
Augustus were envoys from the Seres."

The capital decided his choice of religious Order. The
parable of the talents assumed new force in this city of learning. If he had been endowed with a good intelligence, that gift
must be used in the service of God; and the Order which
above all others directed human learning to spiritual ends was
the Society of Jesus. Father Bencivegni had led the way; his
schooling, his mother's particular affection for the Jesuits, all
confirmed his judgment. On the feast of the Assumption,
1571, three years after his arrival from Macerata, he put aside
Justinian and Gaius's *Institutes*, knocked at the door of the
Roman College and formally asked to be admitted to the
Society of Jesus. A tall, imposing priest, Alessandro Valignano, who was deputising as master of novices, received Ricci
and in a Neapolitan accent questioned him about his education
and family ties. Then Ricci made the solemn promise to
renounce the world, all possessions, all hope of temporal goods,
and to live in any country where his superior might think him
most useful to the glory of God and the good of souls.

Next day he entered the house of S. Andrea at the Quirinal,

opened as a novitiate four years previously. In addition to the clothes he wore, now exchanged for a black clerical habit, his worldly possessions consisted of a threadbare coat, four shirts, some handkerchiefs and a towel, as well as three books : a Latin grammar, the *Mirabilia* and Florus.

That same day Matthew wrote to his father, making known his step and explaining that he could not deny his vocation. Presently he received an answer which confirmed him in his decision. When his son's letter had arrived, Giovan Battista Ricci had at once set out for Rome, determined to remove Matthew from the college. The first evening, on his arrival at Tolentino, he had been struck down by a fever which prevented him from continuing his journey. The illness was as violent as it was unforeseen : the angry father recognised in it the anger of God. He wrote to say he was returning to Macerata and would try to accept his loss.

During his first year at the house of S. Andrea Ricci lived as far as he could away from the world. The hawk was hooded and disciplined before being trained to serve its master. Learning was set aside and the novices alternated between prayer and menial household tasks, designed to foster obedience and humility. Nothing was permitted to interrupt that colloquy between the soul and God, foundation of a dedicated life.

The following May, convinced of his vocation and strengthened in his love, he consecrated his body, mind and will in the three vows of poverty, chastity and obedience. In the late summer he was sent for a short while to teach at Florence, returning in September to resume his course of rhetoric at the Roman College, learning during these first two years the method which would permit him to profit from more advanced studies : the marriage of word and thought, the art of speaking and writing in the manner of Cicero, the sharpening of apprehension through clear expression. An exceptionally retentive memory helped him to excel as a scholar : after reading any page of a book only once, he could recite it without a single mistake.

He came to know the length and breadth of Europe in the person of his friends. They ranged in age from fifteen to forty, and came from Italy, France, Germany, Portugal, Flanders, Poland, England and Spain. The foreign students became his particular favourites : men of different language and customs, history and values, yet linked to him by a common overriding belief symbolised in Latin, the language in which they prayed and spoke to each other. They had come to Rome less for book learning than for orthodoxy, which one day they would take back to their own countries, many heretical. Those from France and Germany had suffered much already and by returning would put their lives in peril. His sympathy and open manner won their friendship, which he valued more than anything else at the Roman College. He was happier than he had ever been.

In 1575 Ricci entered on a new phase of his studies : philosophy and mathematics, Aristotle and Euclid. The more advanced course was taught by a young German, Christopher Clavius, the most brilliant mathematician of his day. From plane geometry Ricci progressed to astronomy and the movement of the stars, still taught according to the Ptolemaic system, and thence to the construction of sundials, clocks, spheres and astrolabes. He showed special aptitude for this course, winning notice as a mathematician of promise.

Out of school, he tried to foresee the life for which these studies were merely the preparation. During his novitiate, the victory of Lepanto had saved Europe from the immediate threat of Eastern conquest. The two great enterprises of his age remained : consolidation of Catholicism in Europe and its propagation abroad. As an Italian, should he choose the first course, his life was predictable. Not for him the heroic sufferings and martyrdom facing his brethren in other countries of Europe, but the tame routine of preaching or teaching, the handing on, with renewed fervour, of an untainted faith, later perhaps a professorship at the Roman College. A good life : even the best, were there not, for him, so clearly a better, a life combining action and intellectual pursuits, for both of which he felt himself equipped. Already in the person of the foreign students he had felt attracted by the challenge implicit in man's diversity. He had been stirred by first-hand reports from missionaries in India, Japan and South America, amplifying the facts and denying the more frequent fictions of contemporary travel books; above all by the apostolic life of Francis Xavier. Conversion of the world's new-found peoples, doing for Christ what He had done on earth : to that ideal he could give himself body and soul. Again the way had been pointed. Valignano, the Neapolitan who had received him as a novice, after a year as rector of the college at Macerata, had asked leave to proceed abroad as a simple missionary. The General nominated so gifted a man Visitor, with plenipotentiary powers, for the whole of India, and gave him picked fellow labourers. In September 1573 he had left Rome for the East. There were other signs, faint in themselves, but all concurring. Had not the apostle Matthew, at the customs house, worked among foreigners and later suffered martyrdom in central Asia? And, as though the baton had been handed on, he himself had been born in the very year when Francis Xavier died, gazing across at the coast of China.

To volunteer for the foreign missions was one thing; to be chosen and sent another. Intense competition meant that only men of outstanding spiritual, intellectual and physical stamina were selected. Ricci pressed his case over a period of years. At first his voice was drowned by others with more influence. He persevered steadily but unsuccessfully until the end of 1576, when the procurator of the Indian province returned to Rome to report and to select new missionaries. Ricci petitioned with renewed insistence and, to his great joy, was finally approved. In the spring of the following year the General of the Society formally assigned him to the Indian province.

In May together with other prospective missionaries he was ushered in to the customary papal audience. At the far end of a high pillared hall sat a man of middle height dressed in a long white cloth mantle, a fine rochet and a red pontifical mantellina down to the waist. His face, with blue eyes, aquiline nose and long white beard, wore an expression of dejected majesty. Silent by nature and rendered still more silent by the burden of his seventy-five years, Gregory XIII nodded to the young members of his favourite order, destined for those missions which he had supported and helped in every possible way. He spoke a few words, drily but affably, to each of them, warning them of the hardships which lay ahead, bidding them God-speed, and raised his hand in blessing. Behind the tired terse salutation Ricci seemed to hear another voice, another text : " Go out all over the world, and preach the gospel to the whole of creation."

The way to India lay westwards. Not only did the Turks block the direct overland route, but the eastern Indies as far as the Philippines had been assigned by papal decree to their discoverers, the Portuguese. Missionaries in that area owed allegiance to the King of Portugal and, if they were not Portuguese by birth, had to submit formally to the civil authority at Lisbon. Moreover, they were obliged to sail from the Tagus in Portuguese carracks, the only ships plying a regular route to India.

In May 1577 Ricci set out by road for Genoa, and thence by sea to Portugal. Reaching Lisbon in midsummer, he was obliged to wait until the following spring before continuing his journey, the annual departure of carracks being timed to catch the monsoon in the Indian Ocean. He spent the intervening nine months at the great university of Coimbra. He lived at the Jesuit college, virtually a seminary for the foreign missions, growing familiar with a country, little more than a million strong, which was now tottering under a top-heavy, world-wide empire; quickly mastering Portuguese and reading theology in preparation for the four-year course he would have to complete in India. Here, as in Rome, he won friends easily : among masters by his intelligence, among students by his affectionate manner.

On March 24th, after a farewell audience with the young King of Portugal, Ricci and thirteen other Jesuit missionaries were accompanied by processions to the same harbour from which Vasco da Gama had set sail. While hymns were sung and prayers recited against the dangerous voyage, the party was divided between the three ships of the fleet, Ricci travelling on the *Sao Luiz* with Michele Ruggieri, a Southern Italian aged thirty-five who had obtained a doctorate in law at Naples

University before entering religion. The *Sao Luiz* was a large two-masted four-decked carrack, with towering poop and prow, a clumsy transport vessel of some nine hundred tons. She carried fifty thousand crowns in silver, part to pay for the cost of government and garrisons in the East, part to be traded, as well as a cargo of woollens, scarlet cloth, crystal and glass ware, Flemish clocks and Portuguese wines. The human cargo, soldiers, merchants and adventurers five hundred strong, were packed as densely and with less care in the interstices of the ship.

To the sound of cheering patriots and wailing wives, of trumpets and gunfire, the fleet cast off and set sail down the slate-grey waters of the Tagus. Five days out, on a southern course, they passed a French corsair off Madeira, but without being intercepted. For the first month, until they crossed the equator, the almost coffined confinement proved the worst of their discomforts. Ricci lived on deck, by day observing the Guinea coast, outline of an almost unknown continent; by night the new southern stars, disorderly chalkmarks on a blackboard, not yet metamorphosed into animal groups.

They drifted into the doldrums, where the stifling, unfanned heat melted the pitch between the pine planks and even the tallow candles on board. Putrid water and lack of food accelerated the outbreak of disease, turning the carrack into a hospital ship without doctors or medicine. The master's whistle, blown to ask prayers for a new victim, became too frequent for notice. Mass which could have given their suffering point was forbidden in such infernal conditions by canon law. For the first time glib words like pain and self-sacrifice uncoiled themselves and struck.

In June, hugging the coast, they rounded the Cape of Good Hope and at the end of the month cast anchor, in the cool season, off the island of Mozambique, where a fortress, pitched among dunes, swamps and coral reefs, asserted Portuguese power. Here six weeks were spent, taking on water and provisions and a cargo of African slaves, big-lipped giants, their black bodies figured like raised silk by searing irons.

The fleet weighed anchor in August and followed the

eastern seaboard as far as the vast mountain stronghold of
Abyssinia, alone in northern Africa to resist the advance of
Islam, where Jesuit missionaries had recently been sent by
Ignatius de Loyola to search for Prester John and to reunite the
local Church with Rome. Thence across the Indian Ocean,
along the course which for centuries had supplied the wealth of
Mohammedan power, to Goa, almost central in the western
coast of India.

Here Ricci and Ruggieri landed on September 13th. They
joined two other Italian missionaries, who made port at the
same time in another ship : Rodolfo Acquaviva, son of the
Duke of Atri, one of the most brilliant and distinguished
noblemen of his day, and Francesco Pasio, a close friend of
Ricci's at the Roman College. Before entering the town, they
walked out among the island's palm trees, exultant at their
release from six months' imprisonment. Choosing a glade, they
stretched out on the grass and began excitedly to discuss what
might happen to them, for Goa was not the end of their
journey but merely the base from which missionaries were sent
to the other coastal regions of India, Ceylon, the Moluccas,
Japan. Pasio turned to Ruggieri, the eldest, and laughingly
designated him Superior : he must assign them their roles.
Ruggieri caught the spirit and after a moment's consideration
said, " I predict that all four of us will work together, Rudolf
as theologian, Francis as philosopher, you Matthew—when
you've been ordained—as mathematician and myself as
lawyer."

" Excellent," Pasio and Ricci cried, " but where?"

" Why, nowhere else but in China," said Ruggieri, and
burst out laughing, for he knew that China was the one country
which refused to admit missionaries, and that their superiors
had no intention of sending them there. Only the intense,
dutiful Rudolf remained serious.

" Don't laugh, Father Michael. The future will turn out just
as you predict."

Later they walked across the mountainous sandy-soiled
island of Goa to the town, which stood on rising hills at the
northern tip. Its walls lacked strength, for two encircling rivers

and a harbour bar afforded adequate protection. By the southern gate they entered the Orient. Turbaned Moslems and
Hindus, Kaffirs from Africa and squat-faced, ochre-skinned
merchants from Indonesia moved in a pageant of dress and
babel of tongues. Every street had its market, the colony
appeared a single bazaar as merchandise from East and West,
gold chains, pearls, rings, spices, gums, coverlets changed
hands at the cross-roads of the world. Yet the atmosphere of
the town was as Portuguese as its architecture. No square,
street or crossing was without its church or monastery : on all
sides were pasted placards announcing religious ceremonies and
processions. Dominicans, Franciscans and Jesuits hurried
through the dusty streets, centre of an archdiocese which extended from Mozambique to Japan. With Rudolf's prophecy
ringing in their ears, they walked up to the church of the
Jesuit college of St. Paul to venerate the body of Francis Xavier,
whose footsteps had marked out the boundary of that archdiocese. From Goa he had set out on his final journey, taking
with him a rich cloak to wear at his interview with the Emperor
of China; to Goa his uncorrupt body, clothed in that same
garment, had been transported a year and a half after his
death.

In the college of St. Paul, which Xavier himself had acquired
from the Franciscans, Ricci began his first year of theology,
and from new acquaintances discovered with a shock, the
dichotomy between his own ideas of conversion and missionary
reality. Closing the *Summa* after his day's reading, he would
walk through the town, finding it no longer a promised destination, a haven from the sea. Close to the cathedral and opposite
the viceroy's palace was held the slave market, where boys and
girls of two continents were sold for a trifle to the common
soldiery. Every Portuguese possessed a servile retinue, administering orders in the form of blows along the lines set by
Albuquerque who, capturing Goa in 1510, had massacred the
entire Mohammedan population. No law curbed their cruelty.
The viceroy, all-powerful representative of the King, was
appointed for three years only, all too short a time to amass a
fortune unless he permitted judges to be bribed, heinous

offences to be condoned, offices to be privately bought and sold. More detrimental still, the fidalgos, resplendent in taffeta and satin, who paraded like conquerors under tasselled parasols, were wholly enslaved to the calculating, full-lipped half-caste women, occasionally to be glimpsed behind the verandahs and shutters of the two-storeyed whitewashed houses, fluttering a fan or strumming a guitar. No Portuguese woman of self-respect, except an occasional governor's wife, privileged and protected by servants, would face the long voyage, and the men, fired by tropical heat and easy wealth, had for the first time crossed black with white. The mestiços, heirs to the worst vices of both, took revenge for cruel humiliation, past and present, inflicted by the Portuguese. Like the luxuriant jungle vegetation across the hills, they were prying apart and overthrowing the intruder's fortress stone by stone.

Portuguese possessions, strung up and down the coast but never extending further inland than a day's march from their boats, had been wrested with unforgettable outrage from Hindu and Moslem, who now, millions strong, awaited an opportunity to drive out the imperialists. Half in terror, half in application of the principle, *cuius regio, eius religio*, accepted everywhere in Europe, the authorities tried to force on the native population the faith they professed but did not practise. In 1540 all Hindu temples in the island of Goa had been destroyed; in 1567 a law was passed forbidding a Christian to keep infidel servants in his house, with the result that thousands were obliged to adopt a religion they neither believed nor understood in order to retain their daily bread. Ricci understood now why Xavier " fled," as he himself put it, from the Portuguese sphere to Japan, where the ruthlessness of European officials could not undo his work.

Conversion meant largely conformity to Portuguese habits. Neophytes were forced to abandon caste, usages and distinctive signs, and adopt the clothes, languages and names of their new masters. Those who could not be bribed were coerced. Nominal rolls of all Hindus were made, a hundred on each list being compelled on alternate Sundays to hear sermons on the benefits of Christianity, sermons delivered through interpreters (to learn the native dialects would have been proof of weakness, an admission of equality between infidel and Christian), the garbled translation rendering *Spiritus sanctus* as *spiritus mundi*. These laws were rigorously enforced by the Inquisition. If an Indian dissuaded another from becoming a Christian, he was liable to death. Denounced by a child, he might spend two or three years in prison without knowing the cause, before being sentenced and taken, on a great feast day, to execution. Prisoners were paraded through the torrid streets in shirts steeped in sulphur and painted in lurid colours with flames of fire, pointing upwards in the case of those to be burned at the stake.

From such scenes Ricci would return to the *Summa*, where St. Thomas urged a far different course : " *Inducendus est infidelis ad fidem non coactione sed persuasione.*" The voice of Christian reason jarred with history. Were not the Crusades the traditional means of dealing with infidel peoples? For centuries Portugal had fought a death-struggle with the Moors, and in Goa considered her present tactics a continuation of that other holy war.

Ricci did not indulge in profitless indignation, for he discovered within his own Order, largely independent of civil and ecclesiastical authority at Goa, another kind of apostolate embodying his ideals. In 1575 Valignano, on his way through India, had directed that conversion must follow upon charity, not force. But charity presupposed understanding, and understanding a knowledge of the native tongue. Missionaries therefore must learn the dialect of their diocese well enough to confess and preach. As a corollary, increased importance was attached to the education of local children at the college of St. Paul. To this work, his first year of theology completed, Ricci was himself applied, being given the unusually arduous task of teaching both Latin and Greek to the more advanced pupils.

Disappointed that he had come so far and with such high hopes merely to teach school, he appealed unsuccessfully for some more active work such as was beginning to engage his friends. Valignano, continuing his tour of the vast Indian province, had spent ten months in Macao, a Portuguese enclave on the China coast, studying Chinese customs and law. He had decided to apply a new technique of evangelisation and called for a missionary to learn Chinese in Macao preparatory to entering the country. Ruggieri, chosen by the Indian provincial, had already sailed and arrived there. One of Ricci's compatriots from Macerata was in Japan, where in the single year 1577 twelve thousand were baptised. Rudolf Acquaviva was preparing to leave at the end of the year as superior of an embassy of three Jesuits to the court of the Mohammedan Mogul Akbar, greatest ruler in India, lord of seventy kingdoms, commander-in-chief of 300,000 cavalry and twenty thousand elephants. The Mogul himself had requested the embassy : he was believed to look favourably on the Christian religion : at Goa the well-informed hoped for nothing less than the conversion of all India.

While great events were being shaped, he alone remained behind, teaching Demosthenes' First Philippic to ebony-headed schoolboys. Final humiliation, even this proved too much for him. Still not fully acclimatised, after a month he fell severely ill and, in the hope that better air might restore his health, in November 1579 he was sent four hundred miles down coast to Cochin, cradle of Christianity in India. Here, beside lagoons fringed with coconut and pepper plantations, he felt remoter than ever from Europe, missing most of all his friends at the Roman College and Coimbra. After a short rest he continued to teach at the Jesuit college, where four hundred natives were given an education not greatly inferior to that which he himself had received at Macerata.

The call he had first heeded as a schoolboy was that summer inscribed beyond defacement, when the Bishop of Cochin, on the feast of St. James, laid hands in silence on his tonsured head, vested him with stole and chasuble, anointed his palms with holy oil and bound them together with linen. Later, receiving bread and wine at the Bishop's side, he participated in the moment of consecration. To the boys at the college, when lessons were resumed, he was now Father Matthew, with power to celebrate Mass and forgive sins.

He had spent a year in Cochin when a letter recalled him to Goa to complete his four-year course of theology. Halfway through his third year, in April 1582, he received the marching orders for which he had been praying so long. His friend Michael Ruggieri, almost broken in spirit by the difficulty of the language he was trying to learn and the discouragement of the older priests in Macao, had insistently asked his superior, Valignano, to send him Ricci as a companion for the proposed Chinese mission. The Visitor, already impressed by his virtue and learning at the Roman college, ordered Ricci, in company with Francis Pasio, to take the next boat for Macao. It seemed that the prophecy of Rudolf Acquaviva would yet be fulfilled.

Eleven days after receiving the order, Ricci and Pasio sailed from Goa on one of the carracks which set out annually for Malacca, Macao and Japan. Since the Chinese for almost a century had been forbidden by their own laws to exchange goods directly with Japan, the Portuguese acted as middlemen, gaining more profit from this carrying trade than from any other Eastern source. A month out they skirted the Andaman Group, where the cannibal islanders traded nuts and the lime called Adam's apple for calico goods. Two weeks later they sailed into the port of equatorial Malacca, on the south-west coast of the Malay peninsula, most abominable and dissolute of all Oriental emporia. Here European curios, Indian chintzes and cotton piece goods were bartered for aromatic timber : sandal, eagle and aloes wood; for sharkskins and deer-hides from Siam; and above all for cloves and nutmeg to season the vapid salted meat served throughout winter on European tables. In July they again set sail, across the typhonic China Sea. On this final lap of his ocean voyage Ricci succumbed to the intense heat and bestial conditions. In his cupboard-like bunk, narrow as a grave, he lay seriously ill for five weeks, until sailing past the temple of Ama, goddess of sailors, who gave her garbled name to the town, the carrack anchored at temperate Macao.

The enclave marked the success and failure of European relations with China. Almost seventy years before, the first

Portuguese ship, commanded by an Italian, had entered the Pearl River and berthed at Canton. On their arrival the new-comers were accorded the same trading rights as Arabs and Malays had long enjoyed, and which the Chinese themselves received in ports as far as Sumatra, limit of their western voyages. The Portuguese, however, accustomed to treat all foreigners as enemies to be plundered or conquered, soon resorted to piracy and violence. Terrified by European seventy-pounders, more formidable than any weapon even the Japanese corsairs could boast, the Chinese forcibly expelled the traders from Canton. Later, learning that Malacca, which recognised Chinese sovereignty, had been seized, they forbade the Portuguese to touch at Chinese ports. But trade entailed such wealth for both nations that soon a compromise was reached. In 1557 the Portuguese were permitted to take possession of Macao, a small peninsula in the Canton estuary. The Chinese walled it off on the landward side and guarded the barrier with strong forces. Twice a year the Portuguese were allowed to sail up to Canton for two or three months under rigorous safeguards. Here they bartered Japanese silver for silk, gold, musk, pearls and porcelain: in January for the Indian and European markets, in June to form next year's cargo for Japan. Since Chinese silk was highly prized in Japan, and silver far more valuable on the continent than in the island kingdom, this trade had fattened a generation of fidalgos.

When Ricci landed, Macao held a population of ten thousand, the bulk Chinese, with a scattering of Malays, Indonesians, Africans and Indians. The Portuguese, all men and many married to Chinese wives, numbered no more than a thousand. To serve their needs and those of their convert slaves, the Jesuits had founded a residence for five priests and the first of the half-dozen churches of the enclave.

Michael Ruggieri, after an affectionate welcome, led Ricci up to the residence of St. Martin to meet Valignano, who had recently returned from Japan and was now waiting to leave for Goa. Novice and novice-master now met on the other side of the world as missionary and organiser of the missions. Valignano then stood at the height of his powers, a very tall figure with foreseeing eyes and forceful jaw, a natural leader of immense presence and authority. Born in Chieti in 1539, after taking his doctorate of law at Padua he went to Rome, hoping for preferment from Pope Paul IV, who during his long term of office as Archbishop of Chieti had become a close friend of his father. He served as auditor to Cardinal Sittich d'Altemps, but soon returned to Padua. Here, at the age of twenty-three, he wounded a courtesan, was brought to justice and banished from the republic. Four years later, a man of exceptional talents who knew the world, he entered the Society of Jesus, where he was presently appointed to high office. Already, during his eight years in the East, he had proved himself the ideal successor to Francis Xavier, everywhere winning the affection and respect of his subordinates, organising dioceses, building churches and colleges along the trail which Francis had blazed. Their gifts and methods were complementary. As a Spaniard, Francis had preached in the agonising belief that all who were not baptised would suffer damnation; he scorned and made little attempt to understand the pagan beliefs he encountered; without time to master local languages, he had converted largely by his miracles, his holy presence and heroic acts of charity; alone in Asia, he had felt obliged to travel quickly from country to country, leaving his neophytes behind with little surveillance. His Italian successor, on the other hand, looked no less to the future than to the present. He believed that lasting conversion would result only from patient understanding of Eastern civilisations. He saw Portuguese and Spanish traders not as privileged imperialists, but as outnumbered intruders who would be expelled when no longer useful. Missionaries, if they hoped to remain, must win the people's affection by adapting themselves as far as possible to local habits and indigenous beliefs. Humility and respect must replace the traditional attitude of righteousness and pride. Above all, Christianity must be presented in a way which Eastern peoples could understand and appreciate.

Arriving in Macao in 1578 he had spent eleven months

studying the government, laws and religion of China, as well as past missionary failures. Since the death of Francis Xavier numerous attempts had been made, chiefly by Jesuits and Franciscans, to obtain a footing, all without success, for the Chinese, cut off for centuries from the outside world, mindful of the recent Tartar invasions and terrified by the aggressive acts of Portuguese merchants, viewed all foreigners as enemies or evil spirits. But with Valignano past failures weighed less than the prospect of converting what he now learnt to be the most populous, fertile and wealthy kingdom of the world, its people industrious and peaceful, its government in the hands of philosophers whose learning, order and prudence won his admiration. After a detailed, empirical study of the difficulties involved, he decided to attempt to realise Francis Xavier's dream along entirely new lines. Missionaries in the past had been arrested as spies preparing another Portuguese attack and, unable to explain themselves, sent back to Macao. Valignano believed China, which practised religious toleration and admired learning, would be naturally well disposed to Christian ideals. These, so far, had been overshadowed by piracy and aggression. Missionaries therefore must achieve an almost impossible feat, which no Westerner had ever before attempted : they must learn to read, write and speak the Chinese language. Only in this way could they explain their doctrine and good intentions, prove themselves men of learning and overcome the xenophobia aroused by the swashbuckling methods of early Portuguese traders.

Having found in Macao neither support for so revolutionary a method nor suitable missionaries, he had written to India for an Italian priest and left detailed written instructions as to his training. He then sailed for Japan, most encouraging of all mission fields. The island kingdom, thirty years after Xavier's landing, boasted 150,000 Christian converts, most of exemplary standard, and Valignano believed they would grow to form the best and largest Christian community in the world, provided Rome would sanction admission of natives to the Society as priests and lay-brothers. After spending two and a half years in the island, the same length of time as Xavier,

Valignano had now returned to Macao with valuable new experience.

Ruggieri had not altogether fulfilled his expectations. After almost three years' study and several long stays in Canton at the semi-annual fair, he still could not speak or understand the language. Moreover, he lacked that presence and suave distinction which the Chinese mandarin class prized so highly. He could at times be intrepid but lacked the force to persevere for long on a bold course.

Ricci, the Visitor soon discovered, possessed not only these qualities but untiring physical and mental energy and a prodigious memory which, in three months, enabled him to read Chinese at least as well as Ruggieri. Valignano arranged for the two men to live alone in a small house in the grounds of the Jesuit residence, devoting all their time to the study of Chinese, while he himself, drawing on his experience in Japan, imparted to them his principles of adaptation, equality and friendship with the governing class.

But when, in December, Valignano boarded the annual carrack for Goa, China still remained a sealed empire. Occasionally an official had been bribed into permitting a short visit inland—Ruggieri had penetrated a hundred miles, as far as Shiuhing, only to be expelled after a few weeks—but even these sorties were stopped when the new viceroy of Kwangtung and Kwangsi provinces, the most important mandarin in southern China, issued an edict threatening severe penalties against anyone who helped foreigners to enter the country. The older priests at Macao nodded their heads wisely. Time spent in learning so difficult a language was wasted; these zealous, gifted young men would be better employed helping to care for the Christian merchants. Easier to scrub an Ethiopian white, they claimed, than to convert the Chinese.

Events continued to justify this attitude until midsummer 1583, when the utterly impossible seemed to happen. A Chinese soldier arrived at the Jesuit house of St. Martin with an official letter from the governor of Shiuhing, a mandarin named Wang P'an. He had heard from Ruggieri of Ricci's skill as a mathematician, as well as of the maps, clocks and spheres he could make. His curiosity aroused, he invited the two men to Shiuhing, where he held out hopes of land on which they could build a house.

At first the Italians suspected a trick, but after verifying the seal and questioning the soldier, they hastened to obtain the necessary money. Their own procurator could give them nothing. Jesuit missions in India and the Orient had since their inception been supported by the King of Portugal and when, three years before, Portugal and Spain had been united under the Spanish Crown, administrative changes had even further delayed the trickle of money from Goa to its dependency, Macao. Valignano had been obliged to invest in the annual carrack from Macao to Nagasaki, in order to raise an additional five thousand ducats a year for the growing Japanese and proposed Chinese missions. This sum was occasionally supplemented by donations and legacies from wealthy Portuguese. Only last year, however, the all-important carrack bound for Japan had foundered off the island of Formosa, causing a loss of 200,000 ducats to Goa and Macao, so that Ruggieri and Ricci, in their search for alms, found most of their supporters penniless. However, they finally persuaded a wealthy Portuguese trader to come to their rescue. Gaspar Viegas had already founded the novitiate at Goa, given a fortune to start a mission in Cochin-China and for several years paid the expenses of the house of St. Martin. Now, with certain friends, he came forward to provide money for their journey and stay in Shiuhing. The Chinese unit of currency was the tael, an ounce of silver, not minted in coins, but cut from bars and weighed on ivory scales. With one tael a European could buy his food for a week. The annual living expenses of a missionary were reckoned at about a hundred, and the cost of a house at five hundred taels.

At the beginning of September final arrangements were complete. Ricci stood ready to undertake the work for which all his past life he had been preparing. From Macao, prison rather than fortress, he was at last setting out, with neither precedent nor model, to enter the least known country in the world, closed, so it seemed, from all ages to the word of God, the most extensive mission field since the days of St. Paul, its territory unmapped, the full limit of its frontiers uncertain, the latitude of its capital undetermined. If he were not at once sent scurrying back, he would be attempting to win men of a civilisation older than his own, whose language he had not yet mastered, to a religion founded in a country of which they had never even heard. This undertaking appeared folly at its most fantastic. Yet it was precisely from this conclusion that hope could be drawn of great achievement.

CHAPTER TWO

Breaking the Seal

RICCI and his companion installed themselves with their baggage, early one September morning, in places requisitioned by the soldier from Shiuhing on the junk which plied between the enclave and Canton. They were changed men. Their hair and beards were shaven smooth and they had replaced their black soutanes with the grey cloth cloaks worn by Buddhist bonzes, as the best way of making clear that they were men of God. Presently they were joined by their interpreter, Philip, a Christian born of Chinese parents at Macao, by the crew and other passengers, baggage and scanty possessions slung from their shoulders, ochre bodies bare to the waist, heads shaded by wide, limpet-like hats. As goats, hogs and baskets of poultry were hauled on board, a lout stumbled against the cowled figures. With a gesture of respect he sheered away and stretched out beside the bronze gods in the stern. The nut-brown matted sail was swung squeaking to the wind, ropes cast off and the junk glided past the familiar Portuguese-style houses, double-tiled and plastered over, the church spires built low against typhoons, into the wide waters of the Western River. The small, hilly peninsula, a forbidding fist thrust out at the entrance to China, was reluctantly unclenched and at last released them.

Eagerly Ricci observed the lie and colour of the land, its crops and trees, sifting them for signs which would help him to understand the people. Across an immense brown delta stretched fields of silt divided by raised earthen dykes and bounded northwards by terraced hills. Peasants were hoeing fields of reeded ginger, rice, sugar-cane and cassia, others deepening part of the network of irrigation canals. One feature was particularly obvious. Every scrap of ground belonged and was under intense cultivation. It offered no place for the in-

truding foreigner, even for his grave. The river was as diligently worked by innumerable sampans and sea-going junks.
Near the banks were moored houseboats, each with its miniature garden, crowded with poor families, young and old herded
to the number of fifty or sixty, rearing ducks for a living.

The missionaries kept their faces hidden and did not speak.
If they were recognised, they would either be subject to contempt and abuse, such was Chinese loathing of hairy devils
and ugly demons, or else—should one or more of the passengers bear a particular grudge against the Portuguese
—be turned off the ferry as aggressive spies, bent on seizing
Canton.

All day the junk continued its course northwards. As the
sun went down, paddy-fields, tepid water and treacly air were
with a single thrust dipped and dyed in blackness : fireflies,
lamps of fishing boats and stars united in a wheeling, blinking
dance to the beat of cicadas and frogs, the occasional leap of a
white porpoise, the intermittent bamboo drumming of night-
watchmen on shore. The last conversation, meaningless to the
missionaries as the duck boats' clangour, came to an end : apart
from the crew only the grey cowled figures remained awake,
shades being ferried across the Styx.

At dawn, they sailed past warehouses and docks under
towering walls. Even here the river was wider than the Po, as
though distended by the press of boats which almost covered
its surface. Canton was not one of the noblest Chinese cities,
yet it seemed to Ricci larger than Lisbon, larger even than
Rome. Here they must obtain leave to proceed on the final
stage of their journey from the Haitao, or Vice-Commissioner,
a mandarin known to be favourable, for Portuguese trade
brought wealth to Canton merchants and tangible forms of
gratitude to himself.

Escorted always by the soldier, they disembarked and, drawing their cowls close, passed through massive brick walls laid
on freestone foundations, crenellated at the top, forty feet high,
by way of large folding gates plated with iron and protected by
portcullises, yet a further sign how foreigners were feared.
Once within the city Ricci discovered the reason for its vast

extent : all the houses consisted of a single story. There were other causes for wonder. The wide, straight streets, better far than any in Europe, were paved with stone and intersected at right angles. They were lined with shops, their goods displayed in front on bamboo tables, and contracted by booths offering bowls of wine, fruit and steaming rice. Before each store stood a large wooden pillar, higher than the eaves of the houses, bearing an inscription in gilt characters and hung from top to bottom with coloured flags, streamers and ribands. The two strangers had to fight a way past coolies carrying loads on bamboo poles, sedan chairs, men on horseback and a dense throng of half-naked buyers and sellers, shouting their wares, arguing, haggling—a mass made molten and hissing by the sun.

The soldier led them through a triple triumphal arch like a huge ideogram, crowned with tiles, to a long low building standing in its own grounds near what seemed the centre of the city. Girded by columns without capitals, its dominant feature was the glazed tile roof, looped up at the sides like an awning. The only architrave was the horizontal beam supporting the roof rafters, the entablature a broad screen of wood fastened between the upper part of the columns and painted vivid blue, red, green and gilt.

After a considerable delay they were led into the audience hall, at the far end of which, behind a table draped like an altar with brightly coloured damask, sat a mandarin, dressed in black, ankle-length sarsenet, a tight, black silk brimless cap on his head, trailing two wide horizontal wings like laurel leaves. The missionaries, their interpreter and the soldier prostrated themselves a stone's throw from the table. Presently the Haitao spoke; Philip replied and at length informed his masters that the mandarin graciously allowed them to stand. Rising, they proffered Wang P'an's letter which the Haitao, having first examined the seal, carefully read. Ricci glanced at the decorative lattice-work of the hall, at its tiled floor and flat ceiling painted with squares, circles and polygons and hung with gilded, inscribed tablets, at the furniture covered with glossy varnish which for all its grandeur seemed decidedly flimsy.

The Haitao, who seemed in no hurry, continued to address Philip, but at last he called an assistant to lead the visitors away. Having prostrated themselves three times, the missionaries left the hall.

While Philip explained that they had been assigned lodgings until passports could be issued and a boat arranged for Shiuhing, the Haitao's assistant led them once more across the city out into the suburbs, stopping finally at an enclosure where a group of buildings in poor repair stood amid a garden gone to seed. Unlocking the courtyard gate the assistant led them into the main building. Rats scurried away at their entrance; an owl flapped heavily through the gaping roof. The place was little better than a cattle barn, dirty, without furniture, holes in the bamboo walls. After a word of explanation the assistant took his leave.

This, Philip explained, was the Palace of the Ambassadors from the King of Siam to the Emperor of China. Here they were lodged every three years, on their arrival by sea, until word came from Peking authorising them to complete their journey. It was evident from the state of the buildings how little respect China felt for her neighbours, and their own presence there showed that she made no more distinction between other nationalities than did the Portuguese at Macao between the different Oriental nations.

Imposing temporary order on the tumbledown building, they lodged the night. Next morning they discovered that the necessary authorisation had not yet been issued and that they would be obliged to extend their stay at the palace. Already the impatient missionaries were growing conscious of a new, exasperatingly slow rhythm, of a world of officials, seals and counter-seals. But at length their passports arrived and they continued their journey up-river, through undulating country, to Shiuhing, which they reached a week after leaving Macao. The walled town lay in the loop of two rivers, picturesquely situated between the low mountains. Ricci reckoned it somewhat smaller than Macerata, but instead of soaring, its horizontal buildings seemed to hug the earth.

The soldier led them through bazaars which showed every

sign of prosperity to a hall like that at Canton, where the governor was holding audience. Here they were forced to kneel down with all the other Chinese who had business there that day. Ricci looked about him. The governor, a man of about forty-five, wore the same black silk gown and winged hat as the Haitao. The wild goose embroidered on his girdle and its worked gold clasp showed he ranked fourth in the nine grades of Chinese officials. Huge parasols behind him were bespangled with gold. On his desk, its damask covering fastened at the corners with buttons and loops, lay brushes on a grooved rest, an inkstand, one side black, one red, with two partitions for water, beside which the inevitable fan lay folded.

When their turn arrived, the governor asked them who they were, whence they came and what they wanted. Philip translated the questions and transmitted Ruggieri's answer. "We are religious who serve the King of Heaven, and come from the farthest parts of the West—that is, from India. Our journey has taken three or four years. We have heard of the good government of the Middle Kingdom, and all we ask is a piece of land away from the commercial distractions of Macao, where we can build a small house and pagoda. There we will remain serving Heaven until we die. We beg your Excellency to help us. We shall give no trouble. We intend to seek alms for our food and clothing and shall remain indebted to your Excellency for the rest of our lives."

When the often rehearsed petition had been translated to Ricci in Macao, he had asked why no mention was made of their intention to preach Christianity. Ruggieri had explained that such a claim would be taken as an unpardonable insult. The Chinese believed they possessed a monopoly of the world's wisdom, all foreigners being considered illiterate barbarians. The idea was present in the names—Chung-kuo, Middle Kingdom or Chung-hua, Middle Flower—by which they had called their country since the second millennium before Christ, when China, restricted to the region of the Yellow River Basin, had everywhere been surrounded by more primitive peoples. Because rebellions and seditions had often originated from the diffusion of revolutionary new ideas, it was essential, and Ricci had accepted the point, that they win entrance and acceptance before proclaiming their doctrine.

The governor appeared satisfied with this speech. " You seem virtuous men," he replied, " so I will help you. You may look about the town for a piece of land that pleases you. I shall see that the viceroy lets you have it. Meanwhile, pray to Heaven for me."

Bowing their foreheads to the ground three times, the missionaries withdrew.

That afternoon they made a tour of Shiuhing and surrounding country. Although extraordinary sights on the river journey had made surprise his usual attitude, it was a shock for Ricci to walk, unheeded in his disguise, about the small town, with time now to observe the low wooden dwellings, their roofs wind-swept waves of a brown river, verandas landscaped with miniature rock gardens and dwarf cedars, past the flat round faces, eyes set obliquely, black hair worn shoulder length, voices high-pitched and nasal. There were children playing, a single tuft on their shaven heads—but not a woman to be seen. There was every sign of order—maintained from a tribunal, unmoated and unwalled, by a soft-voiced scholar with no sword at his side. There was every sign of religion—in the fat-bellied idols of clay or metal at house door and street corner. Beyond the town gate, hung with edicts, vertical columns of sabre-slashing characters, Ricci found more at which to wonder : banyans with vast rooting branches and mulberry trees, their shadow splashed as though with blood; the silt-laden river, where black cormorants, throats fastened with cord below the pouch, darted underwater and returned to disgorge fish at their master's feet; rich men, androgynous creatures dressed like women in ankle-long coloured silk, being carried in sedans like holy statues to or from the town. Gryphons and headless creatures might have startled him more, but for a short while only. Because they could be dismissed as another species, their monstrosity was not reciprocal. These were men, his own sort, yet their totally different ways bewildered and challenged. He had been prepared for the marvellous, the unique—and these he had found—but not for this all-pervading music in an alien mode, setting everything within him off-key. It was his own accepted truths which began to appear curiosities, and he himself a creature outlandish in body and mind.

The part of Shiuhing which best pleased the two Italians lay to the east, outside the walls, where the first story of a brick and stone building was under construction. They learned that the graduates of the town, having collected three thousand taels from Shiuhing and its eleven dependencies, had obtained the viceroy's permission to start erecting an octagonal tower of nine storys, its purpose being to prevent good luck flowing away from Shiuhing in the waters of its two rivers. Close by stood the residences of the governor and viceroy, more than a mile outside the walls, among trees and gardens, commanding a pleasant view across the Western River. They agreed on what seemed an ideal site and, calling on Wang P'an, asked whether they might have land there. "Your presence," he replied, "will prove an added adornment to the Tower of High Fortune. I shall write at once for the viceroy's permission."

It was their practice to spend every spare hour on the Chinese language and, returning now to the private house where they were being lodged, they took from their baggage a collection of manuscript notebooks and grammars which they themselves had composed in Italian and began to hear each other's vocabulary, discussing and often disagreeing over the difficult pronunciation. Michael Ruggieri had been studying the language ever since his arrival in Macao four years before. The first European ever to learn Chinese, he had imbibed it painfully like a child from the merchants of Macao, themselves ignorant of any European tongue.

Instead of receiving direct instruction from master or book, he had been obliged to collaborate. First he had drawn the simple objects of everyday life, tree, horse, ship, then progressed to more abstract terms which had to be acted out or gropingly explained : for each picture or sign his Chinese tutor would paint the equivalent character and teach him how to pronounce it. On a short visit to Canton, he had been shocked to discover that the language he had been learning in Macao was purely local, each part of China possessing its own dialect, in-comprehensible to inhabitants of other provinces. Since none of these dialects were spoken by educated men, all he had so far learned was useless. He had then begun an even more laborious task, to pick up the rudiments of mandarin, *lingua franca* of the official class. When Matthew Ricci joined him they had worked together chiefly from the library of Chinese books gathered in the house of St. Martin, increased their vocabulary and learned to read simple sentences. Matthew had an uncanny knack for languages—almost, Ruggieri would say, to mitigate his own comparative slowness, a gift of tongues. The weird uninflected monosyllables, like Italian only in rarity of consonants and frequency of vowel terminations, were in themselves difficult enough to learn, but what proved almost impossible was to attune their ears to the added dimension of five tones, each of which changed the meaning of the same sound.

Few moments were so humbling as this, when they garbled and faltered : they who had come, masters of Western learning. so wise, so self-confident, to teach a new doctrine, were forced to return to elementary school, painfully, plank by plank to construct a raft to carry across their cargo. Until it was built they were poor, ignorant and helpless as coolies.

Three days later the governor summoned the missionaries. " Since I wrote to you last month I have spent much time con-sulting the laws, trying to find some way of keeping you in Shiuhing. At last I have found an imperial privilege. Here it is." He indicated a musty volume. " ' While the laws of the Middle Kingdom forbid foreigners to live in the country, nevertheless having regard to the brotherhood of man, any stranger who comes from a distant country and either cannot or does not wish to return, may remain in the Middle Kingdom, provided he is quiet, humble and useful to the country. He must take from his belongings sufficient money to lead out his life, and he may be assigned land for his lodging.' " He paused and looked up at the two Italians. " When I found this privilege, I told the viceroy about it and asked all the high mandarins of this province whether or not it could be made to apply. All replied that it could. You, in your turn, must promise to fulfil certain conditions. You must not be joined by other barbarians; you must continue to wear our dress; you must promise to conform to our habits; you must obey our magistrates; if you marry, you must choose a woman of our country. You will become, in all save your physical appearance, men of the Middle Kingdom, subject to the Son of Heaven. Are you willing to make these promises?"

As the governor's words were translated, Ruggieri and Ricci listened with mingled feelings. A loophole which would allow them to live in China : this exceeded their most extravagant hopes. But at so dear a price! Their superior Valignano had given them express orders to adapt themselves as far as possible to the Chinese way of life. Their shaven heads and grey mantles already proclaimed them bonzes; they had intended to speak Chinese and live close to the people. But to transfer their allegiance to a pagan Emperor, whose rights over his subjects were unlimited by law, to perpetuate their kneeling position before Wang P'an by voluntary acceptance of Chinese authority, to replant themselves once and for all in alien soil, that was tantamount to changing their nature, to reincarnation. The two Italians consulted. What counsel would Valignano have given? They recalled his directive : Make every possible concession to establish yourselves within the country. " Are these conditions a prerequisite of our remaining?" Philip translated Ruggieri's question, then the governor's affirmative answer. Again they took counsel and reluctantly decided to acquiesce. First Ruggieri, then Ricci awkwardly repeated promises of submission and conformity. The governor nodded in satisfaction. " Now I can legally assign you a piece of land. The viceroy has given his agreement. To-morrow I will come to the tower and formally hand it over to you." The missionaries paid their respects by bowing to the ground three times, and returned to their lodging.

Next morning they arrived early at the tower and had to wait some time before they spotted the governor's suite winding down from the eastern gate. In front swaggered guards, some swinging bamboo whips, others beating gongs, another holding the seal of office. Then came the governor carried by four bearers on an open litter—for all the world like the Pope in Rome—followed by friends and other guards who bore brightly-coloured tiered parasols and tablets designating his rank. At their approach all who happened to be on the road turned tail and fled. Even children playing far off hurried home and slammed the door.

At the tower Wang P'an dismounted from his litter, carefully arranged his loose clothes and presented two of his suite to the Italians, his own personal assistant and the president of the tower committee.

" I propose," the governor told his friends, " to grant these bonzes land where they may build a house."

His subordinates, who had already greeted the missionaries coldly, did not hide their displeasure.

" If these foreigners remain," protested the president, " they will call others from Macao and drive us out of our town."

Turning to Ruggieri, the governor said, " Yesterday you solemnly promised on no account to summon others of your country from Macao, to observe the laws of the Middle Kingdom and obey its officals. Will you abide by that promise?"

As Philip translated Ruggieri's affirmative reply the governor smiled approval, then glided in slow and stately fashion to a corner of the field in which the tower was being built and with his staff of office marked out a small piece of land barely fifteen yards square. The missionaries looked on in dismay, then persuaded Philip to demur.

" We are honoured," said their interpreter, " that you should grant us land at all, but this piece you have marked out is hardly adequate for both house and pagoda."

Puzzled, Wang P'an replied, " This is not for the pagoda, but only for the house." Then he pointed to several Buddhist temples grouped near the tower. " There you have ample space to worship Heaven."

In consternation Ruggieri replied, " We cannot worship there, your Excellency. We do not adore idols, but only the King of Heaven."

When these words were translated, all the mandarins showed great astonishment. After consulting with his two subordinates, the governor replied, " It is of small importance. You can build your own pagoda and put inside whatever images you like." Thereupon he marked out another piece of land twice as large as the first.

Meanwhile inhabitants of the district and workmen from the tower, silently, in groups of two or three, had gathered round the party, anxious to catch a glimpse of men so curious and to learn the governor's plans for them. The crowd became even more pressing when, as a gesture of gratitude, Ruggieri produced presents for the governor. First he held up a prism of Venetian glass, then uncovered a small painting of the Virgin, which had been sent from Rome. The mandarins and the crowd treated the objects like stars fallen from heaven, fearing to touch, at first hardly daring to look. When Ruggieri showed the governor how to hold the prism to the light and view the eight colours of the spectrum, he turned pale as the glass itself with excitement. Having examined it from every angle, he passed it round his astonished suite.

After experiments at Macao, the presents had been carefully chosen to arouse Chinese wonder. Glass, even in its crudest form, was unknown in this part of the country, where parchment served as windows, so that the equilateral, brightly polished Venetian prism seemed a heavenly jewel, a crystal where the rainbow lay caged. As for painting, the Chinese prided themselves on this more than any other art. They aimed not to represent facts but to suggest a poetic idea, esteeming idealism, achieved with delicate lines and pale water colours, more than material solidity. Europe, confronting and imitating reality, had recently evolved a perspective unknown in China, where height represented distance, so that now the oil painting of the lady in blue, its heavy chiaroscuro giving an illusion of three dimensions, appeared to onlookers a living figure. Some, in awe of what seemed preternatural, had even flung themselves on their knees and repeatedly bowed down to the ground in worship.

When the prism had been passed round, the governor asked,

" May I take these wonderful objects to my house? I should
like to show them to my family."

" They are yours," Ruggieri replied. " We make a present of
them, in thanksgiving for the land you have allotted to us."

The governor smiled and re-entered his litter. As the two
missionaries knelt to pay homage, he motioned them to their
feet, before being carried away to the sound of gongs.

That same afternoon, however, some of their confidence was
spilled, when the governor returned the prism and painting.
Puzzled, Ruggieri sent him instead some elaborately worked
handkerchiefs. But before nightfall these too were returned.
Philip questioned the servant who brought them back. " Were
they too mean a gift for his Excellency?"

" Oh, no," replied the servant. " One of his three ladies was
delighted with them. She wanted to keep them for herself, but
the governor would not hear of it."

Later the knowledgeable Philip provided a possible explanation. " He must have an important reason for so discourteous
an act. Perhaps he does not want the viceroy to suspect him of
having been bribed to assign you that land."

Next morning the missionaries hired workmen to help them
excavate the foundations of the proposed house : a brick building of two storys in European style. Since the builders had
never erected any but single-story wooden houses without
deep foundations, it would be necessary to carry out much of
the work themselves. Near the site, therefore, they rented a
small house where they could celebrate Mass on feast days and
Sundays. During the other days they encamped in a rude
shelter fashioned from piles of bricks to be used in building.
Living conditions were uncomfortable and the workmen recalcitrant, but Ruggieri and Ricci were far more troubled by the
huge crowds of every class who came, sometimes from miles
around, to gaze at the prodigious newcomers—they had never
seen white men before—with those large noses and eyes considered so ugly in China, and to inspect their belongings. They
swarmed over the site, rendering work impossible for much of
the day. In particular they clamoured to see the prism, which
they called " the precious jewel beyond price." In order to

gain their goodwill the missionaries had to down tools and show kindness to all, however rude and ungracious. From morning to night during the first weeks they were largely engaged like museum-curators or toyshop keepers in showing their belongings, while the builders laboured. But the essential work progressed : as they drove the excavations deeper and laid the first bricks above ground, interruptions became less frequent. Under their hands, after so many years, so many frustrations, the first mission house in China was gradually taking shape.

Philip meanwhile culled information. The most discouraging news concerned the graduates of Shiuhing who were supervising the building of the tower. Ricci had already learned the fundamental importance of graduates. They formed three classes : bachelors of arts, masters and doctors, attaining their rank by passing examinations, the chief subjects of which were the classical works of Confucius. Only masters and doctors— men of elegant literary style and traditional learning—could hold official government posts. They were recruited in theory from all classes of society without distinction, in practice from those families which could afford to educate their sons, and since the country's hereditary aristocracy was forbidden to hold office, this intellectual *élite* formed the most powerful group in China, united by its own elegant language, too complex for the masses to learn. Between graduates and those who had not passed an examination lay a gulf wider than that between Italian nobles and peasants.

It appeared that the graduates, already hostile to foreigners, were particularly angry that part of their land should have been requisitioned. They intended their tower to serve partly as a place of recreation, and had planned to lay out pleasure gardens in the surrounding field. Here, outside the town, amid cinnamon and magnolia trees, flowering cherry and plum, they would be able to stroll in the evenings, listen to the lapping river and indulge in a favourite pastime, contemplation of the moon. With aggressive barbarians—suspected spies—in their midst they would be unable to enjoy themselves fully. More important still, according to the principles of geomancy, the new building would deflect auspicious currents of cosmic influence from the tower, thus perhaps invalidating its primary purpose, the retention of good fortune. Their resentment, Philip discovered, grew more plangent with each brick that was laid.

The outside walls were being completed when the graduates intervened. One morning the president of the tower committee approached the workmen and ordered them to stop building. Ruggieri and Ricci at once protested, asking the reason for his interference.

" The builders started work on a day of ill-omen," was the reply. " That is sufficient to blight the pleasure gardens. Later, when I have decided on a propitious day, I shall give orders for work to begin again."

To his puzzled masters Philip once again provided an explanation. A universal superstition held that the position of the stars rendered certain days and hours propitious for work and play, others unpropitious. Every year two sorts of calendar were published by the Government, in which days were marked either lucky or unlucky by the imperial astronomers. No one would dream of starting on a journey, building a house, burying a relative or celebrating marriage on a day of ill-omen, for fear of calamitous consequences.

The missionaries decided to resist. If the president were telling the truth, they could not acquiesce in the superstition. If—more probably, considering his tardy protest—he were lying, to yield once to trickery would create a dangerous precedent. Without providing an explanation, they ordered the workmen to continue. The president walked off indignantly, threatening counter-measures. That same afternoon, however, heavy autumnal rain began to fall, harbinger of the equinoctial storms, making work impossible for the rest of that day.

The Italians decided to confront the anger their resistance would certainly arouse. These graduates were reasonable, educated men, steeped in Confucius, therefore in theory moderate and humane. Very well, they would show them their fears were groundless. Philip had learned that the fiercest opposition came from the bachelors, those graduates not yet appointed to government posts. In Shiuhing, as in every other town, they lived in a school which harboured the local shrine of Confucius, under the jurisdiction of a special mandarin, some acting as tutors, others continuing their studies, all with too much time on their hands, proud as cockerels and very conscious of their new-won rank.

With Philip, Ruggieri visited the school and spoke to the bachelors he found there. He pointed out that the governor had given them permission to reside in the town and that the viceroy had raised no objection. Unable to resist this point, they shifted their ground. The presence of the foreign bonzes disturbed them less than the site of the mission house, which would interfere with their plans for the pleasure gardens. On this point they proposed a compromise. The house should be built not beside the tower but some distance off, where it could be approached from the town without crossing the proposed gardens. The new site, they said, was one of the most agreeable in the neighbourhood, overlooking the river with its continual diversion of boats, towards wooded hills. To this Ruggieri objected that they had already spent much on labour and materials and could not afford to make a second start. As a gesture of conciliation, the bachelors offered several thousand bricks and a quantity of larch wood from the materials assembled at the tower. Ruggieri decided to accept.

The missionaries abandoned the old site and transferred their workmen to the new, where once again walls began to rise. As soon as they had received the builder's first estimate, they had sent a letter to the Portuguese rector of the Jesuit house at Macao and therefore superior of the mission, asking for more money. The superior now wrote back that shipwrecks were ruining Macao and he could not send a single ducat. In these circumstances the missionaries were obliged to pawn some of their curios, including the Venetian prism. This loan enabled them to cover over what had already been built on the new site —a mere couple of rooms. Completion of the work would have to await further help from Macao.

Their joy at owning and living in their own particular house was enhanced by a gift from the governor. On the day they took possession he sent an edict to exhibit outside the door : a proclamation of protection, as it was called. After referring in flattering terms to the bonzes come from a distant kingdom, it said that the governor had given them this land to build a house, at the viceroy's command : no one was allowed to interfere with the inmates or harm them, under pain of severe punishment. Philip showed them how to affix the scroll to their doorpost, where it caused the greatest excitement. Writing, it seemed, exerted an uncanny power, and the written word of a mandarin possessed the force of law. Now all approached the house with a new respect for men who enjoyed not only the governor's company but written, irrefutable proof of his protection. Soon afterwards Wang P'an gave them two documents, one confirming the donation of that piece of land, the other permitting them to travel to Canton and Macao. Both were written as meticulously as medieval Bibles and signed with his seal in red ink. This, Ricci learned, was the distinctive mark of office. On his appointment, a magistrate was carried in solemn procession to the pagoda dedicated to the protective spirits of the town. Here he swore a solemn oath to observe justice and faithfully to administer his office in a ceremony known as " taking the seal." The seal, a gift from the Emperor, he guarded with scrupulous care, for if it were mislaid its holder would not only lose office but suffer severe punishment. When a magistrate walked through the town, his seal was carried in front of him in a box locked and franked with a second seal.

Wang P'an often visited the small house, occasionally bringing with him other mandarins and doing all he could to increase the strangers' reputation. Still mute, Ricci's smile and confident manner asked for and received his friendship. Wang P'an came to feel a genuine affection for him and showed the keenest interest in European beliefs and customs. A doctor of letters, a poet and an expert calligraphist—the Chinese prized fine handwriting almost as much as its sister art, painting— he had, since his appointment as governor in 1580, already won a reputation for incorruptible justice. The missionaries resolved

to retain his friendship at all costs, since without it the graduates' hostility and the people's irrational terror of foreigners
would soon drive them from the town.

Until they had mastered the language, they let their wonderful picture speak for them. They used the larger room of
their new house as a chapel, placing the altar at one end with
the Virgin and Child above it. As an act of politeness all their
visitors, including several bonzes from the neighbouring
pagodas, venerated the picture, genuflecting and bowing in
front of it head to the ground. Before long, however, questions were raised. The foreign bonzes claimed to worship a
single god, yet they solemnly venerated this picture. Could it
be that their god was a woman? Post-haste Ruggieri wrote to
Macao for another picture and within a fortnight received a
fine portrait of Christ, painted by one of Ricci's companions on
the voyage to Macao, who had later sailed to found the first
school of Christian art in Japan. The new painting was
substituted for the old above the altar, and misapprehension
made less erroneous. The foreigners adored a Tartar.

They made far more rapid progress in the language now
that they lived within the country and spoke occasionally with
mandarins. Before the end of the year both Ruggieri and Ricci
could read and write. But their problems now increased rather
than diminished. The Chinese, it seemed, possessed no un-
ambiguous word for a personal God. At first the missionaries
thought they would follow the example of Francis Xavier.
During his first months in Japan, he had been misled by his
interpreter into using the ambiguous word "Dainichi." Later,
when he discovered that the word designated a local fertility
god, he took no second chance and transliterated the Latin
word Deus. In Chinese, however, this could not be done
without awkwardness and possible confusion. They decided
finally to follow the advice of their first young catechumen,
who saluted the painting of Christ with the title "Lord of
Heaven." The choice, they soon discovered, conveyed their
meaning well, for the Chinese, in their earliest books, invested
the visible sky or Heaven with the attributes of a supreme
being : the Christian God, being Lord of Heaven, not only

ranked higher but possessed infinite, intangible and personal qualities lacking in their concept of Heaven. The Virgin they called the Lady Mother of the Lord of Heaven.

Unable at first to comprehend anything so totally unfamiliar as Christianity, the majority of visitors found it easier to treat the newcomers as a peculiar sect of Buddhist bonzes, but what, Ricci asked himself, did that signify and entail? Perusing the annals of China and the religious texts of past centuries, he began to form a clearer picture of himself and Ruggieri as they must appear to the Chinese.

The earliest religion of the country contained far less magic and far fewer logical errors than any primitive creed known to Ricci. A single, omnipotent, supreme Being was worshipped in the form of Heaven, together with various subsidiary protective spirits of stars, mountains, rivers, and the four corners of the world. Virtue pleased, vice displeased Heaven, which rewarded or punished men in this world according to their deeds. So reverent was religious awe that only the Emperor and high officials might perform sacrifice, and the people never attributed to Heaven or other spirits the reprehensible conduct with which Egyptians, Greeks and Romans defiled their gods. This primitive religion no longer existed in its original form. Over a thousand years before Ricci's arrival, its beliefs and practices had already become partially incorporated in three main sects, to one or more of which most Chinese now claimed to belong. Of these the most flourishing, the most highly esteemed and boasting the largest number of great books was Confucianism, the national philosophical system of China, professed—at least in public—by the majority of graduates, and preserving the essentials of the primitive theology, in particular the Emperor's sacrifice to Heaven, more as a state religion than a vital creed. It had been handed down in the most curious fashion, not consciously chosen or proclaimed, but imbibed through education, the essential criterion for passing state examinations being a thorough knowledge of the works of Confucius, whose doctrine became the stamp of the ruling class. Confucius had been born in the sixth century before Christ, an impoverished minor aristocrat, orphaned at an early age. A philosopher rather than religious teacher, he spent his life training students for a political career. His teaching had been transmitted by disciples in the form of a confused, un-scientific collection of maxims and discourses based on reason, capable of various interpretations and twisted out of all recognition by later commentators, the most influential of whom, Chu Hsi, had presented the Master's teaching as atheistic rationalism.

One of Ricci's greatest difficulties was to disentangle the authentic teaching of Confucius from the heteroclite system known as Confucianism. From a study of the *Analects* he became convinced that Confucius had taught a reverence for Heaven, upon which all earthly things depend, and that this religion was untainted by idolatry. Yet while reverencing the traditional Chinese Heaven, Confucius initiated a change from supernatural to ethical thinking, a shift of emphasis from God to man and human relations, which ever since had dominated Chinese philosophy. Almost at the time when Aristotle declared man's supreme happiness to lie in the contemplation of a God whose existence he proved by reason, Confucius was preaching that man's good was in himself and that he should seek the peace of mind which follows from virtue. Paradise could be realised on earth, here and now, if all men followed the way of co-operation and made no attempt to change their place in society. Man's duty to Heaven was satisfied by the Emperor's annual sacrifice; man's duty to his neighbour demanded wisdom, patience and unselfishness every moment of every day. Religion was reduced to the science of human relations. The creation of the world and who sustained it were questions which interested few early thinkers, and the myths they invented as explanations were generally discredited. Confucius too ignored these problems, believing that reason was powerless to establish the nature of God or the existence of life after death.

This failure to provide cosmological truths or to take account of an after-life paved the way for the second most important sect, Buddhism, which possessed a powerful metaphysical structure and did not hesitate to speculate about the supernatural. Buddhist bonzes had travelled overland from India to China in the first century after Christ, preaching a mystical monism—that the world and all things in it formed with their creator a single substance—the attainment of salvation through moral perfection, and transmigration of souls, with ultimate reward for the good and punishment for the evil. They praised celibacy, which Confucius had condemned, and held that not only the Emperor but every creature must worship God. Buddhist bonzes were to be seen everywhere—from books Ricci calculated their numbers at three million—some begging alms, others living in monasteries off their own land. Valignano, fresh from Japan where Buddhist bonzes were highly esteemed, had authorised Ricci and Ruggieri to assume their dress and habits, in order to make apparent to the Chinese, in a way they could understand, that the foreigners too were priests.

The third and least important sect was Taoism, made popular by Lao Tzu, a near contemporary of Confucius and born, according to legend, as a wise old man of eighty. Confucius called his righteous way of life *tao*, but Lao Tzu applied the term to the basic principle of the universe; by abandoning and refining away his passions, the Taoist sage could unite himself with this cosmic force. Originally a form of mystical pantheism, the doctrine was soon corrupted, teaching that union with the *tao* was attained not by self-denial but by quaffing an elixir of life, in search of which alchemy and magical rites were practised. Later it became a religion, raising the spirits of nature to the rank of gods and borrowing the worst features of Buddhism, including its lurid hell. In Ricci's day its priests were celibate and distinguished by a wooden skullcap on their unshaven heads. While Buddhist bonzes had the all-important task of conducting funeral rites, Taoists were summoned only to exorcise demons.

So confused and intermingled were the histories and doctrines of each sect that many Chinese practised them together and thought them really one. The majority, however, wishing to follow all three, ended by following none. In practice the graduates were atheists, while the masses, unable to appreciate the subtle philosophy of the other two sects, worshipped the myriad metal and clay idols to be seen everywhere, in houses, streets, ships and public buildings.

Ricci realised that it must be made quite clear that although he and his companion adopted the dress and habits of bonzes —although, that is, they were priests—their doctrine had nothing in common with Buddhism. But the more eagerly he explained that they worshipped an ineffable, infinite God, the greater his visitors' bewilderment. They would point to the lifelike picture of the Saviour : finer than anything in the Buddhist pagodas, but nevertheless an idol. The foreign bonzes carried rosary beads; they burned lamps and candles on their altar; they spoke of heaven and hell; they venerated a holy woman : but all these practices took place in the nearby pagodas. Clearly the foreign bonzes were Buddhists—perhaps of a new and esoteric sect, but all the same Buddhists. In an unexpected and sinister way, the habit had made the monk.

CHAPTER THREE

Paradise Revealed

SOULS were dependent on silver. At the end of the year Ruggieri decided to visit Macao in order to obtain money for the upkeep of the house and, if possible, for further building. Wang P'an asked him to bring back a clock in a wooden case, for he had learned that they could be obtained in Macao, and in return provided an official boat of thirty oars for the journey, on which Philip would accompany his master. At the beginning of December Ricci waved his friends good-bye.

For the first time he found himself alone among the Chinese. The absence of a single other European made plain the full implications of his position, and the revolution of his life during the past three months. He had become in Western terminology a Chinese citizen; he dressed as a bonze, he wrote, read and spoke the Chinese language and lived in a house furnished in Chinese style. So far he had made all the concessions, without obtaining any in return. True, he had been admitted within the gates— but to what purpose? The Chinese language did not contain words for essential Christian concepts; the people equated all they saw and heard with idolatry; even an act of charity redounded to the credit of Buddhism. He found himself wondering, who is being converted? Would he, in the last resort, be slowly absorbed, like the Tartar conquerors, by the Chinese millions he hoped to win? Heaven preserve his faith! As for the work of apostolate, by all human standards it seemed the most impossible, most presumptuous of dreams.

The days and weeks passed but still Ruggieri did not return. Ricci grew anxious and wondered whether the viceroy, who had refused their proffered presents and shown every sign of coldness, had sent orders to Canton invalidating his friend's passport. Meanwhile he continued to learn, slowly replacing his distorted ideas about the country, accustoming himself to carry his meaning in those leaking pails, Chinese ideograms, adapting himself to jeers and continual contemptuous inspection, to the inland climate, to the use of wands and the bitter golden green drink called *cia*, conforming to the extraordinary in all except one thing. While the mandarins locked up their seals for a month in preparation for the ceremonies of the New Year—the first full moon after the sun entered Aquarius—and the people of Shiuhing set out meats before the god of the kitchen, Ricci, following another star and a newer calendar, celebrated Christmas without festivities, alone.

Towards the middle of January the governor's boat sailed up the Western River and moored close to the mission house. But Ruggieri was not on board. The only passenger was an Indian boy, who handed Ricci a letter from his friend. The carrack from Japan, delayed by storms, had not made port till the New Year. Even with its safe arrival, Macao remained a poor town. Unable to procure the few ducats necessary to have a timepiece made for the governor, Ruggieri had sent an Indian servant from the Jesuit house who knew how to construct clocks. He ended by saying he would return as soon as he could raise the money they needed. Greatly relieved, Ricci explained what had happened to Wang P'an. He seemed satisfied with the new arrangement and sent two local metal-workers to the mission house to help the Indian.

Ruggieri's protracted absence increased suspicion. Rumour had it that he was starting trouble in Macao and would arrive soon at the head of a Portuguese army. Ricci learnt from the governor, himself a native of Chekiang, that the people of Kwangtung province were reputed the most hostile of all Chinese to foreigners. From time immemorial their coasts had been harried by pirates, and since the installation of the Portuguese at Macao their junks had lost much trade. The educated classes, who might otherwise have shown civility, were becoming indignant as more and more of the common people came to believe that, because building on the tower and mission residence started simultaneously, the foreign bonzes were constructing the former at their own expense. They were even beginning to call it the Tower of the Foreigners. Others supposed it to be part of a fortress the missionaries were erecting for the Portuguese.

Soon hostility spilled over in acts of bravado. Under cover of darkness skittish youths would climb the tower, rising now like a full-blown lupin beside the seedling mission, and throw stones, breaking the tiles of the house. One evening, while Ricci was out walking, the Indian servant grew so exasperated that he ran out and caught a boy who had been hurling stones. To teach him a lesson he locked the hooligan up in the house and threatened to hand him over to the governor for punishment. Shortly afterwards three elderly mandarins, attracted by the cries, came to the house and asked what had happened. They then approached Ricci and said it would be more prudent to release the boy. Ricci did so at once.

Two neighbours, leaders of those who opposed the missionaries, decided to profit from the incident. Taking counsel with a relative of the prankster, a young man versed in legal matters, they decided that he should accuse Ricci before the governor of having kept the boy in his house three days by administering a medicine which rendered him temporarily dumb, with the intention of selling him into slavery at Macao. As neighbours and eye-witnesses they would support his charge. The young man, hoping to win a name by driving out the foreigners, agreed. His hair in disorder to signify distress, he staggered through the streets, shrieking and demanding justice for the evil the foreign devils had done the poor boy, whom he falsely declared to be his brother.

Ricci turned to his acquaintances, who next day helped him to draw up a written defence against the calumny. Before the document had been completed, a soldier entered to lead Ricci and the Indian clockmaker to Wang P'an's audience hall. There were no courts and the governor maintained order by following his own judgment rather than written law. The precincts of the hall were packed with angry crowds who jeered as the defendant was led past, and the interior too was thronged with curious bystanders. At the left of the governor stood the plaintiff, his so-called brother and the two false witnesses; at the right, guards with instruments of torture. The Indian at his side, Ricci kow-towed three times and remained kneeling. Wang P'an, who wore the severe wingless cap of judgment, threw a scornful glance at the strongly built figure mantled in grey cloth, his hair and beard shaven but marked as a foreigner by the long face, straight blue eyes and high-bridged nose.

" I have received you kindly, given you a place to live in, taken a great deal of trouble to do you favours—and you repay me by maltreating my people. You proclaim a doctrine of love, yet you secretly steal away a boy who has done you no harm." He spoke so vehemently that Ricci caught only a phrase or two. Still searching for a reply, he saw the Indian fumble in the folds of his wide sleeves and throw forward in the centre of the hall a handful of stones. They rolled along the tiled floor with the ring of truth. A moment of silence, then the Indian and Ricci haltingly began to put forward a defence.

" The accusation is false. The boy had been pelting our house with stones—and broken the roof in several places."

Their words sounded flimsy but evidently the stones had impressed the governor, for when the plaintiff shouted " All lies! I bring witnesses to prove my charge," Wang P'an silenced him and asked Ricci for a full account of the incident. This he gave simply and straightforwardly, but faulty grammar seemed to discredit his words. Even if Wang P'an believes me, Ricci thought, his position will be awkward, for by openly taking my part against his own people, he may be deprived of office. When the governor had listened to both plaintiff and defendant, he said :

" There is no doubt that the black clockmaker seized the boy. He is a ruffian and must be sent back to Macao."

After directing both plaintiff and defendant to be kept in custody, instead of calling the plaintiff's witnesses, whom he evidently knew to be biased, he ordered the president and other mandarins in charge of building the tower to be summoned, for they had visited the site on the evening in question.

Most of that day Ricci spent in an ante-room, piecing together from snatches of conversation the progress of the case. The plaintiff had managed to slip away and visit the president of the tower committee, to whom he had given money and the promise of more on condition that he and his associates supported the false charges. He had also arranged that Ricci's two neighbours should be allowed to come forward spontaneously and give incriminating evidence. The case seemed as good as lost. He foresaw a public bastinado, followed by ignominious expulsion from the town. Distractedly he prayed for himself and also—he hoped with more fervour —for the endangered mission.

In the late afternoon witnesses were assembled. Ricci and the plaintiff were again led in and knelt before the governor. Suddenly disorder broke out at the back of the hall and, to the surprise of everyone present but Wang P'an, three old men clad in the purple robes of graduates entered and knelt beside Ricci. Stealing a glance, he recognised the men who had advised him to release the boy. The governor addressed them.

" Is it true that the foreign bonze stole this boy away?" and he pointed to the snivelling urchin.

In a cultivated voice the eldest answered, " No, your Excellency. The boy threw a great many stones at the foreign bonze's house : for this reason a servant came out and took the boy into custody. We happened to be passing, so we intervened and procured his release."

" Did the foreign bonze keep the boy three days?"

" No, your Excellency, not even three hours."

The governor rose and signalled to the guards. His inordinate authority, like that of every Chinese magistrate, lay not in rigorous laws or the power of beheading, but in a humble bamboo cane, with which he possessed the right to whip any one of his subjects in public audience. Yet, so terrible were the wounds it could inflict, so arbitrary the will which wielded it, that China largely owed her incomparable order and unity to a flimsy-looking piece of wood, five feet long, three inches broad and an inch thick.

At the governor's signal four guards hurled themselves on the plaintiff, led him screaming to the centre of the hall and threw him face downward on the floor. While one guard held him fast by the feet, and another by the head his clothes were wrenched off. A burly executioner, stripped to the waist, raised the bamboo cane above his head. At a second signal he swung the stick down on the back of the victim's thighs. A shriek of pain. " One," cried a guard. Again the weapon was raised and in a whistling arc smashed down on bare flesh. Two, came the count. Three. Four. Five. The victim was turned over, and blows delivered with unabated fury across the front of his thighs. Ricci looked from the squirming prisoner round the hall. Most bystanders were casually conversing; some laughed, few showed interest, none pity. His two neighbours, who had been called to give false witness, evidently frightened by the sudden turn of events, took advantage of the whipping to elude their guards and scurry out of the hall on hands and knees. Ten, he heard the tally cried, and the prisoner was again turned over. What had he been told? That twenty or thirty strokes left permanent scars; fifty required months to heal; a hundred brought death. In supplication he bowed his head to the ground.

" I beg your Excellency to stop these blows. The man was mistaken and meant no harm."

Wang P'an replied above the screams, " This crime deserves no mercy. He has had the audacity to accuse innocent men."

Again and again Ricci interceded, but not until thirty strokes had been administered did the punishment cease. Then, having dismissed the elderly mandarins, he declared Ricci and the Indian boy free. So sickened by the punishment he could scarcely feel relief, Ricci walked home, explaining what had happened to a host of curious questioners on the way, and wondering whether anything but misunderstanding and conflict could arise from this first intimate meeting of two disparate races.

Next morning the governor sent Ricci yet another edict to place outside his house. It proclaimed, " The foreign bonzes have come to this town with the viceroy's permission. One of them, against all the rules of courtesy, has been unjustly accused. No one in future is to molest them : if any are caught doing so, the Indian clockmaker is to bring them to the

governor's hall, where they will be punished mercilessly."
Hostility relented and a few weeks later, when Ruggieri and
Philip returned with sufficient money to pay their debts and
continue building, subsided altogether. Work was started at
once on an additional six rooms, a veranda and a large
separate chapel.

Soon after Ruggieri's return, news reached the missionaries
that a poor Chinese had been pronounced incurably ill by
the doctors and dumped in a nearby field by his despairing
parents to die. Ricci and Ruggieri went out with a litter, found
the sick man and brought him back to the house. Since they
had no place to lay him, they told Philip and the Indian to
construct a small wattled hut in the garden where they could
set up a bed. They fed and looked after him, but it soon
became clear that they could not save his life. Ricci, who knew
something of the Kwangtung dialect, asked him whether he
would accept Christian teaching. The poor wretch was convinced that Heaven had intervened in the shape of these
strangers who cared for him like a son.

He made a gesture of assent and murmured, " If it teaches
you to treat me like this, it must surely be true."

So every day in his homespun Chinese Ricci taught the
dying man the existence of an almighty God, and that although his body could not be saved, his soul could be
redeemed, to enjoy eternal life. But these ideas, so opposed to
the traditional belief in transmigration, were beyond him, and
Ricci was obliged to simplify still further, teaching him the
bare essentials for baptism : to acknowledge the Lord of
Heaven, to repent for past wrongs. When the Chinese gave
his assent, Ruggieri, as superior, poured holy water over his
brow and recited the Latin words of salvation. As Ricci
watched, it seemed that the moment of salvation of a single
soul pointed beyond itself to his own vision : the conversion of
China. But the missionaries' joy lasted only a few days; their
first Christian had been reborn only to die.

Since disinterested charity outside the family circle was
incomprehensible, the town gossips fitted the incident into a
known category. Nodding with worldly wisdom, they said,

" It is obvious the foreign bonzes knew the sick man had a precious jewel in his head. When he died they cut open his brain and took possession of the jewel. How else do you suppose they can afford to enlarge their house?" All but the graduates accepted this story as certain truth.

Wang P'an, however, understood and sympathised with their motives. That spring there arrived with pomp and ceremony two wooden tablets on which were inscribed in gold three or four large, well-formed Chinese characters, a present from the governor, who had engraved them himself. In this way mandarins were accustomed to show their favour, single out friends for particular respect and officially recognise a place of worship, which otherwise remained illegal. One tablet, intended for the door of the house, which also served as chapel, proclaimed " Pagoda of the Flower of Saints " : a tribute to the Mother of God, patron of the chapel. The other was inscribed " They came from the West to bring us knowledge of Paradise." The missionaries had originally been obliged to say they came from India, for the Chinese did not have names for Europe or its kingdoms. Their books stated India to be the furthest western land, and sometimes used that name loosely for the West. India, whence Buddhism had been brought to China, was believed to be a specially religious country where men tried to save their souls, and possessing in the Ganges a river of marvellously holy water. While Europe believed Paradise lay in furthest Asia, China, under Buddhist influence, thought it lay towards the West. Consequently, Wang P'an had identified the Heaven of the missionaries' teaching with the country of their origin.

Both tablets were dated and signed with the governor's name and rank. The missionaries set them up, like vertical captions on a Chinese etching, one beside the bamboo screen of the large room, the other beside the front door, under the shadow of the wooden cross which crowned the house. They and their chapel had been given a name : first stage, so they hoped, towards being understood.

From their own side, too, they strove towards that end, turning likewise to written characters. They had discovered how little trust the Chinese placed in the highly ambiguous spoken word. Only when he had seen the pictographs written down and had studied them was he prepared to give or withhold his assent. A whole sentence might be shut up in a character whose beauties the eye alone could detect. The written or printed word had another advantage : it could penetrate and be understood throughout China, whereas they were restricted for the moment to a single town. They could not adopt the traditional evangelical method, haranguing in the open air or at home, for in China only revolutionary political doctrine was spread in such uncouth fashion. Religion was diffused by the example of a good life and by books. To wander through the streets preaching would be interpreted as the prelude to Portuguese conquest, and before the day was out they would be sent packing to Macao.

Towards the end of their first year in Shiuhing they began to translate the Ten Commandments, Philip and their acquaintances helping them to find equivalents for the Latin. In Chinese style, instead of using pens, they painted the characters with small brushes made from hare fur, dipping them in a mixture of water and ink manufactured from soot and sesame oil. By October the manuscript was ready to take to the local printer's shop. Printing, known to Europe for little longer than a hundred and fifty years, had played an important part in Chinese civilisation since about the eighth century. Ricci had been astonished by the number and quality of volumes, covering every field of human knowledge, most of them well produced except that the flimsy paper, made from bamboo pith, would take ink on only one side. The printer, he found, possessed no movable type, for although the component parts of the characters were sufficiently simple, the difficulty of combining them into a multitude of forms would have been insurmountable. Instead, the written text was pasted in reverse on a smooth, unknotty tablet, made from pear, apple or jujube wood. When dry, the surface of the paper was scraped off, leaving nothing but the black characters on the tablet. Then the printer cut away the wood round the characters until they stood out in relief. From this he could print at great speed and at small expense a very large number of copies, the block being preserved indefinitely.

The Decalogue emerged as a handsome production of sixteen columns, running from top to bottom and right to left. To those visitors who enquired about their doctrine, the missionaries presented copies. Like all written or printed writing, they were handled with almost awesome care : indeed, in the sixth of the ten courts of Taoist purgatory punishment was inflicted on those " who had shown no respect for written paper." The effect far exceeded Ricci's expectations. His Chinese friends said the commandments conformed to reason and natural law, and some even promised to observe them. So successful did this first leaflet prove that they soon produced another containing the Pater, Ave and Credo in Chinese. In return friends brought presents of incense, oil for the altar lamp and alms for the missionaries' food, this being the customary way to repay a master's teaching.

Ricci was touched by this response, however conventional, for as he came to admire the natural virtues, good humour and industry of the Chinese, as he found himself sharing their joys and troubles by way of a sensitive, almost intuitive natural sympathy, he longed to establish warm relations, to help them to the truth no longer as a mere duty but from fellow-feeling.

One day, as an experiment, Ricci exhibited an up-to-date Flemish map of the world he had brought from Macao. It showed Europe, the eastern and western coastlines of North America, the full extent of South America, the outline of Africa, India, Indonesia, Japan; the Kwangtung coastline and, to the north-west, Cathay as described by Marco Polo. One of its chief features was a supposed Great Southern Continent, occupying the lower quarter of the atlas, its two northward projections separated by a deep gulf near the Malay Archipelago. Their Chinese visitors were puzzled. Some thought the map a strange painting, others a Taoist charm. When Ricci explained what it was, they refused absolutely to believe him.

" Surely you are mistaken," they protested, " we have our own maps bearing no relation to this."

One of the mandarins sent a servant home to fetch an atlas and, when it arrived, spread the inferior parchment out on the table. This time it was the missionaries' turn to be astonished. There could be no mistake about the heading : " Picture of All Under Heaven," but practically the entire sheet was occupied by the fifteen provinces. China like a cuckoo had turned all the other countries out of the nest. Into the right-hand corner Korea and Japan were squeezed; at the bottom on the same line as Cambodia, stretched the islands of Borneo, Sumatra and Java; to the west lay India with Arabia underneath it; at the top was written Karakorum. A legend at the north-west corner mentioned that nine barbarian countries lay eastwards, eight to the south, six in the west and five to the north. All the foreign countries put together were smaller than a minor province of the Flowery Kingdom. No wonder, thought Ricci, they are contemptuous of foreigners when they consider the rest of the world so small in comparison with their own country. At the same time, the map brought home the almost unimaginable extent of China, stretching on all sides to the absolute natural limit, its eastern semicircular coast bounded by sea; desert to the north, to the west a rampart of high mountains. Ricci noted that altitudes were marked and that the map was crossed with rectilinear divisions, in accordance with the Chinese view that the world was a four-square plane.

Only Wang P'an believed that the European map might be more than a fiction.

" I want you to translate all the annotations into our language," he told Ricci. " Then we can compare the two maps. If I am satisfied that your version is correct, I shall have it printed and distributed throughout the Middle Kingdom."

Ricci had been taught geography by Christopher Clavius; he had a knowledge of Ortelius and Mercator; at sea and in India he had taken bearings which had enabled him to revise and complete the atlases he carried, even the best of which still relied on imagination for distant Asia. Carefully he drew up a simple and reasonably complete map on a sinusoidal projection, with the prime meridian 170 degrees east to bring China towards the centre, marking the land white and the sea with large black dots. With its parallels of latitude and longitude, the equator and meridians, all the countries with their names written in Chinese, it impressed the mandarins, who had to admit that while amplifying, it also corresponded with their own knowledge. No one in Shiuhing had ever left China, whereas the foreign bonzes had travelled from the distant West. Their map, after all, might represent the truth. The consequences of this admission were revolutionary and highly favourable. If China was merely one among many great countries, if other people knew more of the world than they did, had they been wise in believing that all foreigners were, like their immediate neighbours, barbarians? Moreover, when Ricci pointed out Italy, so distant from China, and the oceans which lay between, they began to lose some of their fear that the missionaries were the forerunners of conquering armies. Ricci took his work to the governor, together with a clock which the Indian had now completed. Wang P'an was delighted and thanked Ricci profusely. He had the map printed at once, with his own name on it, and gave copies to all his friends. The clock, however, he was unable to regulate and soon returned to the missionaries for use in their own house. There he began to resort even more frequently as a consequence of two fortunate events : his wife, who had not yet born him a son, became pregnant and he himself received promotion, three years before the normal date, to the office of Superintendent of the Western Frontier. While still resident in Shiuhing he now had authority in two provinces, and with his increased power could help his protégés even more. Extremely superstitious like all Chinese, he believed his new friends had brought him luck.

The following month they published an even more important work. As early as 1581 Ruggieri had written a Latin catechism which had been translated into Chinese by Philip and others. The following year Valignano ordered Ruggieri to have it printed as soon as possible. As the two Italians made progress in the language, they saw the book's shortcomings and started to improve it. During the past summer, a strange event had taken place. A graduate from Fukien, married and father of a family, came to the missionaries. In a dream he had seen a foreigner, who explained what he must do in order to be saved, but on waking could not remember his doctrine. Having heard of the foreign bonzes, he identified them with the figure of his dream and had come to learn from them the way of salvation. Ruggieri invited him to live in their house to learn Christian doctrine and to help the missionaries with their Chinese writing. It was this graduate who perfected the style of the catechism and prepared it for publication. Its sixteen chapters took the form of dialogue between master and pupil. First, the existence of God was proved from the causal argument, and God's attributes enumerated. Versed in Chinese customs more than Psychology, the Italians made extensive use of simile. "Those who adore Heaven instead of the Lord of Heaven are like a man who, desiring to pay the Emperor homage, prostrates himself before the imperial palace at Peking and venerates its beauty." Then followed a discussion of the soul's immortality, the ten commandments and the purpose of baptism, arguments effective enough to win the young graduate to the new faith during the course of revision. In its printed form the work contained over thirteen thousand characters on seventy-eight pages, bound in blue cloth. Chinese books were authenticated with their author's seal, engraved with name and surname on ivory, brass, crystal or red coral. The missionaries made their own seal from the letters IHS, with a cross above the H, a monogram of the name of Jesus Christ, which Ignatius de Loyola had adopted as the emblem of his Society. They stamped this seal at the beginning and end of the catechism. Twelve hundred copies were printed in November 1584, but the demand proved so great that these were soon followed by an even larger impression from the same blocks.

Meanwhile news of the establishment of priests in China had spread to Japan and the Philippines. In his letters Ricci in particular had suggested that the time was ripe to present gifts from King Philip II of Spain to the Emperor of China. This project had been under consideration for some years and the gifts had already reached Mexico. In Japan widespread conversion had been achieved through gaining the goodwill of the great daimyo; Ricci was not alone in believing that the most effective way to evangelise China lay through the Emperor. Christianity was a reasonable religion : reason appealed to the head, and therefore to the head of state. Now that a foothold had been obtained within the country, the moment seemed opportune.

The optimistic news from China stirred mercantile as well as missionary hopes. Although Portugal and Spain had been united under the Spanish Crown since 1580, each country jealously safeguarded its former spheres of influence. The Spanish authorities now cast envious eyes on the wealth Portugal was amassing from China and which promised, as the country opened its gates still wider, to exceed even their own Mexican and Peruvian treasures. The Governor of the Philippines and the Bishop of Manila decided to set up a Spanish trading base in Kwangtung province, with the Italian missionaries' help. They sent a Spanish Jesuit and the royal exactor of tribute to Macao, carrying money for the Chinese mission and letters which asked the Jesuits of China to obtain permission for a present to be brought to the Emperor by Spanish ambassadors. This present, to the value of 70,000 ducats, would include two dozen Mexican horses, velvet, brocade, Flemish tapestries, Venetian glass, mirrors, clocks, gold, swords, oil paintings, red and white wine. Such a gift, it was hoped, would persuade the Emperor to grant free entry to Christian missionaries. On their arrival in Macao the visitors from the Philippines wrote asking Ruggieri to obtain permission for them to come to Shiuhing and treat personally with the viceroy about the proposed embassy. Ruggieri, unsuspecting, acceded to their request. Both Wang P'an and the viceroy approved the plan of an embassy and it was sent to the Haitao at Canton for his final decision.

Meanwhile the Portuguese traders of Macao learnt that the Spaniards proposed to use their influence to establish a trading post at Canton. The Spaniards possessed unlimited supplies of silver, so highly valued in China; if they came to Canton prices would soar and the Portuguese stood to make a greatly reduced profit. The traders at Macao pointed out that they had largely financed the Chinese mission, which therefore owed them a debt of loyalty. As for the present to the Emperor, they believed that if it was given by Spanish ambassadors, Spain would be accorded more favourable rights than Portugal now enjoyed. To permit such a result would be inconsistent with papal pronouncements and with King Philip's own assurance that the Portuguese should continue to have exclusive trading rights with Macao. Recognising the force of these arguments, the Jesuit superior at Macao wrote an urgent letter to Ruggieri, telling him to let the matter of the embassy drop. This put the Italian in a dilemma, for the petition was now in the Haitao's hands and could not be withdrawn. As chance would have it, the Haitao finally decided against the proposal, saying that only tributary states were permitted to send gifts to the Emperor. Indeed, a well-known prophecy held that the empire would fall if a new embassy was admitted.

Ricci could not share his colleague's unqualified relief. The Haitao's decision had prevented open rivalry between the two Iberian Countries which might have proved fatal to the delicately placed mission. Yet the decision seemed to rule out any embassy in the future; from the Pope, for instance, in order to avoid rousing national sentiment—a scheme in which Ricci had the greatest confidence.

But these grandiose plans affected daily life in Shiuhing very little. Far more important was a decision taken in 1585, second year of their stay in China, when the two Italians made yet another gesture of conformity by adopting honorific names. Until then everyone, even the house-boys, had called them by their Christian names phoneticised. To such scholars as Wang P'an this appeared a barbarous custom because proper names were never used by educated men except, humbly, to designate themselves, or by a high mandarin as a mark of superiority to one very much beneath him in rank. Wang P'an had suggested they follow the Chinese custom. In all China there existed a mere handful of surnames, less than a thousand, ancient and immutable. When a child was born, if a girl, she was known merely by a number—first, second or third sister—but if a boy, he received a first name, usually of two syllables, the surname being monosyllabic. His parents and elders addressed the boy by this first name; others called him by the number he ranked among his brothers. He himself in his visiting books and wherever else he wrote a signature used his first name. If he were addressed by his surname, he would consider it bad manners, even an insult. At the age of twenty-one a local mandarin gave him a middle name, by which everyone except servants addressed him, until later in life he abandoned this for " the great name." Henceforward superiors addressed him by his middle name and everyone else by the great name. It was this " great " or honorific name which Wang P'an suggested the missionaries adopt. Ricci's first name in Chinese was Ma-tou and his surname Li, the nearest monosyllabic equivalent to Ricci, the " r " sound being unknown in China. For a great name, he was now obliged to accept the style by which local graduates already referred to him : Hsi-t'ai, which meant the Far or Exalted Westerner. Ruggieri, who had been known as Lu, adopted the name of Fou-ch'u, the Restorer of the mission which Francis Xavier had in principle founded.

It was doubtful how far the second title could be justified. By the end of 1585 Ricci and his colleague had spent almost two and a half years in China and converted only twenty men : in the same length of time Francis Xavier had baptised a thousand Japanese. True, Ricci could claim they had purposely remained discreet in their proselytising, lest they be expelled for disturbing the peace. But twenty out of a hundred and ninety million Chinese : for that he had become a barbarian! Ricci took recourse from the lunatic figures in the fervour of his few neophytes, in the miracle of conversion.

As the months passed their frustrations grew still more numerous. In an attempt to establish another foothold further inland Ruggieri undertook two journeys. Both proved fruitless, for he seemed unable to win the mandarins' confidence. Increasingly, this task fell to Ricci, who remained at Shiuhing. Time and again Wang P'an grew cold, as enemies tried to drive away the essential otherness, bewildering and challenging, with a succession of trumped-up charges : that the foreign bonzes had aided a Franciscan caught at Canton without a passport; that Ruggieri had committed adultery with a local woman; that their two-storeyed house was an actual or potential fortress—an accusation difficult to refute, for only Chinese town walls or towers were built high and of brick: with tears, written petitions and gifts Ricci had to plead their innocence and bring to the fore Wang P'an's better self; with laughter again and again shatter the brittle edge of contempt. It was a brute life, concerned only with survival. At times, when fury mounted in the town, Ricci would watch from the house the river running down to Canton, to Macao. Why not accept the natural course, drift with the current, leave the Chinese to their idols? In spite of himself the answer would rise indignantly. Yes, it was as simple as that: in giving everything he had grown to love them. However violent their hatred, however often they tried to beat him off, he was condemned to a lifetime of love.

CHAPTER FOUR

Gaining Ground

MANY people in Shiuhing, unable to understand what the missionaries were about, supposed they belonged to the very numerous class of magicians. A firm belief held that cinnabar, a vermilion-coloured compound of mercury and sulphur, could be changed into real silver by means of amber, a resin not native to China and familiar only since its introduction to the country forty years earlier. The missionaries were thought to possess amber and know how to effect the change, because every year the Portuguese purchased in Canton quantities of cinnabar, which they transported to Japan and India. Since their carracks were seen to return from these countries with cargoes of silver, it seemed obvious that the cinnabar had been transmuted by alchemy. Further confirmation was found in the fact that the missionaries lived honestly yet, unlike other bonzes, solicited no alms, neither did they trade or own land. The more vigorously they denied alchemic powers, the more convinced the Chinese became, for since many quacks laid false claim to the art, it seemed probable that those who denied all knowledge really possessed it. The missionaries, in fact, were not displeased at this explanation—an image of the invisible truth—for if it were known that they were being supported from Macao, the Chinese would become even more suspicious of their designs.

No less widespread than the craze for making silver was the desire to know the future. Ricci was astonished by the number of fortune-tellers and their many ways of prediction. Some drew oracles from words; others kept a bullfinch and tortoise to select cards of good or bad import. A man with a small nose and distended nostrils was believed born to penury; a thick hand with a soft red palm betokened good fortune; to dream of the moon falling foretold the birth of a daughter : lives were governed by such auguries and it frequently happened, as Ricci himself had witnessed, that some wretch, for whom serious illness had been predicted by a certain date, would worry himself to death, thus confirming the wisdom of his executioners.

The most esteemed magicians were those who taught the art of living to a great age by ascetical practices, sexual abstinence, rhythmic respiration and especially by the quaffing of an elixir containing what was thought to be gold. Again cinnabar played the dominant role. Easily resolved into its two constituents and easily recomposed, it was taken to be the perfect embodiment of Yin and Yang, the dark feminine and bright masculine principles underlying all creation : not only transmutable into silver but a type of periodic renaissance, holding the promise of immortality. When recomposed, it left traces of yellow sulphuric arsenic and it was this, believed to be edible gold, which formed the basis of the elixirs. The men who administered them, to prove their efficacy, claimed to be immensely old and often, to avoid awkward questions, pretended that most of their life had been spent abroad. Rumour had it that Ricci and his companion knew the art of longevity; that they were far older than they would admit—a hundred, perhaps two hundred years old—and that they did not marry in order to prolong their lives still further.

Lest powerful officials should gain too great an influence over people so ignorant and pliable, possibly leading to rebellion against the central government, the laws of China provided that a mandarin must be appointed to a new post in another province every three years. In 1584 an exception had been made when Wang P'an was appointed Superintendent of the Western Frontier, from which office during 1587 he waited in vain for promotion. He began to fear that his friendship towards the foreigners had ruined his career, but in January of the new year, to his great joy, he was promoted assistant to the governor of Hukwang province. Before his departure, as the customary way of showing gratitude, the people of Shinhing erected a pagoda to one who had governed them like a father.

On either side of his own statue, which dominated the building, Wang P'an insisted on placing smaller statues of Ruggieri and Ricci, in recognition of the good which had resulted to him from their stay. On the day of his departure the whole population, accompanied by drums and gongs, trooped to the pagoda to light candles and burn incense. A leading citizen presented him with a new pair of shoes and solemnly requested his black chamois slippers of office. These he put in a carved box, inscribed with Wang P'an's good deeds, which was locked and placed in the centre of the pagoda, as a relic of his just administration. Special attendants would keep lights and incense burning night and day before the altar of a righteous man whom the people themselves had spontaneously canonised. Ricci paid particular attention to the ceremony, for it threw light on the privileged position of Confucius. Some of his brethren had seen in the veneration paid to the great philosopher a religious sacrifice. But if the same sort of honour, in lesser degree, could be paid Wang P'an, whom none claimed to be more than mortal, the rites to Confucius did not prove the philosopher a god. Ricci had already noted that the mandarins during their fortnightly homage in the school thanked Confucius for his good teaching, which had enabled them to reach their present rank, but they never asked favours as from a deity. The discovery pleased him, for if Confucianism was untainted by idolatry, it would not be necessary to combat all three Chinese sects at once.

With no less regret than the local people, the two Italians said good-bye to the man who had made possible their entrance into China. For almost five years he had given them his friendship and protection at great personal risk. They had found his intellectual attainments equivalent to those of an Italian gentleman : he read his country's classics, could appraise a picture and produce a well-turned poem. For his part, he had lauded parts of the Westerners' doctrine, but remained a religious agnostic.

In order to stay in a country where the local magistrate himself was the law, every three years they would have to win the goodwill of at least one new official. In a European

country that would not have proved difficult, but here government had been reduced to a fine art. Censors from Peking
continually toured the provinces, noting complaints and
irregularities. Every three years all principal mandarins were
summoned to the capital to pay the Emperor homage. On that
occasion their whole career was scrutinised and in the light of
superiors' reports they were either left in office, degraded, dismissed or even severely punished, sometimes as many as four
thousand mandarins being censured in a single spring for
offences ranging from cruelty to acceptance of bribes. Fortunately Ricci was already friendly with Wang P'an's successor,
who had several times visited Shiuhing on official business. He
promised to protect them and soon gave proof of his goodwill.

During early summer and late spring Ricci again had China
to himself, for Ruggieri had returned to Macao to consult
Valignano. By now the objects originally brought from the
enclave had lost their novelty, and in order to draw visitors and
dispel the opinion that all foreigners were barbarians Ricci
turned the knowledge he had acquired from Christopher
Clavius to practical use, fashioning mechanical instruments
which even to the graduates appeared marvels of invention.
Ricci enjoyed this work : he was gifted for it and it recalled his
happy days at the Roman College. With the Indian boy's help
he constructed a large clock, its face incorporated into the wall
of the house so that those passing by could see the movement of
the single hand. A high-toned bell struck the hour, its metal
clapper catching every ear, for Chinese bells were rung with
wooden mallets. The clock was pronounced wonderful rather
than useful. Some of the mandarins possessed clepsydras and
wood-ash or sand clocks, their unit of time being twice the
length of a European hour, but the mass of people were content
to keep tally by day and season. Life dragged a heavy foot :
haggling in the market-place, interminable meals and elaborate
etiquette extended the simplest actions to fill the day. In setting
up the public clock Ricci asserted his own conception of time :
independent of the rhythm of agriculture, urgent, man-made,
with a purpose beyond itself, every hour crowded as a mandarin
day. He also constructed copper and iron globes of the

A Ming Mandarin

sitting in Judgment

world, no less of a novelty than mechanical clocks, as well as sundials. The only Chinese sundial, fashioned for a latitude of thirty-six degrees, proved hopelessly inaccurate at Shiuhing, which lay at twenty-three degrees. Ricci had been astonished to learn that, since the underlying principle was now quite forgotten, the Chinese had not thought of making the necessary adjustment in the angle of the dial.

Every educated man brought on his first visit a present, and by the rules of courtesy expected some return. Since he could not afford expensive objects, Ricci usually gave home-made sundials or globes, so esteemed that their recipients remained greatly in his debt. He also procured by way of Macao a small library of leather-bound books containing engravings of famous European buildings : theatres, palaces, bridges and churches. Even on the illiterate these produced an effect of awe and wonder. Li's country possessed majestic cities; perhaps after all, despite those ridiculous round eyes and large nose, he might be worth listening to when he spoke of the Lord of Heaven.

In midsummer Ricci learned the outcome of his colleague's visit to Macao. Having heard a review of events, Valignano had decided that the time was ripe to send an embassy from the Pope to the Emperor; four Jesuits, preferably Portuguese or Italians, were to meet Ricci in Shiuhing and proceed under his leadership to Peking. Ricci was asked to draw up Chinese letters which, having first been forwarded to Rome for approval, the Pope could send to the Son of Heaven and the viceroy of Kwangtung, as well as a suitable form of passport for the ambassadors, should the Chinese consent to admit them. With the help of a graduate versed in court protocol Ricci composed elegant letters and dispatched them to his superior.

These letters Valignano entrusted to Ruggieri. Only by arousing interest in the mission throughout Europe and especially at Rome could money be raised for the costly gifts befitting so great an Emperor. As a direct participant, taking with him one or two Chinese servants and an array of curios, Ruggieri would attract the necessary attention. Valignano had come to the conclusion that the impetuous Southerner was unfitted for so difficult a mission field. After nine years he still had no fluency in the language; his two journeys had been almost disastrous failures; he was easily imposed on; he lacked the resolution and heroic qualities necessary to withstand constant opposition and disappointment. Ruggieri's sailing date was fixed for November.

In August Ruggieri's successor arrived from Macao. Antonio de Almeida was Portuguese, five years younger than Ricci, a frailly-built, dark-eyed ascetic, burning with zeal for the conversion of China. During autumn and winter he and Ricci were left in comparative peace to continue the task of slowly breaking down prejudice. By the end of the year their converts numbered fifty and in the spring of 1589 they baptised eighteen more, the largest annual total. Among them were the first Chinese women to receive the new religion. Their peculiar status had presented the missionaries with a problem.

The very existence of women had to be deduced. None but the very poorest were ever seen in the streets and even when Ricci had visited private homes, the women of the household always remained in their own apartments, which they were not only prohibited but prevented from leaving. The men had clipped their wings by choosing as the chief criterion of beauty a physical characteristic which made gallivanting impossible : tiny, minuscule feet. From early childhood a girl's feet were bandaged tightly day and night with parti-coloured cloths, ornamented with fringe and tassels. The constriction raised the instep, stunted their growth to half natural size and swelled the ankles wide. In this exquisite deformity their men exulted, rhapsodising about " golden lilies " and " two new moons." It allowed a woman to shuffle and trip about the house—but no further—to serve without distraction father, husband and son, to fulfil Confucius's dictum that beyond the threshold of her apartments she should not be known for evil or for good. Only two classes of women ventured abroad : wives of the very poor, who were to be seen in the fields drawing a plough or harvest-ing rice, and the blind, who lived in a street set apart in every town. By the hour they sat outside their houses, their long black hair caught up with silver ornaments or imitation pink and yellow asters, vermilion on their cheeks, daubs of white at their chin, strumming a lute, summoning to share their darkness men they would know but never see.

Most graduates, especially those of high rank, kept several concubines besides a legal wife, and Ricci had realised early that polygamy might prove an obstacle to conversion of the mandarin class and their women. But at present, although he depended on the protection of one or two officials, his apostolate lay among a lower class, who could not afford concubines : men of goodwill and some intelligence, farmers, merchants, shopkeepers, who, lacking the graduates' pride, were not held back from dealing with bonzes. Many of his converts were men who had for years led devout lives and practised strict fasting according to the Buddhist discipline. Unsatisfied with the theology of that religion, which was running to seed in a multiplication of idols, and sickened by the degenerate Buddhist bonzes, they gladly accepted a religion which more than answered their spiritual aspirations. Their wives, educated only in manual arts, were content in religious matters to follow their masters' lead. Since they could not leave and Ricci could not enter their zenana, women were catechised by husbands or sons. Only for the actual administration of baptism was Ricci allowed to meet them. Since they could not come to Mass on Sundays and feast days, they prayed together in their own apartments. This humble home life Ricci considered admirably adapted to Christian virtue, but it meant that, unlike European women, they could never play the pioneer role of fostering, spreading and supporting Christianity. Congregations at Macerata had been largely composed of women, the churches built by their alms : at Shiuhing no woman had yet entered the chapel. In this respect the seedling mission had already conformed to the climate of Eastern life.

The separation appeared as a paradox at the heart of educated China. Although society was exclusively masculine, its values were so conditioned by the absence of women as to be almost epicene. Without even a preliminary conversation a wife was bought for money, not won by courage and noble deeds; then imprisoned in a home where she must love her husband or languish. Lacking the stimulus of love's rivalry, Chinese men became, in consequence, something less than men. None wore the sword which hung at every Italian gentleman's hip. Sport, hunting, military arts, all the honourable diversions which Ricci esteemed, were here despised and rarely practised. Instead, dancing boys, dressed and made up like girls, were bought in public to serve the swarming sodomites. With no true love to serve, reason had curled in upon itself luxuriously, and life, like the Chinese game of chess, was conducted without a queen.

In the spring of 1589 a new viceroy was appointed, his predecessor, a friend of the missionaries, having died after a few months in office. This official, no less than the governor of Shiuhing, had power to expel them; and they learned with dismay that Liu Chieh-chai had a reputation for cruelty, ambition and greed. At the conclusion of a successful campaign against pirates fishing pearls illegally in the gulf off the island of Hainan, he deemed it suitable that the people of Shiuhing should honour him with a shrine similar to that erected to Wang P'an. When enemies, led by the president of the tower committee, suggested that no site was more suitable than that of the missionaries' two-storeyed house, Liu determined to get rid of the foreigners, on the grounds that they had no right to be in the Middle Kingdom. Through friendly mandarins, Ricci pressed argument after argument in an attempt to remain. He protested that he had been, as it were, naturalised; but that privilege, it seemed, was a dead letter which Wang P'an had had no right to invoke. He then pointed out that more than six hundred taels had been spent on building the house. Liu, unwilling to reimburse so large a sum, more than a new pagoda would cost, decided to offer compensation of sixty taels. Ricci cajoled, implored and finally asked to be allowed to travel to another province, but the viceroy dismissed all his appeals. The missionaries were finally forced to pack their belongings into two sampans which would escort them back to Macao. As they took leave of the small community of seventy Christians, the acting governor came to receive the keys of the house, bringing sixty taels as compensation. Ricci refused the money. He hoped to bring home to the viceroy the injustice of their expulsion and, if that failed, to give himself grounds for returning, when Liu's term of office had expired, to regain possession of the house.

On August the fourth Ricci and Almeida sailed from Shiuhing. At Canton, where they were delayed overnight, they bought black cloth and fashioned soutanes which they exchanged for the ashen cowled dress of the bonzes. The play, it seemed, was over. They resumed European habits and began to speak in Portuguese, but their thoughts remained at the Pagoda of the Flower of Saints. That night they lay awake, miserable and bitter. After such hardships, they were back where they had started, strays sent scurrying from the wrong side of the world, lovers rejected for their physical appearance.

Next morning, as though in answer to prayer, their fortune turned with the estuary tide. As they prepared dispiritedly for the final stage of their journey, a fast boat suddenly drew alongside, summoning them back to Shiuhing. On arrival, Ricci learned that his last hope had been realised : the governor had come to the conclusion that if their house was taken without indemnity, then turned into a pagoda for his statue, everyone would accuse him of expelling the foreign bonzes not merely to enforce the law but for personal reasons.

Ricci was summoned to the viceroy's hall. Since it would have shown lack of dignity to visit an important mandarin alone, he took with him a Chinese servant. Entering the audience hall, Ricci knelt down at the far end, but the viceroy summoned him to his throne.

" Why did you leave without the sixty taels?" he asked, attempting a smile. " I sent them for your travelling expenses. Now I have called you back specially to give them."

" I am grateful for your kindness," replied Ricci, " but I have no need of the money. Once I return to Macao my brethren and friends will provide for me."

The viceroy tried to mask his annoyance. " Surely you are not so discourteous as to refuse a gift from my own hands."

" Your Excellency has expelled me like a criminal from the

Middle Kingdom. I have no obligation to accept your presents."

The viceroy rose to his feet struggling to contain his anger. "No one transgresses my will," he shouted. Not daring to lay hands on Ricci, he turned to the Chinese servant. "You've taught your master these tricks. Put this man in chains."

The servant cried out in terror. "I'm not to blame, your Excellency. The Far Westerner refused the money because he is sad at being forced to leave."

Ricci saw that the viceroy had lost command of the situation. "My servant speaks the truth," he interposed. "Your Excellency has no cause to be angry. If your Excellency were really well disposed towards me, as he claims, instead of offering money which I do not need, he would let me settle elsewhere in the Middle Kingdom."

The viceroy, caught unawares, pretended not to hear and asked an aide to repeat Ricci's words. Then he struck a new attitude. "That was my first proposal to you, but you yourself refused it."

"Is your Excellency willing, then, to provide me with a passport for Kwangsi or Kiangsi?"

"I cannot do that. Those provinces lie outside my jurisdiction. Take the sixty taels and go to some other place in Kwangtung—anywhere but Shiuhing and Canton."

Wishing to enter as far inland as possible, Ricci chose a town on the Kwangtung-Kiangsi border. "Will your Excellency agree to Namyung?"

"If you like, but I think either the monastery of Nanhoa or Shiuchow would be more suitable. Travel that way and see whether you do not prefer one of them."

When he agreed, the viceroy handed him the sixty taels. "Take these—they will help to pay for your new house."

Ricci accepted the silver—to have refused now, after the viceroy's essential concession, would have been effrontery—and the mandarin's good humour returned. Ricci prostrated himself, head to the ground, to show his gratitude, then made to withdraw. The viceroy detained him. "Here are a number of books—straight from the press. The full story of my success-

ful expedition against the pirates of Hainan. You are the man
to appreciate them."

Ricci accepted a pile of gaudily bound volumes and murmured a polite formula. " It is fitting that so glorious a campaign should be handed down to posterity."

The viceroy smiled and bowed to the departing figure. " May
your way be peaceful, Far Westerner."

Provided with passports, on August the fifteenth Ricci and
Almeida again left Shiuhing, this time their heads high. They
travelled by boat—China's waterways were her roads—first
down the Western River, then up the Pekiang, through increasingly mountainous country. Rice terraces alternated with
woods of cedar and oak, with groves of bamboo, their tawny
yellow or emerald stems crowned by waving plumes of duller
green. Chinese maps had revealed the vastness of the Middle
Kingdom : now this knowledge became bewilderingly actual
on the broad river which looped as though it had lost its way
among the limitless paddy-fields and tiered hills. They
covered the distance from Rome to Florence without traversing
the full breadth of a single Chinese province. Over such stages
the galloping post-horses of Italy would have been hard pressed
to make headway, but here time was no less ample than space.
They travelled passive to nature, at the whim of wind and
water, as though man's activities scarcely mattered in such a
gigantic environment.

After eight days, arriving at a pass in the mountains, they
were halted by a servant of the third collateral, acting governor
of Shiuchow, with orders to lead them to Nanhoa. His master,
it appeared, was merely giving effect to the wishes of Liu the
viceroy who, making no clear distinction between the numerous religious sects, considered it both logical and convenient
that the foreign bonzes should reside at this large Buddhist
monastery. Ricci, for the moment unable to see a way out,
acquiesced.

Escorted by two bonzes, after an hour's walk they arrived at a
level, well-watered valley between hills, rich in fruit trees.
The fields on either side of a clear stream were sown with
rice. On sloping ground, flanked by brick bell-towers, stood

the rose-red building of Nanhoa, blue and red glazed roofs billowing like dancers' skirts.

Their guides explained that all the land around belonged to the monks of Nanhoa. The name meant Pagoda of the Southern Flower, the first shrine having been erected in the sixth century. A Buddhist monk who had travelled overland from India bent to drink water from the stream. Because its taste reminded him of his native country, he decided to remain there preaching. The monastery grew to its present size in the following century during the lifetime of a holy monk called Lu Hui-neng. The two bonzes retailed the local legend. Lu had been nurtured not with his mother's milk but with dew which a genie gathered every night. He first entered the monastery as a scullion pounding rice for the community. He wore chains as a belt and his flesh was covered with vermin. Whenever one of these vermin fell, he would replace it under his chain saying —the two bonzes exchanged a glance and giggled—" You still have plenty to eat." Such asceticism found its reward : pilgrims arrived from far and wide to consult the holy man. Many remained, until, at Lu's death, the monks numbered a thousand.

The monastery was divided into twelve houses, each with its superior, the whole being governed by a prior, who, at their approach, came forward to meet the visitors with exaggerated signs of joy. " We are delighted you have chosen to live among us. The whole monastery is at your disposal."

Ricci discounted the welcome, for the bonzes, being subject to civil authority, were bound to carry out the third collateral's wishes with good grace. The community probably resented his presence no less than the Buddhists in Shiuhing. He noticed that the prior snatched at every occasion to show the inconveniences of the monastery and seemed delighted whenever Ricci emphasised their differences of belief or practice.

The prior took Ricci through the buildings. In grotesque contrast to its idyllic surroundings, the place seemed in the last stages of dissolution. The monks were shifty-eyed, almost illiterate and, in the words of the proverb, stupid as black lacquer. From time to time, as they stumbled on women, some of them suckling infants, the prior in embarrassment would draw his guest's attention to a curious idol or finely carved bracket. Ricci remembered hearing that many monks, although vowed to chastity, had wives and children; others were highwaymen and murderers. Unclean corridors and cells were crammed with dusty bronze and wooden idols. In enclosures freaks were penned : pigs, sheep and ducks on which the superstitious could detect the rudiments of a human foot : proof of metempsychosis.

The central temple, a sumptuous hall, was crowded with statues, at least five hundred, wooden, stone and metal, covered with gilt and dominated by the three towering Precious Ones, different incarnations of Buddha. Veneration was being paid only by smoking lamps and cloudy thuribles. On the walls were depicted scenes from the Buddhist hell, more gruesome than any German painting of the Christian judgment. Some of the damned were being roasted alive, others fried in boiling oil, some sawn in half, others lacerated by dogs; yet a fifth group were undergoing a transmigration of soul according to the nature of their crimes, the cruel into tigers, the lecherous into swine. To each crime its punishment, and to each an inscription stating the means to forgiveness : whoever called upon one or other of the idols a thousand thousand times, would be pardoned for that particular offence.

As they left the temple, the prior turned to Ricci. "Naturally you will occupy a position of authority among us. We have heard of your ascetic life and were wondering, my colleagues and I, whether you would feel obliged to impose your own stricter discipline?"

Ricci detected anxiety behind the casually worded question. Repressing a smile, he asked, "You believe I have been appointed to reform the monastery?"

"Why else should you come?"

When Ricci explained that, far from wishing to stay, he was seeking a pretext for leaving, the prior dropped his strained manner and offered to help him obtain land in Shiuchow. Almeida, it was decided, should sail up to the town, while Ricci travelled there on horseback next morning.

That night the monks gave Ricci a farewell feast, after which he slept in the guest room reserved for potentates. Next morning he was taken up a winding staircase to a niche in the temple wall. Here the body of Lu was preserved : a shrunken mummy covered with varnish, surrounded by ninety-eight lamps. Ricci noticed that the prior and other monks genuflected as though to a god and that they were astonished at his refusal to kneel.

Ricci, accompanied by the prior, arrived in Shiuchow at noon. Received in audience by the third collateral, he explained why he could not reside at Nanhoa. First, it was far from the city and, therefore, from the mandarins and graduates with whom he wished to associate. Moreover, it would be imprudent, even dangerous, for foreigners to live among cut-throats.

When the prior, too, had pointed to other inconveniences, the third collateral finally offered to let the Westerners live in Shiuchow. Ricci accepted eagerly. Since they had found welcome here, there would be no advantage in visiting Namyung, five days' journey away to the north-east.

That afternoon, when Almeida arrived, the third collateral presented the newcomers to the chief mandarins. They proved far friendlier than at Shiuhing : here, further north, people seemed less afraid and suspicious of foreigners. While a suitable site was being sought, the missionaries were sent to live in the local pagoda, which, here as in every town, offered unfurnished lodging to travellers as a means of supporting the bonzes. The group of buildings—the Small Buddhist Temple of the Beautiful Pagoda—lay near an anchorage on the western of two rivers which almost encircled old Shiuchow. The town, however, which counted twice the population of Shiuhing, had spilled on to the outer banks on the western side, and a bridge of sixty boats, bound by heavy chains, linked old Shiuchow to the western suburb.

Unloading their belongings from the sampan, they installed themselves in their room at the pagoda. They replaced the idols with their own paintings and set up an altar for daily Mass. Directly in front of the pagoda, close to the river, lay a field which Ricci judged an ideal site. Making enquiries, he discovered no drawback and next day suggested it to the acting governor. The mandarin was delighted because the field formed part of the pagoda's estate and no group were easier to coerce than the bonzes. He wrote to the viceroy asking permission to assign the land and suggested to Ricci that, in order to pacify the owners, he should purchase the field with his own money. Ricci was obliged to deal with agents who, in league with the bonzes, demanded eighty taels for property worth no more than eight. Ricci refused to pay their price.

Six weeks passed, but no word arrived from the viceroy. Ricci began to doubt whether, having had his way with the sixty taels, Liu would fulfil his promise. They continued to live in the cramped room of the pagoda, ill-treated by the bonzes who hoped to drive them away by unkindness. Once again, as in the first months at Shiuhing, they and their belongings became the object of curiosity: all day long visitors of every class streamed in to gaze at their uncouth faces, to listen to their barbarian tongue (as though they were performing gibbons), to inspect their books and pictures, their astrolabes and globes. As the plum trees turned yellow, the weather grew more miasmal. Many of the bonzes fell ill and Ricci learned to his consternation that every autumn at least a quarter of the population suffered from malaria. The mortality rate was high; visitors, it was pointed out with relish, unaccustomed to the climate, were especially susceptible.

Mist laid low the mountains, leaves fell into stagnant water, the death of all creation seemed near. In the first phases of the Chrysanthemum Moon Almeida, never very strong and weakened by severe, self-imposed penances, caught the disease. For six days he lay gravely ill in the pagoda, without servants, medicine or proper bedding. At first Ricci did not summon help, knowing that the disease must take its course, and having little faith in Chinese doctors. On his arrival in Macao he had made a point of discovering how local medicines differed from those he had watched his father dispense. Chinese *materia medica* comprised herbs, roots, barks, twigs, leaves, flowers, seeds, grasses and fruits, an immense variety ranging from coriander seed and betel-nut husks to galangal and apricot kernels. Herbal books were better and more complete than

Dioscorides, the standard European work. All treatment was gentle : disease had to be wheedled away, not openly attacked with a knife. Blood was never let, a tooth never extracted by force. Ricci's esteem for Chinese pharmacy did not extend to its practitioners. Men of intelligence devoted themselves to moral philosophy, the prerequisite for government posts, with the result that sciences were neglected. A few mandarins dabbled, but in general only the stupid and unambitious practised the art of healing : picking up scraps of knowledge from old women and older books, for schools of medicine were unknown.

Almeida grew weaker and Ricci decided as a last resort to summon the most reputable doctor in town. He turned out to be a peasant with airs. On his arrival he felt the sick man's pulse : three in each wrist, from the beat of which he could determine the organ requiring treatment. Chinese doctors believed the human body was built up, like all the universe, from Yin and Yang; etymologically, dark, coiling clouds and bright sunshine. Excessive Yang evoked heat; excessive Yin cold. In addition, the five constituent parts of the body— muscles, blood, flesh, skin and hair, bones—corresponded to the five elements, wood, fire, earth, metal and water, which in turn produced symptoms of wind, heat, moisture, dryness and cold. After examining Almeida, the doctor pointed out that his fever sprang from an irregularity of the blood : he must be given liquids containing herbs with the property of quenching flame. Bleakly Ricci waited while he set the groaning man's disease in its cosmic context, prescribed according to magical analogies, and administered a rare and expensive electuary. When the doctor left, Ricci knelt beside his friend and put his trust in other formulae.

Two days after Almeida's illness passed its crisis, Ricci himself began to feel unsteady. Since his arrival at Macao he had enjoyed perfect health. Physically no less than mentally he had become acclimatised to China, rejoicing in its hot summers and mild winters after the exhausting humidity of southen India, and finding adequate the staple diet of rice and pork. But against the mosquitoes of Shiuchow even a robust constitution proved no defence : he had malaria. Almeida was still too ill to look after him. He lay alone, sweating and shivering, more than ever conscious of solitude and impuissance. Every third day the fever would break within him like torrential monsoon rain, flooding his consciousness, sweeping away the parapets of prayer, the dykes of resolution, annihilating him by fire and water. He believed he would die, and in the interstices of delirium pleaded he might be spared until the new house had been founded—if it were destined to be founded at all—and some visible form given to the mission. As though in answer, five days after he was struck down he received a visit from the acting governor. The viceroy had written at last, granting licence to build and, still better, making the field theirs without payment. More effectively than any herbal prescription, this news helped him to health. He forced his body to respond to the best opportunity he had ever been offered. Presently spirit and will had their way. By the end of the month he and Almeida had recovered sufficiently to walk down to the field and mark out the site of their new house and chapel.

From their lodgings among the Bodhisattvas, a galaxy of star gods and the deities of thunder and lightning, every day they set out, under the malevolent gaze of their neighbours, to clear the ground, to saw and nail together larchwood planks. At the pace of the surrounding crops the house steadily rose and beside it the second church of the Middle Kingdom, different from any that had ever been built, unrecognisable for what it was. To avoid charges of constructing a Portuguese fortress and to illustrate that his religion was not tied to western forms, Ricci had chosen to build in Chinese style.

CHAPTER FIVE

Bonze into Graduate

THE following autumn, as soon as building was finished, Ricci and Almeida set up house, together with two young Chinese from Macao whom Valignano had attached to the mission as candidates for entry into the Society. They were called Sebastian Fernandez and Francis Martinez, for converts in the enclave were given not only a Christian name but also a Portuguese surname. The site of their home was more isolated than at Shiuhing and overlooked a river much less wide and crowded with boats, yet its view of paddy-fields and mountains, the nearby pagoda and tower, was reminiscent of the southern town. The exterior of house and church (secular and ecclesiastical architecture did not differ in form) was indistinguishable from neighbouring buildings—wooden pillared structures with glazed tile roofs like canopies of battle tents—the interior more spacious than at Shiuhing.

Here they began to repay the hospitality of the past year, especially towards a graduate named Ch'ü T'ai-su. On the death of his father, poet, historian and one of China's most distinguished Academicians, Ch'ü, a young man of brilliant promise, turned from Confucius to alchemy. He not only squandered his inheritance but fell into debt and was obliged, with his young wife, to trek round the country in search of wealthy friends, on whose behalf he used his winning manner to influence magistrates. The previous year, hearing that the foreign bonzes possessed an uncanny knowledge of alchemy, he had profited from a visit to the viceroy to meet Ricci. They had become friends and, when the missionaries moved to Shiuchow, Ch'ü, who meanwhile had settled in Namyung, chose Ricci as his master : a great honour, for Ch'ü was three years his senior. The ceremony followed a precise protocol. While the master sat at the north end of his room, the disciple entered from the south, prostrated himself four times in deep humility and offered a present. Next day at a public dinner the disciple announced to his friends that he had chosen a master. Even if he received instruction for only one day, during the rest of his life he must address his teacher as master, sit beside him in company and acknowledge his superiority. Ricci was well content with the arrangement, for through Ch'ü he came to know the local mandarins.

Ricci had soon discovered that the young graduate was intent on learning only one thing: how to change cinnabar into silver. However, as their lessons progressed, he was able to interest his pupil in other more marvellous if less rewarding subjects. He began to teach Ch'ü mathematics, a subject which, like medicine, the Chinese had no incentive to learn and which had remained at a rudimentary stage. In particular, Chinese arithmetic, conditioned by the abacus, was clumsy and slow. If a mistake were made, since previous calculations were effaced, the whole reckoning had to be started again. Ricci, who had been surprised to find that China had always used a decimal system, showed that by means of written numbers, for which ideograms already existed, more complicated problems could be solved. He then expounded the first book of Euclid, inventing Chinese terms for each stage of the argument from the definition of a point to the theorem of Pythagoras. Logical deduction from definitions and axioms revealed a new world to Ch'ü, for Chinese geometry had not advanced beyond practical mensuration.

Ricci enjoyed imparting, for the first time, knowledge which had been handed down by the Arabs, Greeks and Egyptians, opening horizons to the Chinese, who believed that because the good life had been discovered their education need never change, and had made thought itself stereotyped by an unalterable literature. He took pleasure in weaning Ch'ü from the magical properties of infinite and infinitesimal and reducing the world to the measure of man. Teaching, too, proved a means of self-defence, preventing Oriental methodology from becoming habitual.

Every day during the mathematics lesson Ricci found an

opportunity of mentioning Christianity. Ch'ü listened atten-
tively but made no comment. One day he brought a notebook
in which he had listed his principal doubts so that Ricci might
reply to them, point by point, as he did in the field of science.
As he scanned the list, Ricci smiled. Instead of the usual
difficulties—surely the idols will be cross if we desert them;
why may we not continue to cast lots and observe lucky
and unlucky days?—his pupil had raised fundamental questions, ranging from proofs of the existence of God to the
problem of evil. Ch'ü, in his turn, was no less surprised at
receiving answers which seemed to him to resolve the problems
he had believed insoluble.

Convinced of the truth of Christianity, he wanted to be
baptised, but one difficulty held him back. His first wife had
died and he was living with a concubine of low birth, whom
he refused to take as his legitimate and only wife. He had no
male descendant, a very great dishonour, and if the concubine
could not give him a son he would be obliged by the most
hallowed of Chinese traditions to take others until a child was
born to carry on his name and venerate his memory when he
died. Ricci was deeply disappointed. He had come to the conclusion that, given the size of China and the small number
of missionaries, he must win the graduate class, intelligent
enough fully to appreciate Christianity and with sufficient
influence to make it popular. In Ch'ü he had found a typical
graduate, convinced him of the truth of Christianity, yet failed
to overcome the ingrained belief, fostered by Confucianism,
that a man's paramount duty was to beget a son. Social tradition had proved an even more formidable obstacle than atheism
and the lack of common philosophical principles.

In their second autumn at Shiuchow, Almeida again fell
victim to malaria. After a week's fever, on October 16th it
became clear that he could not long survive. Ricci heard his
confession and sat at his bedside, watching the flushed frail
body, like one of those coloured kites their neighbours loved to
fly, sink and rise and sink in a failing breeze. Almeida, who
had a fervent devotion to the Blessed Sacrament, was possessed
by a single thought—to receive viaticum before he died. Since

for reasons of prudence the Blessed Eucharist was not reserved, it would be necessary to wait until Ricci could say Mass. Every few minutes, while an eighth corner of the night was ploughed, he enquired the time. " Remember, Father," he said, " If I'm unconscious by morning, I may still receive viaticum, because I ask for it now with my wits about me." Ricci reassured him. At half-past two Almeida said, " You can begin Mass, Father. As long as you finish after sunrise, you fulfil Canon Law." But long before dawn, at three o'clock, he felt his fluttering body plunge. He motioned that he wished to kneel before the crucifix. Ricci helped him to the ground, where, lacking the strength to balance, he fell forward and died. To the last moment his soul had outrun his body. Gently Ricci took the light figure in his arms and laid it on the bed. At dawn he vested in black and, without consecrating a fourth host, celebrated Requiem Mass.

For the second time Ricci suffered the loss of his only European colleague but he kept his grief to himself. His friends were shocked that he did not show open signs of desolation or wear mourning. They did not fully understand his explanation that in entering religion he and the catechists had already become dead to the world and, so that no offence should be given, during the few days when friends came to view the body, Ricci dressed his servants in white, symbol of pale cheeks, colour of mourning. One of Almeida's acquaintances presented a coffin of cedar wood, three inches thick, twice as large as those in Europe, beautifully carved and varnished mirror-smooth. Burial presented a problem. Ricci did not want to lay Almeida in the church, for the Chinese would have considered the building defiled, nor to bury him with the dead of Shiuchow in unconsecrated ground up on the mountain-side. Until he reached a decision, once again conforming to local custom, he retained the coffin in the house. The Chinese dead were kept at home in varnished coffins, the chinks sealed with bitumen, for as long as two or three years. Filial piety demanded the physical presence of the dead person for most if not all the period of mourning. This allowed time, also, to choose a grave in touch with favourable influences and currents, with invisible winds and streams: "a place on the terrace of night."

During 1591 Ricci was occupied in proselytising among Ch'ü's friends and in teaching Almeida's successor, a young Italian, the four most important of the nine Chinese classics: the *Great Learning*, which laid down man's duty to seek perfection, know and will the good, correct his passions, order his family life aright and so contribute to national peace; the *Doctrine of the Mean*, which defined the principle of righteousness as "nothing too much," counterpart of cosmic order; the *Cencius,* apophthegms of one of the Master's disciples; and the *Analects*, ethical phrases of Confucius, the first of which—" Is it not pleasant to learn with constant perseverance and application?"—in counterpoint with filial piety made up the anthem of Chinese civilisation: conformity with the past. From these texts he must be able to quote as freely as a Roman gentleman from Virgil and Horace. Since they formed the basis of the state examinations, they would also give him insight into the graduate mind.

If most of Ricci's time was spent studying and teaching, there were also compensating hours of recreation and enjoyment. He relished his meals, preferring rice, bamboo shoots and local rice-wine—served slightly heated—to the bread, beef and grape vintages of Europe. Kwangtung rivers abounded with excellent fish, many varieties of which he had never tasted before. He appreciated the view across to the mountains and a climate which pleached the months in an unbroken garland. He enjoyed occasional open-air plays performed by a travelling troupe, the feast of lanterns when the whole town seemed to be on fire, the dragon-boat races along the nearby river. He learned Chinese chess, both the usual form and a more complicated game, in which 278 pieces were moved on a board of 361 positions. He grew to love blue and white porcelain, and to laugh at the antique bronze vases prized by rich graduates only when they were covered with authenticating rust. But his greatest joy came from Europe in the form of annual letters, two or three years old, from friends in another world which did not reject. He delighted, too, in the company of the Chinese

Brothers, their enthusiasm such a pleasant change from the studied gravity of their Confucian counterparts who tried to be old before their time, and in the fervour of his few converts.

Ricci found difficulty in restraining the younger ones from their favourite occupation, entering pagodas and breaking hands and legs off the statues. Once, in defiance of his strict prohibition, a newly baptised houseboy stole an idol and brought it back secretly to the mission house. He waited till late at night, then cast it into the kitchen fire to burn in hell. One of the Brothers, making a last round before going to bed, detected a strange smell of perfumed wood and discovered the idol in the grate, half-consumed. Next day he told Ricci about the incident, adding that he had no doubt who the culprit was. What should he do, dismiss the boy or give him a severe reprimand? Ricci burst out laughing and replied that, for once, such zeal should be overlooked.

The following year, 1592, marked the tenth anniversary of Ricci's disembarkation at Macao, the third since his arrival in Shiuchow. China counted less than a hundred Christians; Shiuchow only fifteen. In comparison with other missions, diverse as Brazil, the Philippines, Japan, he could not profess to be sowing : he was still breaking arid ground.

At times it seemed doubtful whether even that claim was justified. During the course of 1592 he had occasion to return to Shiuhing for a few days. Although some of the Christian community had occasionally visited Shiuchow or Macao to consult a priest and strengthen their faith, most had given up their good practices. Parodies had begun to creep in. Ricci walked down to the Pagoda of the Flower of Saints. Its garden which had once boasted tree peonies and azaleas, was overgrown with weeds. He pushed the creaking door and accustomed his eyes to the dim light. The myriad eyes of gleaming gilt idols gazed back at him. In the centre a drum, wooden fish and tongueless bell hung before the Buddha to come, his belly exposed to view, on his thin lips the shadow of a smile. After only three years rank reversion everywhere.

Ricci baptised five children born in his absence but foresaw that, without the support of educated men, the community would soon revert to type.

Back in Shiuchow, an attack on the mission house by a gang of drunken gamesters, during which Ricci was wounded on the hand by a hatchet blow, shattered the last remnants of complacency. Present methods were proving ineffective and must be revised. Anxiously Ricci began to reconsider first principles, the most important being the adoption of the role of bonzes. He broached this matter to Ch'ü, who put into words Ricci's own experience : the mandarins considered bonzes the scum of the earth and to consort with them put immense demands on their natural pride. As bonzes they could never acquire sufficient respect to prevent ever-recurring malicious charges and open attack. Thirdly, unable to treat with the mandarins as equals, it was exceedingly difficult to win that favour which was the condition of their remaining in China. When the decision had first been taken, it was believed that bonzes enjoyed as high a status as in Japan, where they were venerated almost like Christian priests in Europe. Experience had not only proved this assumption false but seemed to invalidate the whole equation. Most bonzes, whether Taoist or Buddhist, were idolaters and magicians, noted for their vices, uneducated and recruited largely from ne'er-do-wells. When the word " foreigner " was linked with these associations, abuse and hostility were naturally aroused.

Were there alternatives? Throw off their grey habit and be themselves, with long hair, beard and soutane? Even if such a course were not forbidden by Chinese law, experience had proved that it would be self-defeating. First, by asserting European habits they would increase the sense of challenge, dare to suggest that other kingdoms existed as equals, appear to mock ingrained national pride, and associate themselves in Chinese minds with the hated Portuguese who had already conquered Malacca and parts of India. Secondly, they would be presenting themselves under an incomprehensible form. Bonzes, merchants, ambassadors, farmers, artisans, the three ranks of graduates, mandarins—these were the accepted divisions of

man; to be otherwise would be to elude classification and therefore integration in the Chinese pattern of life. Not only they
but their religion would remain exotic, a local cult transplanted,
which could never thrive.

Another more daring plan had occurred to Ricci. In birth,
education, manners and intelligence he and his companions
most resembled the graduate class. Moreover, the doctrine of
Confucius, which they professed, was in its original form
monotheistic, therefore more akin to Christianity than the
idolatrous form of Buddhism practised by the bonzes. Would
he not be nearer the truth in equating himself to the graduate
class? The struggle merely to exist in the Middle Kingdom
would then be far less difficult, and the way to Peking, which
led through the hierarchy of mandarins, open at last.

But cogent reasons opposed such a change. First, Valignano
had given unqualified approval to Ruggieri's original assumption of Buddhist dress, and it was not for him to question the
decision of a superior with far greater missionary experience.
Secondly, if he were to criticise methods, he would in some
degree be relieving himself from blame for unprecedentedly
slow progress. Thirdly, the pattern of ten years seemed to show
that they were meant to triumph through humiliation and outrage, not through the authority and respect they would command as members of the graduate class. This remained his
greatest doubt : that impatience with suffering secretly prompted the plan.

While considering this problem and waiting for advice from
Valignano, Ricci brought to completion a work on which he
had been engaged since 1591 : the translation into Latin of the
four classical books he used as a teaching manual. Although
he was now familiar with five thousand out of a total of fifty
thousand ideograms—the most to which even a Chinese
scholar could pretend—the work presented formidable difficulties. Equivalents had to be found for numerous concepts, some
unknown to the European mind, others overlapping or narrower than the obvious Latin counterparts. The Chinese
Master himself had emphasised the importance of naming
things correctly as a prerequisite of true thinking. Often Ricci

had to master etymology. The structure of the character *Hsiao* showed an old man seated on the shoulders of a younger. Thus filial piety, with its notion of the son subjected to the father, was something more than *pietas*, and provided a valuable clue to a society which for two millennia had not changed. Obscure gnomic utterances, depending for their force on a knowledge of history and social life, had to be unravelled and presented in intelligible form. Proper names had to be phoneticised for the first time (Ricci now originated the Western rendering of the Chinese K'ung Fu-tzu—repectable master Kung—transliterating it in Latin as Confucius). Finally, the stiff style of the uninflected original had to be moulded into plastic Ciceronian Latin. This first translation of Chinese books into a European tongue remained in manuscript as a textbook for his colleagues.

Detailed study of the Classics prepared the way for Ricci's next work. Valignano had ordered him to compose a new catechism to take the place of Ruggieri's which, although widely read in Japan and several times reprinted, was not only incomplete in its apologetic and refutation of idolatry, but heavy and unattractive in style. Appeal had been made to concepts which the Chinese could not accept as self-evident. Ricci decided to make his catechism lead on naturally from the first principles of the Classics, just as Christian apologetic in Europe utilised Plato and Aristotle. Christianity must justify its claim to be not a local superstition, but a universal religion based firmly on natural wisdom.

Meanwhile Lazzaro Cattaneo, a Ligurian of thirty-four, had been appointed Ricci's colleague in Shiuchow. Arriving in Macao in 1593, after studying the problems presented by the Chinese mission, Cattaneo had come to the same conclusion as Ricci. He had proposed the change in dress to Valignano who, in the light of Ricci's comments and slow progress at Shiuchow, now sent orders that, as soon as convenient, the missionaries were to dress like graduates, in purple silk with a blue border, and with a square black hat. Valignano added that he took responsibility for the changes, of which he would inform both the Pope and the General. After the loss of his second colleague Ricci had asked for permission to travel north to found a new house : Shiuchow had proved a death-trap and besides, since the latest attack, people were badly disposed and seemed certain to remain so. To this plan Valignano gave unqualified approval. Ricci received these orders with the suppressed excitement he had felt on his first journey up the Western River. At forty-two it was less easy to adopt the totally different role entailed by a change of costume and scene. Against this he pitted the hope that, with the Emperor present, he might be granted a speaking part.

Not until the following spring was it possible to effect the transformation. A high official called Shih Hsing, Vice-President at the Ministry of War, had been summoned to Peking from his home near Shiuhing. Three years before a Japanese army of three hundred thousand men had invaded Korea, for the first time using firearms against a foreign enemy. Korea, the founder of whose ruling dynasty had been invested by the first Ming Emperor, was a tributary Kingdom of China. Although Chinese troops had been sent to help the invaded country, the Japanese were advancing rapidly and had captured Seoul. In alarm, the Emperor had now placed Shih in command of a new army of eighty thousand men, for civil mandarins directed the war, with authority over the highest generals. On his way through Shiuchow Shih sent an officer with a present to the missionaries, asking one of them to visit his barge. Though only a few steps distant, he sent a beautifully caparisoned horse for his guest. Ricci decided it would be more courteous if both he and Cattaneo went. They were still dressed in ash grey cloaks, for they had decided to adopt graduate robes elsewhere than at Shiuchow.

Ricci was astonished and excited by the Minister's barge, an immense ironwood vessel, carved and varnished with gold, the apartments hung with silk and costly paintings. Shih, a distinguished man of middle age, a crane embroidered on his dress and a jade girdle-clasp, the insignia of highest mandarin rank, received them with every politeness, mentioning that a magistrate of the town had sung their praises. He asked about their country and its customs ; what gods they adored and how they worshipped them. Only after these formalities did he come to the point.

"I have a son of twenty-two, who recently sat for his first examination. He failed and since then has been a prey to grief and shame. He has worried himself ill. I love the boy and have tried every remedy. Now I am taking him with me to Peking to see a famous doctor. I wonder whether you, with your prayers, can help him back to health."

Ricci made a rapid decision.

"Your Excellency, I understand, is staying in Shiuchow only a few hours. In that time I can do nothing, but if I remain with your son some days I believe that the Lord of Heaven in His mercy may grant him peace of mind. If your Excellency is willing I should like to accompany him. On the journey we can discuss the best means of helping your son."

The Minister, delighted at this proposal, ordered the governor of Shiuchow to issue the necessary passport. They agreed that Shih should travel ahead while Ricci, when his baggage and documents were ready, was to join him at Nanan, the first town of Kiangsi province.

On the following day, April the eighteenth, Ricci set out with two servants and two young Chinese catechists, John Barradas and Dominic Fernandez, sons of leading citizens of Macao who had come to live with the missionaries on probation before being admitted to the Society.

At Nanan they overtook Shih, who provided them with one of his boats. In return, Ricci presented the Minister with a sand clock and two finely worked handkerchiefs. During the journey Ricci was often summoned to his host's boat to describe the customs and beliefs of Europe, especially when, on their passage through a town, mandarins came on board to pay their respects. So numerous were these visits that Ricci was given no time to speak to his host's melancholy son. Shih kept postponing their interview, and seemed to have become more interested in showing off the foreigner's ability to quote appositely page after page of the Classics.

Ricci was very impressed by the interior of Shih's great boat, which he now had leisure to explore. He walked through apartments holding twelve tables and as many chairs, admiring well-appointed kitchens with capacious pantries, and high-ceilinged cabins which put those of the *Sao Luiz* to shame. Europe could boast nothing like this floating palace. It was a pity having no colleague to share his enthusiasm, but he would describe the vessel when he wrote home in the late summer.

By day trumpets and drums, by night lanterns at the mast-head, signalled a Minister's barge, with right of way through the traffic of sampans. Along the route were stationed round-shouldered but muscular coolies. Whenever the wind fell, the fleet of boats was tracked by these gangs, retained at govern-ment expense. A tracking rope was fixed near the top of the principal mast and joined to another attached to the prow. To this main rope were fastened cords formed into loops, one of which each tracker, throwing it over his head, placed round his breast, often protected by a piece of wood. The men, who united their steps in song, were driven forward by the sting of a lash. A hundred straining trackers were required to haul the heavy state barge at the pace imparted by a breeze.

A few hours out of Kanchow the river, receiving a tributary, grew very wide and dangerous. For twenty miles or so rocks rose up in mid-stream; from the principal hazards the whole stretch took the name of Eighteen Rapids. As they approached the crew of the rented boat became nervous. They told Ricci that many shipwrecks occurred in those waters and that unless the pilot was very skilful, their boat might well end up on the rocks. Ricci noticed that before traversing the rapids Shih entered a pagoda on the river bank to beseech the idols for a safe passage, and concluded that in time of stress even the most rational Confucian acknowledged the supernatural. On Ricci's boat cruder safeguards were taken. The master, holding in his hands a screeching cock and surrounded by his crew, came for-ward to the forecastle. Wringing the victim's neck, the master cut off the head and threw it into the river. He consecrated the boat with the blood spurting from the body by sprinkling it upon the deck, the masts, the anchor and the doors of the cabins, and stuck upon them a few of the bird's feathers.

Several bowls of meat were then ranged in a line across the deck. The brazen drum was beaten, lighted tapers held towards heaven; papers, covered with tin or silver leaf, burned and crackers fired off in great abundance. The captain made libations to the river by emptying into it from the prow various cups of liquids, last of all throwing in a bowl of salt. The crew then fed on the meat and with less trepidation launched out into the current.

Ricci watched Shih's barge successfuly negotiate the first two rapids. The next barge, carrying his three wives, other women, relations and children, also shot the first rapid and headed for the second, " the rapid of the celestial column." As his own boat approached, Ricci understood the sailors' alarm. For almost its whole width the river bed fell steeply away as though below a mill-wheel in a churning welter of foam and boulders. The pilot steered close to the bank, where water ran slower and submerged rocks were more easily detected. As they slipped safely through, disaster overtook the boat in front. A sudden eddy dashed her against mid-stream rocks : in an instant her hull was stove in and she began to sink. The river being comparatively shallow, her high forecastle was not at once submerged. On to the tilted deck clambered crew, children and tiny-footed ladies, some with babies in their arms, screaming, not for help, which none expected, but in terror.

The sailors on Ricci's boat became panic-stricken, for one shipwreck augured a second. Someone remembered an irregularity in the libation ; others besought the captain to turn back. None gave a thought to the women perched on the bow, in danger any moment of heeling over. In the general indecision Ricci took command. Rushing to the stern, he directed the pilot to head for the shipwrecked barge and to bring his boat about as close as possible. The pilot protested that in such seething water the manœuvre was impossible, but Ricci made him attempt it. Her hull grinding against the rocks, tossed this way and that, the boat held her course to within a few yards of the wreck. A rope was thrown and the rescuing boat drew alongside. At once the terrified crew leapt on board, while Ricci crossed and helped the white-faced shrieking ladies and children to safety. The boat cast off and made for deep water.

Shih, anxious because the second barge did not follow but unaware of the shipwreck, had anchored a mile ahead. When Ricci's boat drew alongside, the great mandarin threw aside all dignity of office. What had happened to the other barge? Where were his wives and children? A gangplank was thrown across and the Minister lurched aboard the rescuing boat. Ricci bowed and led him into the cabin where his three silk-clad wives, still sobbing, knelt down before their master.

Learning the full story, Shih thanked Ricci profusely and, rarest thing of all, with emotion. Since it would have been an intolerable breach of etiquette for him and his party to remain with the women, Ricci offered to travel in the wherry which acted as forerunner, indicating the route across the rapids. Shih agreed, promising to make one of his other boats ready for Ricci, and meanwhile sent back a messenger to summon another barge for his family. This arrived the same afternoon, but since it would have been improper for the ladies to show themselves, they were kept on the rescuing boat until nightfall. At the same time Ricci, with John Barradas, transferred to one of the official cargo boats.

Next morning a strong wind sprang up. The pilot of the boat in which Ricci was travelling ordered sail taken in, but in the fast-running current his command proved unfeasible. A few minutes later a sudden gust directly abeam capsized the boat, as well as another unwieldy cargo vessel directly behind. Ricci, who had been on deck with Barradas, was thrown wide into the rapids. Recovering from the first shock, he struggled to the surface, but the swirling waters again and again forced him under, flinging his feet against a sandy bed which yielded no support, thrashing a mill-race through his throat and lungs. As he thrust out for leverage, a rope swept against him. Finding it taut he hauled himself up to regain his breath. It proved to be part of the ship's rigging, still attached to the wreck. Presently he managed to grasp a spar wedged between rocks, then a wooden writing-desk swept out of the cabin. A sailor gave him a hand to regain the stern of the boat which, like the forecastle the previous day, jutted above the surface. The crew, who had reached safety, clung there jibbering, but of John Barradas there was nothing to be seen. Fearing he had been pinioned, Ricci looped a rope under his shoulders and, attaching the end to the upper part of the stern, again entered the plunging river. Now and again he stood in his depth; for the most part he was obliged to grasp the hull with one hand and edge his way along the length of the boat, looking and feeling for his friend. Another barge anchored alongside and for most of that day joined in the search. But they found not a trace of Barradas, alive or dead. The Minister, in condolence, sent Ricci a present of money to burn incense for the dead youth, a token all the more generous since most of his possessions had foundered with the other capsized ship.

The loss of his companion, when everyone else from the three wrecks, even children in arms, had been saved, struck Ricci, half dead with exhaustion, as a sign. Providence appeared to have intervened to check a pointless journey. All that evening he wondered what to do. Only when Dominic Fernandez rejoined him and instead of lamenting Barradas's loss gave thanks for his master's escape, was the balance righted. He had been ordered to found another house : nothing but his own death must turn him back. He sent word to the Minister that he intended to continue the journey.

They sailed into calmer water. At each town Ricci took bearings with a sextant and entered them for future maps. Along the route at set points provisions were provided at government expense for the whole fleet : fresh fish and meat, fruit and vegetables packed in ice, muddy local wine and clear drinking water. At the large town of Kian another high wind sprang up by night and scattered the convoy, again almost capsizing several boats. Interpreting the repeated winds as a sinister omen Shih decided to transfer to sedan chairs. He wanted to send his guest back to Shiuchow, explaining that the overland journey which only he and his family could undertake at government expense would be beyond Ricci's means. In fact, Ricci discovered, he was becoming frightened at the prospect of introducing a foreigner to Peking in time of war. While horses and litters were being obtained for the overland journey, Ricci, who had already taken pains to con- ciliate the mandarin's suite, invited Shih's secretary to visit his boat and, producing a prism, showed him how to hold it up to the light.

" I want to give your master this present," he said. " But I cannot return to Shiuchow without it, having lost most of my other possessions in the wreck. I must therefore first know for certain whether your master intends to take me to Peking."

Ricci was well aware that Shih's suite had been informed of their master's plans, but, as he foresaw, the secretary, aston- ished at the iridescent jewel, informed Shih of the offer. The Minister, torn between covetousness and fear, decided to com- promise. No longer mindful of his sick son, he said he would allow Ricci to travel with his baggage by water as far as Nan- king and offered to provide a passport.

In importance the southern capital almost equalled Peking, but it was not the Emperor's city. Ricci stifled his disappoint- ment and accepted the offer with a good grace, presenting Shih with the prism. It so exceeded his secretary's description that at first the Minister refused to accept a gift worth, so he claimed, at least two hundred taels. In the end Ricci had to beg him to keep it.

They parted on friendly terms, the Minister, his wives and children in thirteen sedans, protected by horsemen; while Ricci, Dominic Fernandez and his servants proceeded by water, across the eighty-mile extent of Lake Poyang, into the Sky Blue River, the Yangtze, largest of three great basins draining the mountains of China. As they sailed into Nanking province, the country became alluvial and flat as a worn coin, while space assumed a new form. By night, the unpropped sky bent down by the weight of its clustered fruit, so that it seemed China had been endowed with more and brighter stars than any other land. By day, as far as the eye could see, thousands upon thou- sands of boats crowded the river, in places two or three miles wide, their matted sails silhouetted against what seemed the edge of the world. Each of the numerous islands boasted a shrine, and every few miles, among the wheat which Ricci saw for the first time since leaving Europe, stood beacon towers, used to signal important news. The sailors considered the river extremely dangerous, and at dusk, or whenever the wind rose, hastily put in to one of the tributary streams.

On the last day of May, six weeks after leaving Shiuchow, Ricci sighted the suburbs of Nanking. The city was considered by the Chinese the largest and most beautiful in the world and when he first glimpsed its massive outer wall, forty miles in circumference, overtopped by pagodas and towers, Ricci felt inclined to agree. In order to attract the least possible attention he took lodgings in a house on the outskirts. After unloading his baggage and leaving Dominic to guard it, he hired a sedan chair and began to explore the city.

The outer wall, protected by a deep moat, reared fifty feet high and extended twenty feet at the summit. Within lay estates, each mansion standing in spacious gardens, surrounded by groves and lakes. In half an hour he arrived at the second wall, eighteen miles in circumference, even more formidable than the outer rampart, crowned at every gate by long five-storeyed brick towers and guarded by primitive artillery and troops. Here began wide, regular streets, laid out at right angles, shops, houses and public buildings. Horses, sedan chairs and pedestrians forced a way through to the din of street-criers and musicians. In no other city had he seen so many towers and pagodas, nor so many bridges, for the city was brocaded with a silver thread of canals, all linked to the Yangtze which flowed along its western length. At the eastern end of Nanking proper, within the third wall, six miles in circumference and strongest of all, lay the palace, to which only imperial officials had right of access. Two centuries before, the Emperor had transferred his court to Peking, the " Capital of the North " founded by Kublai Khan, in order to withstand Tartar invasions. To avoid giving offence to Nanking, he allowed the " Capital of the South " to retain its imperial palace, privileges and ministries, which were duplicated at Peking. It was in keeping with her different logic that China should possess two capitals, the northern boasting the imperial court, the southern being the larger, older and more beautiful city, burial place, too, of past emperors.

Shortly after his arrival, Ricci decided to call on an acquaintance, fifth son of Liu, former viceroy of Shiuhing, and for the visit to vest himself as a graduate. In preparation, he had allowed his hair to grow almost to his shoulders, as the Chinese wore it, and his beard fell well below his breast, thicker and longer than the few straggling hairs even the highest mandarin could boast.

He lifted the precious garment from his baggage. After his coarse grey rags, the well-cut silk felt smooth and cold as the manner he must now assume. Shuffling off in a single action the despairs of a decade, he now put on the ankle-long silk robe with loose, flowing sleeves in the Venetian style, which all graduates wore on formal visits : purple, with a pale blue border two inches wide at the neck, lined and with a belt of the same colour : almost the red and blue of his coat of arms, folding the wide ends across his breast and tying them at the side with long bows. No less than for the larvae on their mulberry leaf, the silk in which his body was now enclosed would be the means and condition of metamorphosis. As he picked up the high square black hat which went with the dress, he smiled, for it resembled nothing so much as a bishop's mitre. A fan and softly embroidered silk slippers, so impracticable as to be a symbol of leisure, completed his attire.

In two details he refused to conform. He would not spend half an hour every morning combing his hair, and he would not let his finger-nails grow. Some mandarins aspired to nails like razor-shells, six inches long, which they protected with slivers of wood or silver cases.

Ricci, knowing the value placed on suave politeness as an aid to peace of mind, had studied details of graduate etiquette. He had had his own visiting books made, twelve pages of thick white paper, six inches by four, inscribed in small characters with his name in its humblest form : Li Ma-tou. The book was carried in a red case, colour of good omen, by one of his servants, also dressed in a long fine tunic. When Ricci arrived in a sedan chair at Liu's house, a visiting book was

handed to the gateman, who carried it up to the door. Later
Liu appeared and, hiding his surprise, welcomed Ricci as an
equal. Joining his hands with the long sleeves, then raising
and lowering them several times, he repeated the formal greet-
ing : " Ch'ing ch'ing." As gravely as he could, Ricci recipro-
cated, finding it strange no longer to have to prostrate himself.
At the threshold each made way for the other, Ricci finally
leading. In the room prepared for guests Liu took a chair in
both hands, placed it in the position of honour at the north
end, made sure it was solid and removed a speck of imaginary
dust. Ricci then took another chair for his host and, placing it
opposite his own, repeated the polite gestures. They sat down
and began conversation. Ricci explained how he came to be in
Nanking, and his change of dress. Liu showed no displeasure.

" You have become one of us," he said.

" I should like to think so," replied Ricci, " but is there an
accepted category to which I can belong?"

"Certainly. You are what we call a graduate theologian, a
bachelor of arts who instead of taking office devotes himself to
the study of theology, discussing and writing about religious
matters. It is a recognised grade."

Ricci willingly accepted the new designation, noticing with
pleasure that Liu showed no sign of his former supercilious-
ness. He then explained how anxious he was to be allowed to
live in the capital. Liu promised to help, but pointed out that it
would be even more difficult to reside there than at Peking, for
the southern capital was continually suspected of revolutionary
designs, and none of the magistrates dared relax the laws, least
of all during wartime.

A servant carried in tea and set it on a lacquered table between the two purple-clad figures. He filled first Ricci's bowl,
then Liu's : in both lay crystallised fruits which, after sipping
the tea, they ate with silver wands. Hampered by flowing
sleeves, this proved as awkward as to express the simple truth
in flowery, formal phrases of polite conversation.

The visit completed, Ricci rose and bowed. At the door of
the house Liu made to accompany his guest. Ricci, according

to etiquette, insisted that his host should not cross the threshold. After an exchange of bows Ricci walked to the freestanding gateway, while Liu withdrew a few paces, reappearing at the door just as Ricci's sedan was taken up. At this moment a final " Ch'ing ch'ing " was exchanged. Presently a servant arrived at Ricci's lodging to bid him goodbye in Liu's name, a compliment which Ricci was obliged to return through one of his own servants.

Ricci was elated by this first successful call. He had evidently fulfilled the demands of urbane ceremonial, for he received amiable visits from Liu, who introduced him to important friends. After enquiries they discovered that Hsü Ta-jen, a mandarin Ricci had known at Shiuhing, now held a post in the Court of State Ceremonial. Ricci remembered him, an upright, conscientious old man, concerned with one thing only, advancement in his career. They had become good friends and Ricci had given him a sphere, a globe of the world and a sand clock.

Again he wore graduate dress and was carried in a sedan chair. Outside the mandarin's house stood a specially fine arched gateway, signifying that the owner had passed the doctoral examination. But the house itself was austere and meanly furnished : Ricci recalled that his style of living had won Hsü the reputation of being a saint.

Before the completion of formalities, Hsü Ta-jen, unable to contain his astonishment, broke out, " How do you come to be here, my dear friend?"

" Shih, the Minister of War, provided me with a passport," replied Ricci, and after explaining the circumstances added, " I am delighted to find your excellency here, and have only one desire : to remain in Nanking with you as my protector."

The well-mannered mask remained impassive, but Ricci observed Hsü's pupils dilate : how often a similar question had evoked that response.

" You have made a mistake in coming here," said Hsü. " A capital city is no place for foreigners. And your visit to me was ill-advised. I shall be accused of inviting you to Nanking."

" Surely not," said Ricci, showing his passport, " since I am authorised by a Minister."

Although Shih far exceeded him in rank, Hsü was not appeased.

" The laws forbid foreigners to enter the country," he said. " No magistrate, however powerful, has the right to set them aside. Besides, Shih is far away now; it is I who will be held responsible. Where are you staying?" he demanded.

When Ricci gave the address, the mandarin called guards and told them to arrest the landlord. Ricci protested.

" It is an offence to harbour foreigners," replied Hsü. " In order to vindicate my character which your visit here has compromised, I must enforce the law." Relenting a little, he said, " I am sorry I cannot help you. Your best plan is to leave Nanking at once." Ricci pleaded, but his charm of manner, which usually overcame anger or fear, left the austere Hsü unmoved. The old man led Ricci to the door where they took formal leave of each other.

On his return, Ricci found the house in disorder. The guards, in order to extract a bribe, had painted his case in the darkest colours. Ricci explained what had happened and tried to reassure the house owner, who that same day was led before Hsü, threatened with torture and accused of plotting revolution. The landlord defended himself by saying that Shih's servants had introduced the foreigner. Finally he was released on sole condition that next day he put Ricci on a boat sailing south. At this news, Liu and his friends proffered comfort and indignation. Those who had insisted he visit Hsü now pointed out that he had a very niggardly and timid nature, and that Ricci had been mistaken to trust him. They told him to defy Hsü by remaining in or near Nanking, and at first Ricci resolved to do so, even at the risk of imprisonment. Only the landlord's dangerous position forced him to change his mind. Reluctantly he decided to withdraw to a smaller town and from there strive for permission to return. He chose Nanchang, which Shih had recommended to him. Next morning, after only a fortnight in the capital, he boarded the public ferry and, utterly dispirited, sailed south.

Nanking, its size, the great river on which it stood and its numerous bridges : these Ricci pondered during the journey. He had by now traversed half China and extended the boundaries of the world known to Europe by thousands of square miles. Everywhere he had taken bearings, noted mountain ranges, estimated population, described climate. Yet, engaged on his discovery of China, he had been searching simultaneously for another country which eluded his grasp : Cathay. Chinese tribute-lists, histories, maps, the scholars he had questioned— all were ignorant of the country. Yet, in the West, that name was on the lips of every geographer, occupying on atlases a vague and vast position east of Persia and north-west of China, itself a mere fringe of coast around Macao. Very often he felt puzzled that so vast a country should have no relations with China. Now, with Nanking fresh in mind, memories of Polo's book came back. Polo had not so much as mentioned the name of China ; for him Cathay was the most important country of the East, and he had noted that the greatest city of Cathay contained 12,000 bridges. Ricci estimated that there were well over a thousand in Nanking, and other figures in the Venetian's book, checked by later travellers, had proved to be greatly exaggerated. Could he have been describing Nanking under another name? Polo also mentioned a great river dividing Cathay from east to west. Could that be the Yangtze, which separated the seven northern from the eight southern provinces? The different appellations were difficult to explain, but it might be that the Mongol conquerors of Polo's day had provided names from their own tongue. For the moment the identity of Polo's city with Nanking was no more than a bold hypothesis, but he decided to take every opportunity of putting it to the test.

On the eleventh day of the voyage, shortly before the ferry was due to arrive, Ricci was standing on deck, turning over events and gloomily surveying the future, when suddenly a shadowy figure approached and spoke to him.

" So you are travelling to destroy the ancient religion of this country and establish a new one?"

Ricci started. He had always taken scrupulous care to hide

from everyone his ultimate intentions. Certain that the figure
was more than human, he fell back and whispered, "Are you
God or the devil, that you know my secret?"

"I am not the devil. I am God."

Ricci fell on his knees and cried, "O Lord, since You know
my plans, why don't You help?"

Carried outside himself, the pressure of disappointed hopes,
of difficulties surmounted in vain, became too much. Tears
streamed down his cheeks. The stranger began to comfort him
and promised to help him reach both the capital cities. For a
moment Ricci had a vivid glimpse of storied gate-towers he
had never seen before. In astonishment and gratitude he
looked up to the river and a landscape of squat tea-bushes.
Had he been dreaming? No, he was certain the figure had
actually stood in front of him, and the deck was clear now.
Never had he experienced anything similar, and he was not
the sort of person to imagine things, even under stress. Always
in the crisis of deepest depression, at Shiuhing, at Canton, it
had seemed to him that Heaven intervened. Now, perhaps, he
had been given a more personal pledge for the future, like the
vision and promise of help Ignatius had been granted at Storta.
Convinced of its reality, he hurried to Dominic, no less downcast than he by events at Nanking, and described the incident.

They entered Nanchang the following day no longer discouraged by past failures but certain of supernatural help. A
travelling companion, fan-bearer of the local viceroy, recommended lodgings in the south-west corner of the town, where
next day Ricci was able to celebrate Mass. It was the feast of
Saint Peter and Saint Paul; he saw a special significance in the
fact and in the Introit: "Lord, thou hast proved me, and
known me: thou hast known my sitting down, and my rising
up." At last, perhaps, he was destined to begin a fruitful
apostolate.

CHAPTER SIX

Up the Imperial Canal

NANCHANG lay on the River Kan in perfectly flat country. Larger than either Shiuhing or Shiuchow, and the capital of the province, it was not an important trading city. Its inhabitants were parsimonious and content with little; many lived a life of fasting and abstinence in accordance with Buddhist teaching. For learning no less than piety it was famous throughout China. It possessed the right to award more degrees than any other place of its size, and boasted some of the wisest men in China. The streets of no other town contained so many triumphal arches in honour of citizens attaining high rank.

For several days after his arrival Ricci kept to his room, resting and sending out Dominic to make enquiries. He had hoped to find at least one mandarin promoted from Kwangtung province, but was disappointed. He therefore paid his first visit to a doctor who had travelled in Shih's suite, a wealthy man consulted by all the local dignitaries. Ricci was received with the courtesy due to a graduate and shortly afterwards was invited to a banquet at which the guests would include two princes of the blood royal.

Ricci learned that sons of past Emperors were given the purely honorific but hereditary title of Wang, originally signifying King but now bearing the force of Prince, and a large income from public funds, which permitted them a life of untroubled luxury, honoured but with less jurisdiction than a mandarin of the ninth rank. They were not allowed to hold office. None but the heir to the throne was allowed to live in Peking, nor to travel out of the city in which his estates lay. More than sixty thousand persons of royal blood were supported at public expense.

The Princes of Chien-an and of Lo-an, who were present

at the doctor's dinner, proved to be cultivated but effete men of middle age. Neither was related to the reigning Emperor. They began to form a favourable view of Ricci : he knew the fine points of etiquette, could quote appositely from the classics and had amusing ideas about geography and mathematics. Ricci for the first time found himself among men of the highest rank who had never known him as that scurrilous being, a bonze. Intuitively catching and adapting himself to the mood of this new company, he was able to converse and laugh as though he had always belonged. At last he felt accepted : first stage towards making the Gospel acceptable.

During the course of the five-hour banquet the doctor said that Shih, the Minister of War, had been astonished by the Far Westerner's memory. He turned to Ricci, who, as a stranger, sat in the place of honour.

" Will you be so good," he asked, " to prove to my guests that I have not exaggerated?"

Ricci demurred, saying that the gift was not uncommon. This only increased curiosity and finally Ricci agreed to a demonstration. For the Chinese, who judged by externals, his spiritual authority must be backed by worldly prestige.

The doctor sent a servant to his library for a book. Handing it to Ricci he said, " I should be most grateful if you would deign to learn one of the poems and recite it to my guests."

It took Ricci only a few minutes to read the short book, containing four or five hundred characters, a single time. Then he handed it back.

" You decline?" asked the doctor in surprisee.

" I think I have memorised it already," replied Ricci.

The guests smiled.

" Impossible," said the doctor. " You have scarcely had time to read it through."

In answer Ricci rose to his feet. His figure, tall by Chinese standards, with its thick beard and forceful nose, dominated the room. For a moment he was back at the Roman College, about to declaim Cicero; then, visualising the columns of hieroglyphics, he began to read them from his memory with as much ease as from the book. When he had recited not one but all the poems, for some time no one spoke. Then the doctor said in embarrassment, " You must have seen the book before."

" I set eyes on it for the first time to-night," replied Ricci, but he noticed that the guests remained dubious. To avoid the impression of cheating, he continued, " If you will write down a list of characters with no connexion between them—as many as five hundred—I will repeat them from memory."

The guests welcomed the idea; paper, a brush and ink were brought in, and everyone wrote down in turn the first words that came into his head. After several pages had been covered, they were handed to Ricci. He read the nonsense through a single time and gave back the papers, so that the doctor could check his recitation. Then he repeated it word for word, his authoritative voice almost lending meaning to the Chinese gibberish.

" Not a single mistake! " exclaimed the doctor.

This time the guests, convinced beyond doubt, applauded the extraordinary display, and clamoured for another. Ricci declined, but they would not be put off, and finally he proposed to repeat the nonsense backwards. Unhesitatingly he recited the formidable list of disconnected characters, from tail to head, again without fault. The other guests crowded round his table to congratulate him. How was it possible? Did all men in the West possess such a gift? Would he teach it to them—and to their sons, for it would be a great help in their examinations? When the clamour had subsided, Ricci explained how much he wished to remain in Nanchang. As the guests were hopeful of learning his mnemonic method, they approved his plan and offered to help.

Next day Ricci's fame had spread and he received countless courtesy visits. From among his acquaintances he set himself to win one of the most influential, who had already shown himself sympathetic. This was the Prince of Chien-an, who invited Ricci to his palace, received him wearing his robes and crown, and gave him tea to sip from bowls painted with the imperial dragon. In his palace Ricci for the first time saw

wealth comparable to that of the Italian nobility, for the mandarins, even the highest, were poorly paid and though they
lived comfortably in houses provided by the government, few
could afford to surround themselves with beauty. China in her
wisdom permitted only a handful of princes scattered across the
country to spend extravagantly as the surest means of rendering
them powerless. The palace was filled with antique jasper
vases, scroll paintings and lacquered furniture, which, Ricci
noticed, was as flimsily constructed as the houses. The prince
loaded his guest with magnificent gifts; unable to afford an
equivalent expense, Ricci was obliged to fashion presents with
his own hands. He offered a globe of the world, a geometric
quadrant, a sphere, various pictures and prisms, and out of
local black stone constructed a sundial, marked with the twenty-
four periods of the Chinese lunar year and appropriate moral
axioms. The prince set it up on a pedestal of pink stone in
his famous garden, where he showed it off to Ricci.

The garden had been conceived as an ideal painting, according to the principle that nature should aspire to the condition
of art. The naturally flat surface had been made undulant,
raised into hills, scooped into valleys, roughened into rocks;
distances pencilled; colours intricately matched as on a robe
of brocade; bright-leaved trees contrasted with those of a
dusky foliage wherein from time to time specially reared birds
sang like mechanical toys. Goldfish flashed perpetual sunset on
the waters of artificial lakes embossed with lotus and relieved by
well-sited islands, their banks indented. Each had its character, some smooth and level, some steep and uneven, some
gloomy with woods, others festooned with flowers. Around
dead tree-trunks fretted like fossils, blue and white peonies
clustered : between which, as though to re-dye their plumage,
paraded cranes and peacocks. Porcelain lions and tigers
defended palatial pavilions, sited to enjoy the most intricate
view and subtlest mingling of scents. Here, from bowls of
agate and porcelain, cool juices were sipped, that every sense
might be sated. It was no less a terrestrial paradise than the
actual Garden of Eden, bounded by fiery walls, supposed to lie

in furthest Asia : and as such the pleasure-ground was treated by those who enjoyed its fruits. Since they possessed Eden, heaven did not matter.

At the palace intellectual pursuits were followed with the same end. Every mood had its truth, which could be blended one against another like the features of a garden, to titillate, not to command assent, let alone engagement. The prince listened with attention to Ricci's mathematics and religion, savouring them like exotic blooms. He esteemed more than any other gift an atlas beautifully bound in Japanese paper (a Latin work from Macao with names of the continents and chief countries translated) and the manuscript of a book Ricci had composed during his stay in Nanchang on the subject of friendship. Ricci prized nothing in life so much, seeking and making friends spontaneously. Time and again he had been hurt when his overtures had foundered on the rock of xenophobia. By writing such a work he fulfilled his own affectionate nature and hoped to dispel one of the chief obstacles to missionary progress.

The book took the form of a dialogue, the prince asking Ricci what Westerners thought of friendship, and Ricci replying with all that he could remember from European philosophers and saints. Entitled *A Treatise on Friendship*, the main body of the work consisted of seventy-six sentences, short and to the point, like the axioms of Confucius. It was written on alternate pages in Chinese and in a transliteration from the Italian original, so that the reader could enunciate for himself the curious barbarian language. Its success surprised Ricci, the simplest statements, truisms in Europe, being hailed as profoundly original discoveries. The manuscript aroused widespread interest and copies were transcribed by several of the prince's entourage.

Through the late summer and autumn Ricci continued to pay and receive visits, quite accustomed now to his plum-coloured silk robes and mitred hat, to the new respect and elaborate politeness. His grey habit had been ashes damping the fire which now flickered and blazed. His way of life came to be admired—even by casual acquaintances, for the Chinese considered good-humour the better part of goodness. Accepted as an equal, even as a friend, he won the favour of leading mandarins and obtained permission for other graduate preachers to join him.

His success in Nanchang convinced Ricci that if only permission could be obtained from Peking to preach Christianity openly, in a short time millions of converts could be made. Without such official sanction, the mission stood in constant danger. When, in the following year, Valignano visited Macao, Ricci wrote to the Visitor, proposing that he be allowed to travel to Peking and win the Emperor's goodwill. The arrival of his letter coincided with news from Europe that Ruggieri had failed to win support for a papal embassy to the Son of Heaven. War had broken out between Navarre and France; Spain, her trade routes increasingly harried by English ships, could scarcely provide for essential needs. No one had time for this new Lazarus, or money for his remote world. Valignano, therefore, at once approved Ricci's plan and, since it would no longer be feasible at such a distance to consult Macao on important decisions, appointed Ricci Superior of the mission within China.

Ricci responded vigorously to the challenge of his new orders, convinced by his experience on shipboard two years before that he would be given all necessary assistance. Gifts had been collected at Macao against the proposed embassy: these were now dispatched to Nanchang. When they arrived he showed the clocks and paintings and other European objects to the Prince of Chien-an, asking whether he would help to present them. To his surprise, the prince declined. Ricci persevered, but despite numerous attentions and kindnesses, met with an absolute refusal. Only then did he learn from one of the mandarins how close he had come to ruining the mission. Applying European categories to Chinese society, he had supposed the surest way to approach an Emperor was through a prince of blood royal. In fact no class in China was viewed with greater suspicion, for in the past many rebellions had crystallised round usurping princes. If the Prince of Chien-an had even hinted that, in league with Ricci, he intended to approach the Emperor, so nervous was the central Government that the incident would have been considered a threat to internal security and the legal succession, a plot to hand China over to the Portuguese.

A less dangerous opportunity soon arose, when a former acquaintance, Wang Chung-ming, passed through Nanchang on his way to high office in Nanking. Learning that a month after his arrival Wang would be visiting Peking for the Emperor's birthday, Ricci asked leave to accompany him. At first Wang raised difficulties, but when Ricci pointed out that he simply asked protection and that he and his friends would pay their own expenses, the Minister agreed.

Under the Dragon Moon—in the month of June—Ricci left for Nanking with Cattaneo and Brother Sebastian. Though his party had its own hired boat, for much of the ten days' journey Ricci travelled on Wang's barge, discussing the best way of offering gifts to the Emperor. Ricci increased Wang's obligation to him by making the mandarin a present of one of the two clocks.

Nanking they found in a state of extreme alarm and suspicion. Just as hostilities in Europe had baulked the plan of an embassy, so now the Korean war seemed to threaten the alternative scheme. Already the imperial exchequer was drained and Chinese forces could not resist much longer. A few days before, Japanese spies had been caught in Nanking: as a result all lodging-houses received orders to turn away suspicious-looking persons. Unable to find a room, the travellers were obliged to live on their small boat, in squalid conditions, during a period of very hot weather. Worse still, fear of delation was once again proving stronger than natural kindness. However, Ricci's presents had indebted Wang so greatly that he feared even more the discourtesy of sending his guests back. He agreed to let them travel to Peking by water with his baggage, while he made the journey by land. He put at their disposal a light " horse boat," so called because of its speed, carrying a cargo of *gianmui*, fruit of the arbutus tree.

In mid-July Ricci set sail from Nanking, down the Yangtze into the Imperial Canal, constructed three centuries before to link Peking with the southern provinces. It was crowded as a city centre with fleets of barges carrying tribute in kind and in silver to Peking for the expenses of government and the Emperor—all land was held direct from the crown—and with barges of mandarins sailing up to the capital for the imperial birthday. Ricci counted over a hundred boats pass every hour, and this procession lasted all day long. A system of lock gates kept the water at the required level, but so dense was the traffic that sometimes vessels had to wait days before passing the sluices. In the narrow strip of water sail could seldom be used, and most boats were tracked by coolies. In addition, more than a million men were continually employed in repairing and deepening the vital artery. When he asked why the sea route was not used, Ricci was told that, although it was shorter and quicker, typhoons and pirates rendered it unsafe.

The canal was lined like a street with towns and workmen's houses. Among the sights that interested Ricci were huge beams, tree-trunks and wooden columns, bound together, sometimes to the length of two miles, and dragged by many thousands of coolies. These, he was told, were being conveyed from the province of Szechwan to rebuild part of the imperial palace, damaged two years previously by fire. So slow was their progress that Ricci reckoned the total time of transport would amount to almost three years. In addition to tribute, the best fruit and fish, tea and rice, silk and cloth were each year carried to the Emperor's court. The perishable food was kept in ice, supplies of which were collected from deep cellars at points along the canal.

Along the five hundred miles of artificial waterway, straight as a Roman road, Ricci took bearings which would add yet more of a sub-continent larger than Europe to Italian maps. More than ever he and Cattaneo were astonished by the vast extent of the country. As they sailed on week after week without arriving, it seemed as though their destination must be eternity. Gradually paddy-fields began to disappear, the weather became more temperate, coal instead of wood was used to cook meals, the people became taller and heavier, with coarser, larger faces and higher cheekbones. Yet officials still spoke mandarin, received the same education and owed the

same allegiance as their colleagues in Kwangtung : northern
and southern characteristics were united in a single nation, a
reason perhaps for her stability and advanced civilisation.

In early September they arrived at Tungchow, port for
Peking. A large canal led up to the city walls but was reserved
for boats going to the imperial palace. All other merchandise
was carried in carts, on horseback or by coolies. Disembark-
ing, Ricci and Cattaneo took a sedan to the capital fifteen
miles away, with the intention of visiting Wang's house. As
at Nanking, the most striking feature was the circuit of immensely powerful brick walls, guarded by four-storied gate
towers. The buildings perhaps betrayed less ostentation of
carving and colour, the city was less extensive than Nanking,
but climate above all marked the difference. The southern
capital had been humid and sweltering, whereas now the
travellers could believe themselves under European skies.
Against windswept dust everyone in the streets wore black
veils : a custom Ricci decided to follow as a means of con-
cealment.

The imperial palace lay within the second wall, at the south
gate, and extended for a mile across the whole length of the
city to the northern wall. The sedans were lowered close to
the magnificent gates and their occupants told to dismount in
homage. This was the meeting-point of Heaven and earth,
symbolised on painted scrolls by low clouds merging with the
palace courtyards. That day there were no clouds to interrupt a
view extending northwards across gates and pavilions for over
a mile. As he scanned the glazed roofs of imperial yellow
gleaming like gold, Ricci felt a stir of triumph at the completion of a journey which, from his first landing in China, had
taken sixteen years. He had arrived : it remained only to meet
the Emperor.

Ricci, however, was soon shocked to learn that the distance
between Peking and the palace was more formidable than that
between Macao and the capital. The Emperor was surrounded
not only by his palace ladies but by an army of ten thousand
eunuchs, who controlled the palace and all access to it. The
custom originated in the punishment of certain crimes by

castration *à la Turque* and perpetual service in the imperial palace. Later these prisoners gained such power that the office was prized. Parents castrated their small sons and even adults submitted to the operation as a means towards influence and wealth. For although officially all power lay in the hands of the mandarins, the eunuchs played at least as important a role. They came from the lowest classes, were uneducated and having passed most of their lives in slavery were abject, resentful and greedy for power. Having adopted the role of a graduate in order to win mandarin support, Ricci now found himself confronted with yet another group opposed to all that graduates represented. The eunuchs would perform favours only when bribed with enormous sums, far beyond Ricci's means. The resident mandarins in the Ministries, compelled to buy the eunuchs' services, extorted money from the provincial mandarins under threat of removing them from office. They in turn were forced to accept bribes in their own provinces. The city, in short, seemed to Ricci a veritable Babylon of confusion, the elements of natural religion which he had observed elsewhere being submerged under a welter of corruption, injustice and intrigue.

At Wang's request one of the palace eunuchs inspected Ricci's European curios, but made it clear that, with the Japanese in Korea and threatening the Middle Kingdom itself, presents from a barbarian would not be welcome. He hinted that he would exert his influence only if Ricci revealed to him the secret of changing cinnabar into silver. After spending two months in unsuccessful attempts to offer his gifts, reluctantly Ricci decided to withdraw from Peking. He would await the end of the war and obtain further introductions before returning for a final assault on the palace.

Without difficulty he found places in one of the boats returning empty. Since the captain could not afford trackers, they drifted slowly and in December were halted altogether by the frozen canal at Lintsing, an important trading centre, crowded with merchants but unsuitable for a mission residence. The logical course was to remain there until the canal thawed in April, then continue to Nanking. But six fruitless months had heightened Ricci's sense of urgency. He decided to leave Cattaneo and the rest of his party with the presents and baggage, which it would be impossible to transport by land, while he travelled south to find a suitable town for a new house. Because Ch'ü T'ai-su, his " disciple," had often said that he would be glad to help Ricci settle in Nanking province, he decided to go to Soochow, where Ch'ü was now living.

In mid-winter the journey, of some five hundred miles, proved a formidable undertaking. He travelled cross-country on horseback. Since the network of rivers and canals provided adequate cheap communication, little care was given to roads, which remained vague, sometimes indecipherable vestiges across the limitless plain. The horse's unshod pace was slow and, after so many mild winters, the sharp weather began to tell. Near Yangchow he contracted dysentery but refused to delay. When the pain became insufferable he would dismount and lie for a time on the snow-covered ground, then force himself to resume.

At Soochow, a Chinese Venice, he was told that his friend had gone to stay at a pagoda in the nearby town of Tanyang. Drawing on his last reserves of strength, Ricci covered the fifty miles in a state almost of collapse. Reaching the rose-red walls with their cap of snow, he dragged himself across the threshold. Not since his attack of malaria had he felt so ill. As though in delirium he heard Sutras being intoned to the tinkling of triangles and beating of the wooden fish, and smelled the acrid incense which, despite his struggles, slowly wrapped him in a winding-sheet of darkness.

CHAPTER SEVEN

A Banquet in Nanking

FOR several days Ricci lay at the point of death in his disciple's room. Ch'ü had given him the single bed, while he slept on the ground—never for more than an hour or two at a time, for like a son he tended Ricci untiringly. His welcome had been worthy of the journey: as warm, Ricci thought, as any in Italy. No remedy, no food was too difficult to procure, nothing too much for his comfort. Most efficacious of all was Ch'ü's affection, which ended his exile, made him once more belong on this far side of the world. By the end of January 1599 he had recovered sufficient strength to make plans. Ch'ü promised help in establishing a residence at Soochow, where, he claimed, foreigners would be treated with less suspicion than at Nanking.

At the beginning of February, during the Holiday Moon, master and disciple visited the southern capital, to obtain from Wang and other important officials, friends of Ch'ü, letters of favour to the Soochow magistrates. As they were about to enter the north-east gate, Ricci stopped in amazement. It was the very image of one of the storeyed portals he had seen in his vision almost four years before. He felt certain, then, that despite his plans for Soochow, he was destined to remain in the capital. When they passed into the city, he found the old atmosphere of alarm and suspicion gone. News had just arrived of the death of Hideyoshi, the militant Japanese minister who had unleased hostilities in Korea. An armistice had been concluded and Japanese troops had withdrawn from the peninsula.

They took lodgings in a pagoda near the centre of the city. Ricci's visit to offer presents to the Emperor was the talk of Nanking. Most people approved the attempt and thought that only the state of war had prevented their being received.

Wang was very favourably impressed by Ricci's courage in travelling south alone and by the praise he received from Ch'ü. Aware that the foreigner was making a name and that to pose as patron would redound to his honour, Wang urged Ricci to remain in Nanking, ordered two of his suite to look for a house, and invited him to his home for a few days during the festivities of the lanterns, on the tenth of February.

To welcome the first full moon of the new year the Flowery Kingdom spoke the language of the stars. Every building, boat and trinitarian gateway became a constellation; every living thing was recreated in light. Cocks, sinuous fish and horses on wheels, asters and dwarf trees, the goddess of mercy with a child in her arms—all were refashioned, as though for an aeon of darkness, in paper and silk lanterns, red, pink, blue and green—every colour but yellow—each with its flame-like soul, to be trailed in procession throughout the rejoicing city.

The mandarins devised more complex sport. At Wang's garden Ricci watched a display of fireworks, those of Nanking being the most famous of China, and found himself transported to a mythical realm of metempsychosis and shifting truth. Dragons ascended and were changed into fire-breathing lions; a huge spotted crake fluttered in the air and its beak gave birth to a flaming serpent; a chest was hoisted high only to dissolve in countless strings of lanterns; finally Wang's house became the mandarin himself seated in his sedan between equerries, banners and fans—a picture nailed to the night by hissing, multi-coloured flame. In this way the abundant salt-petre, which in Europe would have been turned into gun-powder, was used for no more harmful purpose than the bombardment of moon and stars. Putting the truth into figures, Ricci calculated that in a single year at Nanking alone more saltpetre was consumed for fireworks than during a three-year war in Europe.

This third visit proved as successful as the other two had been vain. He was visited by the very highest mandarins, including the Minister of Finance, the President of the Academy of Nobles and, most important of all, the Censor, who already knew Ricci's little book on Friendship. All insisted that he remain in Nanking. Every day he received offers of suitable houses, where seven months before not even a lodging had been available. Ricci recognised the hand of God. He told Ch'ü that, despite the attractions of Soochow, it seemed better to stay in the southern capital. As soon as an opportunity arose, he would start once again for his ultimate goal, Peking.

Until the arrival of Cattaneo, Ricci rented a small house where he could receive visitors. He would test the strength of his position : if the welcome were more than ephemeral, he would be justified in buying a larger building. Meanwhile Wang lent him furniture from one of his palaces.

Drawing on his experience at Nanchang, he now began a form of apostolate which aimed to convince his friends of the superiority of European science, in order to give authority to his religious doctrine. So great was Chinese pride, so inbred their hostility to foreign teaching, that until they were convinced empirically that they had no monopoly of truth, they would dismiss superciliously a theology and revelation which could never be proved to their senses. At Shiuhing, even at Shiuchow, he had hoped single-handed to spread the wild-fire of Christianity. He knew now that the conversion of China would probably be a long process; that his role was to sow rather than harvest. Repressing his eagerness to speak of the one paramount subject, he let it be known in Nanking that he would teach mathematics.

The Chinese picture of the world took as its first premise a sentence from the oldest astronomical book : " What is square belongs to the earth; what is round belongs to heaven : for the sky is round and the earth is square." Cosmology, eclipses, the movement of sun and moon, were explained by a similar mixture of myth and magic. There were said to be five elements, metal, wood, fire, water and earth, one born out of the other, called the five travellers, because in continual movement. Air was considered simply a vacuum.

Ricci now began to teach that the earth was a globe, exceeded in size by the sun; that there were ten celestial orbs, superimposed, each with its inlaid stars, and moving according to the different principles; that the altitude of the pole varied according to the zones of the earth. In a short book entitled *The Four Elements* he corrected their views about the nature of matter.

His first pupils were two graduates. With the more brilliant, a young man sent by a doctor of letters and amateur mathematician who wished to learn Ricci's views but was unable to attend in person, Ricci became intimate, even confiding that his ultimate purpose was to refute Buddhism and replace it by Christianity. His pupil replied, " It is unnecessary to refute Buddhism. Simply continue to teach mathematics. When my people learn the truth about the world, they will see for themselves the falsity of Buddhist books." This was becoming Ricci's own opinion, for the Buddhist scriptures were full of palpably untrue myths about the universe. Thus, in order to explain the alternation of day and night, they claimed that at night the sun hid under Mount Sumeru, which had its roots twenty-four thousand miles under the sea. This holy mountain, a variant of Olympus—for the Greek myth had spread across Asia—formed the axis of the world, at the corners of which lay four continents, of which only the two southern ones, India and China were habitable.

On the day of a solar eclipse, as Ricci had himself witnessed, the mandarins, warned in advance, paraded in their robes and all the inhabitants of China were assembled by townships, prostrate on the ground, to frighten away with cymbals, drums and an outroar of yelling the monster that would otherwise swallow the sun. While official opinion sanctioned the myth of a monster, the Buddhist held that one of the Lohans caused an eclipse of the sun by covering it with his right hand, of the moon with his left, and many of the graduates believed that during an eclipse of the moon the planet, coming face to face with the sun, grew dim with fear.

If Chinese theories of the world were fabulous and their mathematics rudimentary, a passionate belief in astrology had produced a reasonably practical astronomy. If no one cared how and why the stars moved, it was important at least to know and predict their courses. Both Nanking and Peking possessed colleges of mathematicians, attached to the imperial palace where between twenty and thirty eunuchs, paid by the Emperor, continually observed the stars. Maintained as astrologers rather than astronomers, they had very little social standing. Whenever a comet or other strange phenomenon appeared, they wrote to the Emperor stating what had happened and explaining its significance. They also predicted eclipses, usually inaccurately, and when events did not correspond with their forecasts claimed that they had been correct and that the disturbance, occasioned by some fault of the Son of Heaven, augured national calamity. On these occasions the Emperor—in whom the cosmos and all men's destinies met—was required to examine his conscience.

As Ricci's reputation grew, members of the Nanking college began to worry lest he render their existence superfluous. One day they approached his favourite pupil and asked Ricci's intentions. The young man, with all a disciple's fervour, replied, "The graduate preacher is so great a man in his own country that he would not deign to accept the highest office in the Middle Kingdom, far less so insignificant a one as yours." At this the eunuchs grew less afraid and even paid Ricci flattering visits, careful, however, not to reveal their ignorance by speaking a word of astronomy. In return Ricci was able to obtain an invitation to their observatory, a group of old buildings on a high hill within the city. Here, night after night, the timid, underpaid eunuchs watched for shooting stars and comets, reading the destiny of the Flowery Kingdom in that other supremely important firework display.

When he entered the observatory, Ricci received the surprise of his life. Instead of the pretentious semi-magical charts he had expected, there stood four magnificent heavy instruments of cast bronze, decorated with coiled imperial dragons, finer than any he had seen in Europe : a sphere for determining eclipses marked with degrees according to the European system but in Chinese characters, an armillary sphere, a gnomon and, largest of all, a complex sphere composed of three or four astrolabes, fitted with alidade and dioptra. Ricci turned to the chief eunuch.

"Who made these fine instruments?" he asked.

"A Mohammedan astronomer—about two hundred and fifty years ago, under the Tartars."

Again Ricci was astonished. He already knew that Mohammedans from Central Asia had settled in China, but not that scientists had been among them.

"I did not imagine you were so well equipped," he said.

After examining the armillary sphere, he pointed to one of the graduated arms. "Is that where you read the shadow?"

The eunuch approached, dwarfed by the huge instrument. He looked puzzled, then nodded. Resisting the astronomer's efforts to lead him away, Ricci continued his inspection. He noticed with approval that degrees were indicated by a system of knobs which could be read at night by touch. Then he made a startling discovery.

"Surely Nanking stands at 32 degrees?" he asked.

The eunuch agreed.

"But these instruments are set for 36 degrees." The eunuch did not answer and tried to divert his guest's attention. Intrigued, Ricci put two or three simple questions about the gnomon, to all of which he received evasive answers. At last, seeing that Ricci had found him out, the chief eunuch turned away from the gnomon.

"They're beautiful instruments," he said unhappily, "but we don't know how to use them." He added, "Two sets were made, one for Peking, the other for Pingyang. These have come from Pingyang."

Then Ricci understood. Evidently Pingyang stood at 36 degrees, and the instruments had never been adjusted. They were no more than museum pieces.

He learned from the eunuchs that some astronomical knowledge had come to China by way of the Arabs. The imperial college was divided into two schools, one following the few surviving translations of Arab books, the other ancient Chinese teaching. China, then, had acquired its preliminary knowledge of the Ptolemaic system from the same source as Europe, and at about the same date. Whereas in the West it had been enthusiastically received and developed, here, where science, unconducive to the good life or good government, was not included in the approved list of studies, it had declined to such a point that fine instruments were mere relics, their purpose not even understood.

Although during these first months in Nanking most of his time was spent teaching mathematics, Ricci took occasion to discuss more important topics. Familiarity with the writings of Confucius, of Buddhism and Taoism, had convinced him that his best hope of spreading Christianity was to ally himself with Confucianism, which in almost all respects harmonised with Christian principles. Its lines, like those of a Chinese building, were horizontal : a system of right conduct between men, it had little to say of man's relations with God. Ricci therefore presented Christianity as an essentially reasonable theology completing and perfecting those principles in Confucianism which conformed to natural reason.

Buddhism and Taoism, on the other hand, as they were practised in China, were idolatrous religions with their own pantheons, which could less easily be adapted to Christianity. While praising many of the principles of Confucius, at the same time Ricci continued to attack Buddhist and Taoist superstitions. This surprised the graduates. In their history books were stories of Indians and Mohammedans who had preached in China : but all had attacked Confucianism and praised the idolaters.

One day a certain Li Pen-ku, a Buddhist of seventy-four with a reputation for sanctity, invited Ricci to dinner, the recognised occasion for serious argument. The invitation took the form of a visiting book in which Li wrote that he had washed the goblets and prepared a modest repast of herbs for the next evening. " I should be pleased to hear the Far Westerner express his ideas, from which the company will certainly gather some jewels of wisdom." Ricci excused himself, saying it was a day of fasting, for he did not want to prejudice his delicate position by disputing in public. But Li was insistent and twice sent a servant to say that he was expecting Ricci, for whom he had special food. Ch'ü advised Ricci to go, otherwise Li would take the refusal as an insult.

Li had also invited a famous bonze called Huang San-hui, a distinguished-looking man of fifty-four, with a high brow, burning eyes and square jaw, dressed, a trifle ostentatiously, in the poorest clothes. He had published several volumes of poetry and possessed a good knowledge of the three main sects. While the other guests were arriving—some twenty-five had been invited—Ricci was introduced to Huang. The bonze suggested that they should discuss religion. Ricci agreed.

"However," he said, "before we begin, I should like to know your beliefs. Whom do you consider the first principle of all things, the Lord of heaven and earth and all creation?"

Huang replied, " I believe there is such a creator, but he is not omnipotent. Each one of us is, in every respect, as great as that Lord."

In some surprise Ricci answered, " That is a claim for which you must surely give proof. Can you do the things the creator has done?"

" Certainly," boasted Huang. " I am able to create heaven and earth."

Ricci smiled and reflected a moment or two.

" I don't want to give you the trouble of creating another heaven and another earth, but I should like to see you make— let us say, a brazier, like that one over there." He pointed to a metal vessel holding burning charcoal, installed to warm the guests.

Huang looked at him disdainfully, " You have no right to make such a demand. Do you think I'm an artisan?"

He began to lament that foreigners really were too gross, that his claim had been put forward only in a spiritual sense.

Ricci, raising his voice above Huang's, said, " You should not promise what you cannot fulfil."

Other guests, sipping their tea before dinner began, enquired the drift of the argument. Ch'ü, who had been listening to every word, repeated the conversation and Ricci's challenge, which the majority of guests said was justified.

Huang began to explain his position. " I have heard that you are a great astronomer," he said to Ricci in starched language. " Are you also a mathematician?"

" I have some knowledge of that science."

" When you speak of the sun and moon, do you go up to heaven where those planets are, or do they come down into your breast?"

"Neither one nor the other," Ricci answered. " When we see something, we form in our minds a copy of the thing seen. Later, when we wish to think or speak of it, we look in our minds at these images we have already formed."

Huang rose triumphantly. " There you are. You yourself have created a new sun and a new moon. You could do the same for all other things." He tossed his head proudly and looked round the company.

Ricci sought for a way to reveal the ambiguity. Finally he said, " That image in the mind is not the sun or moon, but a copy only : there is a great difference between the two. For if we had not first seen the sun and moon, we should be unable to form that copy or imagine it, much less create the actual sun and moon."

Neither Huang nor the other guests seemed able to grasp an argument so opposed to both idealism and naïve realism. Ricci gave an illustration.

" Take a shining surface for instance. When it is placed opposite the sun or the moon, it reflects those planets. But no one would claim that the surface creates the sun and the moon or the other objects it reflects."

This the guests understood and approved, but Huang grew angry and in a loud voice began to declaim his idealist theories. Fearing discourtesy, their host Li came up and gently drew him to another part of the room.

When all the guests had arrived, they were invited into the banqueting hall, a long room furnished with pictures, vases of flowers and antique cabinets. Some twenty-five tables, four feet long and three wide, were set in a line. The uncovered tops gleamed with glossy varnish, the sides were hung with silk to the floor. At each stood a chair, carved and varnished and decorated with gold figures. The guests having gathered at the threshold, Li filled a silver bowl with wine and placing it on a silver salver bowed deeply to Ricci. Going into the courtyard he faced south and poured out the wine on the ground as an offering to Heaven. Then he came back, placed another bowl on the salver, and again bowed to Ricci, who accompanied him to the place of honour in the centre of the line of tables. He set the bowl on Ricci's table, carefully arranged beside it ebony eating-sticks tipped with gold and dusted the adjacent chair. Returning to the centre of the room he bowed and escorted each guest in turn to his table with similar courtesy. Then Ricci, as guest of honour, escorted Li to a table facing his own and the others. Each of the guests in turn approached and with both hands arranged the table, the chair and the sticks, as though to set them even more conveniently, while Li stood aside with a deprecating gesture. Having bowed to each other, all the company took their places. Following Li's example they raised their bowls, small as nutshells, in both hands and sipped wine together. The drink, mild as beer, was served warm—one of the explanations, Ricci believed, of Chinese longevity. When the goblets were emptied, the first course of food was carried in, each guest being provided with a separate dish. All the company raised their sticks in their right hands, like an orchestra waiting for the first beat of the conductor's baton, then, following Li's movements, lowered them slowly so that all touched their food at precisely the same moment. Meat and fish were served in no apparent order, mixed with herbs and bamboo shoots and cooked in sesame oil without rice, all cut up so as to be daintily eaten.

After a few minutes, at a signal from Li, all laid down their sticks to resume drinking and conversation. The graduates began to discuss an age-old question, whether human nature by itself is good, bad or indifferent. Ricci listened to the arguments : one said, if human nature is evil, whence comes the good men do; another, if good, whence comes the evil; a third, if it is neither good nor evil, who teaches man to perform right and wrong? As the Chinese received no training in rigorous logic, and made no distinction between moral and natural good, the argument turned in circles for over an hour. As Ricci remained silent, the guests thought the conversation was beyond him. Finally Li politely asked whether he had anything to say.

Ricci, who had been waiting for this opportunity, first summarised their arguments, then said, " All of us here will agree that the Lord of Heaven and earth is in the highest degree good. If human nature is so feeble that it doubts whether its own self is good or evil, how can the honorable Huang be correct when he maintains (as he did not long ago) that human nature is the same as God, creator of Heaven and earth? If it were the same, it surely could not doubt its own goodness?"

A young graduate turned to Huang. " What answer do you give?"

Huang smiled superciliously, as though Ricci's words were unworthy of attention. But Ricci and the others insisted that he should answer. Finally he burst out with a torrent of quotations from the Buddhist scriptures, to the admiration of the whole company.

When he had finished, Ricci said, " I do not believe the religion you profess, and therefore your quotations have no force for me. I too could bring forward authorities from my religion. I purposely refrained from doing so because this evening our discussion is based on reason."

But Huang continued to dogmatise, concluding that although something which was good could also be evil, God was neither the one nor the other.

On these points Ricci challenged him. " The sun," he said, " is light and cannot be dark, for its proper nature is to be light. Similarly the Lord of Heaven, whose nature it is to be good, cannot be responsible for evil."

Then he went on to distinguish between substance and accidents. Imbued with Buddhist mysticism, Huang was not prepared to admit either that being and non-being were mutually exclusive or that the nature of the highest good must be simple. Taking not marbled substance but the shifting nature of man as his norm, he believed in a universe made up of contradictory principles : man was both good and bad; the year both warm and cold; God therefore must combine in himself similar opposites. To Aristotle's clear-cut world of sun and shade he opposed a moonlit masquerade of subtle moods and indefinable spiritual change, where everything altered from hour to hour even to the same observer. Unable to agree about first principles and working from different basic analogies, the poet bonze and the Far Westerner remained, as lamps were lit and gleamed on the varnished tables, a world apart.

Until the early hours of the morning the talk continued, growing more excited and less to the point as goblets were filled and refilled. Dish after dish was brought in and, since none was removed, they stood piled up on each table like miniature castles. The guests ate moderately, the entertainment being more a symposium than a banquet and friends " men who drink together." Ricci eschewed the best dishes. At Nanchang he had discovered that the Christian manner of fasting was considered not in the least penitential, for Buddhists dispensed with meat, fish, eggs, milk, butter and cheese. He was not obliged to adopt the stricter form—indeed he felt tempted not to, for he was a hearty eater and, as his life became busier, stood in need of large meals. But he made the sacrifice, and ate only rice and vegetables on Fridays, Sundays and during Lent.

Though the rice-wine was mild, so long did the banquet last that when the party broke up, servants had to assist some of the guests as they staggered to waiting sedans.

The story of the dispute spread through Nanking, and most people believed Ricci had got the better of the argument. Few, however, understood his scholastic theory of perception, and it was rumoured that the Far Westerner carried in his breast the heaven of heavens and had eyes which permitted him to see other worlds beyond the earth.

Shortly afterwards Ricci's friendship was sought by another poet-bonze, one of the most original and famous authors of China, at that time an old man of seventy-two. Some twenty years earlier he had abandoned a brilliant official career in order to devote himself to Buddhism. First he had tried to reconcile his creed with Confucianism, then, discarding all human learning, had turned to contemplation. He admired Ricci's book on Friendship and although usually too arrogant to pay courtesy calls, he surprised his disciples by going in person to visit the foreigner, presenting him with a fan on which he had inscribed one of his finest poems. Fans, carried by everyone, men and women, rich and poor, no matter what the weather, corresponded as objects of elegance to the gloves of European gentlemen. Frames might be of bamboo, wood, ebony or ivory, the material of paper, silk or cloth, the shape round, square or oval. Among graduates the most prized form was the semi-circular, pliable fan, bearing a moral sentence or poem inscribed on its wing. It formed the usual gift between friends. The poet-bonze's lines were addressed to the Westerner Li:

Like a stork, now you fly towards the mists of the north,
And now direct your course towards the regions of the south.
Above every high pole of the pagodas your name unfurls
And every mountain recounts your storm-tossed voyage
    by sea.

Turning your head, you gaze back on ten times ten
    thousand *li,*
And, raising your eyes, before you see the empyrean city,
You marvel at the splendour of the country in its zenith,
While the sun blazes down in full meridian.

Ricci had already given and received a great number of inscribed fans, but few of their verses could compare with this poem, remarkable for its sense of space and the subtle portrait of Ricci as astronomer and man of God.

At the beginning of May Cattaneo arrived from Lintsing with Brother Sebastian, to Ricci's profound relief. For five months now he had remained alone, not in comparative quiet as at Shiuchow, but every hour of the day and much of the night meeting the most intelligent men of China, powerful mandarins and influential Buddhists, sustaining alone wave after wave of argument, scientific, religious, magical, jeopardising his integrity for love. Now at last he was able to speak with someone who shared his principles and loyalties, speak a common language, leave the asylum where his religious beliefs were treated as curious delusions, find assurance and support. He welcomed Cattaneo, too, as the surest corrective to that creeping, insidious pride which lay within the pleats of his purple robes, as despair had been associated with the bonze's ash-grey cloak. The greatest mandarins hailed him as one of the sages of China, a prodigy of learning, and gravely repeated his *obiter dicta* : he could smile, he could repeat prayers of humility, but not every unworthy thought could be repressed. Yet he knew that all depended on the opposite virtues, China's salvation as well as his own, for when the novelty of Western learning wore off, when his astrolabes and quadrants were no longer one of the sights, only that would remain to turn the scale. It was good, therefore, that Cattaneo knew all his mathematics had been learned from the so much more eminent Clavius; it was good, when he described his by now famous controversy, to be told that he had used quite the wrong arguments against Huang.

It seemed feasible now to buy a house, but although he had looked at many Ricci could find none that satisfied him. In May, however, he received a visit from an official of the Ministry of Public Works who had taken Ricci's part in certain religious disputes.

" I have heard," he said, " that you are searching for a house. Two years ago I had a large mansion with about twenty rooms built for officials of my Ministry. As soon as it was finished, ghosts and spirits began to appear. Several graduates who tried to live in it were frightened almost to death. No one could be persuaded to stay there, so I decided to dispose of it, first at cost price, then for even less, but as you can well understand, no one will buy a haunted house. I have been thinking—you are a holy man, and so demons and ghosts cannot harm you. If you want the house you may have it."

" I'm afraid so large a building would be beyond our means," said Ricci.

" Don't let that worry you. I will accept what you care to pay. The Ministry will be only too pleased to get rid of it."

There and then the official took him to see the house, number three in the Street named Ceremonial Rites, in the best quarter of the city, near the imperial palace. It proved to be more suitable than any Ricci had been shown by house agents and was built on high ground, an important factor in a city so liable to floods. It would be large enough for ten missionaries, and it was a measure of his new confidence that Ricci did not consider the size excessive. The official offered to sell it at half cost price, but as the missionaries were short of money, he agreed to wait for half the payment until the following year. In three days negotiations were completed and on May the twenty-fourth the house was theirs. They sprinkled the rooms with holy water and replaced the pictures of devils, drawn with black ink on yellow paper, which Taoist priests had set up to exorcise the house, with a painting of Christ. They took possession and continued to live there without losing their wits, to the astonishment of all Nanking.

With a base firmly established, Ricci now made plans to reach his ultimate goal, Peking, for he believed that peace in Korea would prove lasting and make it possible to win the Emperor's ear. Money and further gifts were sought from Macao. These reached Nanking in March of the new century which, with new hopes, had been born from the dying year. At the same time Ricci was joined by another missionary, Diego Pantoja, a serious young man of twenty-nine with sharp iron-grey eyes, the first Spaniard to work in China.

That spring saw the publication of the second edition of Ricci's map of the world, prepared at the request of a friend, secretary to the Ministry of Civil Appointments, a circular projection twice the size of the one he had made sixteen years before. Ricci added the peninsula of Korea, absent from the Flemish maps which had been the basis of his first edition. For clearness' sake, the parallels were omitted; according to Chinese convention the sea was represented by formalised waves instead of dots, and for the first time a phoneticised equivalent for Europe appeared. In an elegant preface the secretary wrote: " Tradition has it that the south-eastern chain of the Kunlun Shan runs into the Middle Kingdom : hence all the rivers flow east. But no one has been able to map the north-western chain. . . . We know the frontiers of the Middle Kingdom : it is bounded to the south-east only by sea, to the west by the Kunlun Shan, to the north by the Gobi. But what of the frontiers of the world? Experience shows it to be quite small, whereas speculation suggests it may be vast. Both views are false. The Westerner Li, who has come from the continent named Europe, has published a Complete Map of Mountains and Seas, which he has presented to graduates, and many copies of which have circulated. I have studied it and found it has been compiled with the help of old books published in his country. In fact his fellow-countrymen and the Portuguese love long voyages. Whenever they pass through distant regions, they write about them and hand on their discoveries from generation to generation. Having through the years accumulated observations, they know the general shape of the earth, apart from the regions of the south pole, still unexplored.

" This graduate preacher is a modest man, not bent on gain; he is content to practise virtue and to honour Heaven. Morning and evening he resolves to avoid unkindness in thought, word and deed. Although his theories about the sun, moon and stars are difficult to understand, until more learned men than I are able to verify them I shall continue to believe that they are based on sound evidence." The map was printed at the Ministry's expense : it proved immensely popular and other blocks soon had to be cut for new impressions.

This success increased his friend's desire to lend Ricci all possible assistance. Although the palace eunuchs had usurped many of its functions, the Ministry of Rites—embracing the three fields of religion, education and foreign affairs—was still officially responsible for the presentation of gifts from foreigners. The Censor, fearing also lest he be accused of failing to expedite the Western curios, was only too glad to help Ricci on his journey to Peking. In the late spring he took the initiative in providing a passport, made out exactly as Ricci wished, as well as letters of recommendation to friends in the northern capital.

Ricci succeeded in renting two rooms on board a fast boat sailing for Peking, part of a convoy of five carrying silk to the Emperor. The captain, a eunuch, refused payment for the cabins, because Ricci was a friend of the Censor—a favour he was able to repay by obtaining for the captain carrying-trade worth double the fare. As a farewell present Ricci gave the Censor the large prism which had been left at his palace and which even he considered a very precious jewel. On May the nineteenth, in company with Pantoja and Brother Sebastian, Ricci embarked. The great Censor, their other friends, and the small group of Christians Ricci had baptised during the past year came to the boat to wish the travellers a peaceful journey.

CHAPTER EIGHT

Prisoners of the Eunuch

IMPELLED by love and the need for propagation of the faith, a second time Ricci leapt the falls along five hundred miles of water. Chinkiang, Yangchow, Hwaian, the stages were familiar now, his movements no longer surreptitious. He received continual visits from officials travelling to the capital, and at Tsining in Shantung province stayed a few days with the Commissioner of Rice Transport, whose son he had come to know in Nanking. This great mandarin gave him letters of recommendation and revised the draft of a memorial he had drawn up for the Emperor.

The eunuch was pleased with his passengers: not only had they done him a good turn and consorted with high dignitaries, but their presence helped at the lock gates, where tribute-bearing and official boats always had the right of way. He would invite other captains to see Ricci's presents, then, in return, receive permission to go ahead of them.

At the beginning of July, under the first phases of the Lotus Moon, their ship approached the outskirts of Lintsing. Ricci viewed the town with anxiety, for he had heard not only from Cattaneo, who had personal experience, but from the Censor and other friends about a certain Ma T'ang, who as Collector of Taxes at Lintsing had acquired a notorious reputation. During the Korean War, in 1596, the Emperor had dispatched eunuchs throughout the country, first to discover and develop gold and silver mines, secondly to collect a new two-per-cent sales tax. Two or three eunuchs were assigned to each province with almost unlimited powers, exempt from the jurisdiction of local mandarins. Increased power of eunuchs was a classic symptom of a declining dynasty, but in few other periods had they shown themselves so ruthless. They conspired to make all the money they could; in the words of official complaints "they sucked the marrow and drank the people's blood," yet not a tenth part reached the exchequer. Those who had been ordered to mine gold operated not in the mountains, where gold had formerly been discovered, but in the cities. Selecting a wealthy man's house, they claimed it stood over a profitable seam, and proposed to destroy the building in order to obtain the metal. Only by paying an enormous bribe could the owner retain his home. Some cities and provinces, to be rid of such depredations, had decided to pay an annual sum to the eunuchs, as " money from the mines." The mandarins of both capitals repeatedly informed the Emperor that such brutality and injustice had brought the country to the verge of revolt, but he had already begun to reap the fruits of their plunder and refused to listen. When several mandarins resisted, he even took the eunuchs' part : many mandarins were deprived of office, some imprisoned. This increased the eunuchs' insolence and they began to murder anyone who made a stand. None was more cunning and cruel than Ma T'ang, hated throughout China. The previous summer a mob of ten thousand had risen in exasperation and burnt his house, killing thirty-seven of his staff. The incident had roused him to retaliation and new excesses.

On arrival at Lintsing the eunuch captain went several times to visit the Collector of Taxes in one of the magnificent palaces he had built for himself, but on each occasion was turned back, as Ma T'ang did not consider his presents sufficiently magnificent. The captain was at his wits' ends : he could not afford finer gifts yet must obtain Ma T'ang's consent to continue his journey. If he arrived late at Peking, he would lose money and perhaps even his life. In this dilemma, calling on members of Ma T'ang's retinue, he informed them of the foreigners and their presents, adding that they possessed quantities of jewellery and knew how to fabricate silver. If he had a hand in their introduction their master would increase his influence over the Emperor. Pleased at the news, Ma T'ang presently sent word that he would come on board in the near future to inspect the presents.

Foreseeing danger, Ricci decided to consult a friend he had

first known in Shiuhing days, now military superintendent in Lintsing. When Ricci arrived at his house and explained what had happened, the military superintendent shook his head.

" My poor friend," he said, " you have no hope of getting out of Ma T'ang's hands. He and his kind are the real masters of our country. The Emperor acts only on their advice."

" I shall take my stand on the Censor's passport," said Ricci. " That no one has a right to contravene."

The military superintendent was not impressed. " The greatest mandarins have failed to withstand the eunuchs. What can you hope to do—a foreigner without money or power or influence? No, resistance is futile."

" What course then do you advise."

" Be very pleasant to him : thank him for the favours he proposes. He is weak and effeminate at heart—and susceptible to flattery. But don't try to escape; you will fail and even risk your life."

During their conversation a messenger arrived in haste.

" My master Ma T'ang," he announced, " is making his way to your boat. It is most important that you be there to receive him."

As Ricci prepared to leave, his host said, " Tell Ma T'ang that the far Westerner is in conference with me. Explain that I would not let my visitor leave for anyone else in the world."

When the messenger withdrew, the mandarin turned to Ricci. " He respects no one in the city but me : if you are late, he will think only that I have done him a favour."

Ricci returned to his boat in time to see a palatial barge glide down the canal, long as a European galley, a little broader and far higher, all the woodwork finely carved, gilded and varnished. When it drew alongside, Ricci was escorted on board. Wide verandahs surrounded a dozen cabins and halls, hung with silk and furnished with antiques. He was received by a short, stout, middle-aged man, powder and vermilion on his beardless face merely accentuating its incisive lines, unmistakable as the ideogram for greed. The eunuch waddled towards Ricci with an incongruous, effeminate fluttering of his fan. After an exaggerated show of courtesy,

" I hear you have something to offer his Imperial Majesty," he said in a shrill uneducated voice. As Ricci inclined his head, he continued, " I shall lend you every assistance. Meanwhile, I should like to examine the presents."

" It will be a pleasure to receive you," replied Ricci.

The eunuch frowned. " Your boat is—a trifle small. I prefer to have them carried here."

He shouted the necessary orders, while Ricci tried to control his annoyance. One by one the presents were carried in and taken out of their cases. The prisms particularly excited Ma T'ang.

" Excellent," he said, rubbing his hands together. " These are truly worthy of the Son of Heaven."

Last of all a picture of the Virgin with the Christ Child and St. John the Baptist was unveiled. Astonishment forced the eunuch to his knees.

" Fair lady," he said, " I promise to give you a place in the Emperor's palace. I shall write a letter at once to his Imperial Majesty."

Ricci, however, was not deceived. He had had dealings with eunuchs and knew them to be utterly selfish, without a spark of conscience or the least shame. Despite his assurances of help, Ricci did not doubt that he intended to turn the presents to his own advantage.

" I pray you not to put yourself to such trouble," said Ricci. " You are a busy and important man. In Peking I have many friends—high officials, who have promised their help."

Ma T'ang laughed derisively. " None of the mandarins has as much power as I," he boasted. " Why, when I present a petition to the Emperor, he takes action the following day, whereas anyone else either waits weeks or does not receive an answer at all. No, I am the man to take charge of the gifts."

Remembering his friend's advice, Ricci acceded gracefully. " The Lord of Heaven, Whose picture you are helping to present, will reward you for this good work you are doing Him."

Ma T'ang's face clouded at the implication. " I shall soon be travelling up to Tientsin," he said, " two or three days' journey from the capital, to take the money collected during the past half-year. Sixty thousand taels." His tongue caressed the figures. "I should be pleased if you and your party would accompany me."

Seeing no way out, Ricci again accepted. Interpreting this as weakness, Ma T'ang then said he would have the presents carried to one of his palaces.

Ricci, however, was determined to keep the gifts by him. "I don't think that would be convenient," he said. "The clocks are difficult to regulate. I am afraid they might be damaged."

"The pictures at least I will take."

"We prefer to keep the pictures, to venerate when we say our prayers."

For the moment Ma T'ang did not press the point. As a return for putting the foreigners into his hands, he gave orders that the eunuch captain should be excused the customs' duty, amounting to thirty taels. Ricci and his party transferred to one of Ma T'ang's boats, where they were supplied at his expense with rice, wine and fuel for cooking. Here they received several visits from the military superintendent, who spoke to his friends of the esteem in which the foreigners were held at Nanking, hoping that the news would reach Ma T'ang's ears.

During their short stay, Ma T'ang invited Ricci to a great feast, at which the other guests were eunuchs, in one of his magnificent palaces. While dinner was being served Ma T'ang's own private troupe of performers came in, conjurers better than any Ricci had ever seen at home, contortionists more resilient than the fakirs he had watched in India, and acrobats who made a mockery of nature's laws.

As guest of honour, Ricci was invited to select from a repertory book several historical plays to be performed that evening. Later a troupe of fifty-six "youths of the pear orchard," all young castrati, introduced themselves to the spectators in appropriate speeches, and began to act the first play. The villain's face was painted white, as custom dictated, while warriors wore thick red and yellow paint. All were robed in

gorgeous silk. They declaimed their parts in recitative, inter-
rupted at intervals by shrill, harsh music of wind instruments,
while long pauses were filled with a loud crash of gongs and
kettledrums. The actors improvised their own scenery. A file
of soldiers, piling themselves on a heap across the un-
curtained stage, represented a wall, while a general, to undertake a distant expedition, mounted a stick and circled the stage
two or three times, brandishing a whip and singing a song.
Even actions were stylised : moving the hands slowly across the
eyes signified weeping, while standing stiffly up against a
pillar was the sign of hiding. When their part was done,
dead men rose and walked away.

The faithful concubine, the poor scholar, the stern father,
the husband who dresses up to test his wife's fidelity : round
these stock characters a weak pantomimic plot was woven, in
which the virtuous hero and villain invariably received their
deserts. Neither an indigenous nor ancient art form, the
drama had been introduced by the Tartars and remained at the
level of crude entertainment. Indeed, its essential conflict
between persons was hostile to traditional Chinese thought.
Although he had chosen the plays himself, Ricci preferred the
acrobatics.

The banquet lasted more than eight hours; during that time
the entertainment, which included puppet shows and jugglers,
never ceased. Ricci recalled the politeness, elegant manners
and good humour of dinners at Nanchang and the southern
capital : then looked round at the neutered company, stuffing
themselves with sweets, gulping their wine, some making eyes
at the young actors, others shrieking with laughter at an ob-
scene joke, dedicated to a life of luxury day and night, for
which only depredation and murder could pay. The mandarin
class, after all, was less omnipotent than he had once believed :
their tenuous civilising influence continually challenged from
beneath by these barbarians, leagued not by respect for reason
but by their common vitiation.

A few days after the banquet, it was decided that Ricci
should leave for Tientsin at the end of July. A servant carrying
Ma T'ang's letter to the Emperor accompanied the missionaries

on the eight-day journey, together with four soldiers to see that the ship had right of way. A week later Ma T'ang joined them.

Not until mid-September did a messenger arrive from the capital. Convoking all the local mandarins to his tribunal, Ma T'ang told Ricci to appear in coarse cloth and wearing a small round hat, sign of humility. When Ricci appeared Ma T'ang solemnly announced that he had received a written reply from his imperial majesty : supreme honour which few mandarins could boast. At this, lackeys came forward and made Ricci kneel as a sign of reverence to the imperial word. Ma T'ang then read the rescript, a gilt-edged scroll emblazoned with dragons. Its contents, though scarcely justifying such excitement, were not unsatisfactory : the Emperor placed the whole matter in the eunuch's hands and asked for an inventory of Li Ma-tou's presents. Ma T'ang ordered Ricci to write out the list there and then. More than ever distrustful of his intentions, Ricci purposely did not include everything. When the inventory was completed, the eunuch read out " Three paintings, two small, one large ; two clocks, a large one with weights, a small one which sounds the hour by itself, and two prisms." He scowled. " You must add to the list the jewels I have been told you possess."

" You have been misinformed," Ricci replied. " I have no jewels, and even if I had, no one would oblige me to offer them as gifts."

To temper this rebuff, he invited the eunuch to look at their other belongings in case they should include some object worthy of the Emperor. Mounting a palanquin carried by eight bearers—thus usurping honours due only to mandarins of the second rank—in company with all the city magistrates, Ma T'ang came to the boat and inspected the presents a second time. He selected the clavichord, an illuminated breviary, a well-bound copy of Ortelius's *Theatrum Orbis Terrarum* and seven books of mathematics, most by Clavius. These Ma T'ang transferred to his tribunal ; when Ricci protested, he said the law laid down that gifts which were the subject of a letter to the Emperor should be kept in custody.

Ma T'ang's second letter, forwarding the inventory and asking for permission to offer the gifts, was presented on September the twenty-third, the Emperor's birthday. Weeks passed without an answer. The eunuch took fright and regretted having meddled in an affair involving foreigners. He no longer invited Ricci to his entertainments and soon refused to exchange a word with him. He ordered the travellers to leave his ship and take up uncomfortable lodgings in a pagoda within the walls of Tientsin. Here six soldiers kept guard day and night, but they had freedom at least to say Mass, which they offered daily for a favourable reply. In November Ma T'ang sent a curt note that he would be returning shortly—before the canal froze—to his post in Lintsing. He sent back the pictures and the large clock; the other presents he claimed to have deposited with certain mandarins for safe-keeping.

The following day he came to visit them unexpectedly, with the military superintendent, and a bodyguard of two hundred cut-throats. Entering the pagoda he approached Ricci, his hands restless with disappointed rage.

" My friends at the palace," he cried out, " have written to say you possess quantities of jewellery. Exactly as I suspected. You still refuse to offer it to the Emperor?" His oblique look was confronted by piercing blue eyes; his effeminate face by a bearded, incisive profile, his flabby body by a tall compact figure.

" I have already explained," replied Ricci, " that we have no jewellery."

Ignoring this, Ma T'ang shouted to his men to carry everything from the lodgings into the courtyard. Meanwhile, pacing in agitation, he caught sight of Pantoja in a corner of the room.

" Who is this barbarian?" Ricci hastily presented the young Spaniard. " Why haven't you brought your friend to visit me? Do you think that was a courteous action?"

" Precisely out of courtesy he did not come to your palace," replied Ricci. " For he knows neither your language nor your etiquette."

Ma T'ang scowled and went out to inspect the baggage and furniture. First he opened all the cases and writing desks, scrutinising each object and paper, then flinging it aside. Ricci watched helplessly, his only compensation a look of sympathy from the military superintendent, as if to say, " You see how these eunuchs behave : they will be the country's ruin." Every time Ma T'ang found something which had not been shown him, he complained furiously, as though the object had been stolen from his palaces. If he fancied an engraving or curio, he handed it to one of his suite. When he had rifled all the drawers without finding jewellery, he became even more angry.

" I know you have precious stones hidden somewhere," he cried, looking round the courtyard. Ricci was most anxious that he should not inspect the case containing religious articles.

" You have looked everywhere," he said and tried to distract Ma T'ang's attention. But this only increased his suspicions : determined to justify his claim, he continued the search and at last came on the precious case. Opening it, he found a beautiful crucifix enclosed in a wooden box. Puzzled, he lifted it out and caught sight of the five wounds painted a realistic red. " So ! " he cried. " A fetish to kill the Emperor ! " His look of astonishment and horror told Ricci that he really believed the charge. " I suspected you were up to no good—here is the proof."

Ricci thought quickly. The Incarnation was a mystery which Chinese converts took months to grasp. If he said the figure was the Lord of Heaven whom he adored, the ignorant Ma T'ang would fail to understand and accuse him of lying to escape a heinous charge. Ma T'ang's thugs, muttering furiously, had already begun to crowd round : he must provide an explanation in familiar terms.

" This figure," he said, " represents a great saint of the West who willingly suffered death for us on the cross. We paint pictures of the scene and carve crucifixes, so that we may always have him before our eyes and thank him for suffering on our account."

" Nonsense," shrieked Ma T'ang. " It's a fetish made to inflict a terrible death on his Imperial Majesty. You will be taken to Peking under arrest."

The mandarin on the other hand seemed satisfied by Ricci's explanation. " All the same," he said, " it is cruel and improper to keep representations of such a scene."

Believing he had discovered a cache, Ma T'ang continued his search into the case containing all the missionaries deemed most sacred. Distractedly Ricci and Pantoja prayed for deliverance. After a few moments the eunuch found two other crucifixes which, to Ricci's surprise, seemed to damp his suspicion. He examined them and compared them with the first, then said petulantly, " No one ever makes more than a single fetish. They may, as you claim, be representations of a saint." Next he found and set aside two reliquaries, one an ebony cross containing bones of saints, the other in the form of a triptych, as well as a gilded Mass chalice, which had been sent that same year from Macao. These he said he would forward to the Emperor. Finally he took possession of a bag containing two hundred taels, set aside for their expenses in Peking.

Concluding his search, the eunuch sat down, motioning Ricci and the mandarin to chairs beside him. With a grand gesture, he returned the bag of silver to Ricci, as though it were a present. " You see, I am an honest man," he swaggered. Ricci thanked him, then asked for the reliquaries, but with these the eunuch refused to part.

" At least give me back the chalice," Ricci begged. " With that we sacrifice to the Lord of Heaven. It is a sacred object which no one but we who are consecrated may touch."

The eunuch, sensing a challenge, lifted the chalice and began to turn it over and over in his stubby, plump hands. " What do you mean?" he asked in a slow, insolent voice, " no one but you may touch it?"

Furious, Ricci threw down the bag of silver in front of the eunuch. " Take double its weight—or more if you like—but give us back that holy vessel."

The eunuch clasped the chalice to him: it was evidently more costly than it looked. Moved by Ricci's appeal, the man-

darin intervened. " Evidently they want the goblet only because
they consider it holy. Since they offer double its weight in
silver, you had better accept."

The eunuch glanced from Ricci to the military superintendent, puzzled and on ground where he felt unsure. Ricci
held his breath. For a moment sacrilege hung in the balance.
Ma T'ang looked down at the cup : his palaces, after all, were
heaped with more valuable treasures. With an ill grace he
handed the chalice back.

After ordering an inventory to be made of all the presents,
which were to be transferred to the government strong-room
in the city, Ma T'ang left the pagoda, saying that since he had
sent a new letter to the Emperor, they could hope to reach
Peking shortly. Two days later he returned to Lintsing, leaving
Ricci and his party under guard.

November passed, in a cloud of winnowing and perfume of
harvest. In the pagoda which served as their prison Ricci and
Pantoja began to pray and fast, begging God, for the sake of so
many million souls, to grant them safe passage to Peking. But
the year drew towards its end, a cold winter set in, freezing the
canal, and still they heard nothing from the eunuch or Peking.
Ricci therefore dispatched two letters. The first, to Ma T'ang,
asked him to write again to the Emperor, because they were
suffering from the extreme cold, the lodgings having no form
of heating. The second, to the military superintendent at Lintsing, asked for advice and begged him to use his influence with
Ma T'ang. The servant who delivered the first note was
severely beaten and sent back without a reply, while the
military superintendent, afraid to correspond with Ricci, also
turned him away. Later, however, he sent secretly for the
servant, to whom he gave a verbal reply : " Your affairs have
gone from bad to worse. Ma T'ang intends to increase his
reputation by launching a formal charge against you as fetish-
ists bent on murdering the Emperor. He has already spread this
rumour here in Lintsing and says you ought to be sent back
in chains to your own country." In a secret written note he
advised " Save your lives while you can. Return to Canton,
even though it means losing all your belongings. Above all,

destroy those crucifixes. If you are afraid to increase the danger by leaving, submit a memorial to the Emperor by way of your friends in Peking, asking permission to leave the country."

Ricci had supposed their situation desperate, but not as desperate as this. He refused, however, either to destroy the incriminating crucifixes or to abandon his attempt to see the Emperor. Smuggling him out of the pagoda by night, he sent Brother Sebastian to the capital, two days' journey away, with some small presents and appeals for help to his few acquaintances and those to whom he had letters of recommendation. A week later he returned to confirm Ricci's doubts : rumours spread by Ma T'ang had alarmed Peking : his friends were too frightened to intervene. They advised Ricci on no account to submit a memorial, for the Emperor did only what the eunuchs proposed. Instead, he and his party should throw themselves on Ma T'ang's mercy and beg for their lives in exchange for the presents.

Since the eunuch already possessed their presents, barter was out of the question, and Ricci had no illusions about his mercy. Guards surrounded the pagoda. A tribunal was presumably being found competent to judge and execute foreigners who had tried to kill the Emperor. Ricci was furious with himself for allowing the trap to close. Now their only escape lay overhead. While all around giant inscrutable idols were invoked to grant release from the wheel of life, they prayed they might be spared, not for their own sake—even Brother Sebastian was eager for martyrdom—but to establish the Church in China.

CHAPTER NINE

Within the Forbidden City

THE year turned and with it their fortune. In mid-January a letter was dispatched to Ma T'ang, the contents of which Ricci learned a few days later. "Having considered the memorial submitted by Ma T'ang, Collector of Taxes, concerning the gifts which the distant barbarian Li Ma-tou desires to offer, His Majesty orders the said Li Ma-tou to present his gifts at Peking. At the same time the Ministry of Rites is commanded to examine the matter and submit a further memorial."

Six months had passed since they had fallen into Ma T'ang's hands. For eight weeks they had been in imminent danger of their lives: everyone, mandarins, eunuchs, even their guards believed they would die. And now deliverance. It seemed certain to Ricci that Providence had intervened. All that he could ever learn about the reprieve was that one day, when the second memorial had been dismissed to an obscure palace limbo, the Emperor suddenly remembered that "certain foreigners wanted to present His Majesty with a striking clock." Petulantly he asked, "Why don't they give me that striking clock?" The Emperor's private secretary, a eunuch, replied, "The foreigners cannot enter Peking without a licence, and your Majesty has not yet replied to Ma T'ang's second memorial." The Emperor called for the memorial and at once issued a rescript.

Ma T'ang was displeased because his charges against the foreigners had been ignored, and because the Ministry of Rites, a hated mandarin body, had been ordered to take the matter out of his hands. But with an imperial rescript he could only comply. Reluctantly he commanded the gifts to be removed from the strong-room and given back to the foreigners, who were to be provided with horses and porters at public expense for the journey to Peking. When the gifts were restored, for safety's sake Ricci opened both the reliquaries and removed the pieces of the true Cross. He left only minor relics such as pieces of saints' clothing and soil from the Holy Land, carefully altering the inscriptions in case they ever fell into Christian hands. The pieces of the true Cross he concealed in his own personal baggage.

On January the twentieth Ricci and his party set out with eight horses and more than thirty porters, in charge of a mandarin who informed them that this was the usual way of escorting ambassadors from tributary kingdoms. As foreigners wishing to present gifts, they had been provisionally placed in that category. They changed horses at every town and spent each night in the Governor's house as guests of honour. After shivering all winter, it was luxury to sleep on brick *kangs* kept warm by an interior charcoal fire. As men " summoned by the Emperor " they travelled at a slow pace conformable to their new dignity, taking four days to reach Peking, where they were lodged outside the walls in a house belonging to the court eunuchs.

Ricci had hoped to be able to offer the presents himself, but now he was informed that foreigners were not admitted to the palace, and he must submit them through the Director of the Office for Transmitting Letters. This news was a severe blow, for he had brought the presents only to win an audience. However, each moment he spent in the country was a contravention of age-old custom, and he believed that the palace gates, like those of China, would yield to prayer and perseverance. Meanwhile, he drew up a complete list of the presents in Chinese :

    1. A small modern painting of Christ.
    2. A large antique painting of the Virgin.
    3. A modern painting of the Virgin with the Christ Child and John the Baptist.
    4. A breviary, with gold-thread binding.
    5. A cross inlaid with precious stones and pieces of polychrome glass, containing relics of the saints.
    6. An atlas—the *Theatrum Orbis Terrarum* of Ortelius.

7. A large clock with weights, and a small striking clock of gilded metal worked by springs.

8. Two prisms.

9. A clavichord.

10. Eight mirrors and bottles of various sizes.

11. A rhinoceros tusk.

12. Two sand clocks.

13. The Four Gospels.

14. Four European belts of different colours.

15. Five pieces of European cloth.

16. Four cruzados.

He scanned the items : toys to win an Emperor. They were not the magnificent valuables of the embassy he had once planned, but in the clocks he had special faith. As for the rhinoceros tusk, it was believed to be a unicorn's horn, giving protection against poison and every disease. Most of the objects had already aroused mandarin curiosity and covered such a range that one at least would surely interest the Emperor, whatever his tastes. On this point Ricci, despite discreet questions (for the Son of Heaven was never the subject of idle gossip), had obtained no exact information. His gifts were being offered, like prayer, to the invisible and unknown.

Next Ricci drew up the draft of a memorial to accompany them, balancing as far as possible humility with an essential petition. He carried the draft to a highly qualified scholar whose profession it was, for a very high fee, to turn mundane thoughts into ethereal language suitable for the Son of Heaven. Every phrase had to be elaborated in a special way which even many graduates did not know. Having copied out the memorial on two separate sheets in special calligraphy employed only for such occasions, he read his version to Ricci :

" Li Ma-tou, your Majesty's servant, come from the Far West, addresses himself to your Majesty with respect, in order to offer gifts from his country. Your Majesty's servant comes from a far distant land which has never exchanged presents with the Middle Kingdom. Despite the distance, fame told me

ALEXANDER VALIGNANVS SOC: IESV. GENERALIS INDIA=
RVM VISITATOR. ALTER A XAVERIO ORIENTIS APOSTOLVS.
OBIT MACAI. XX IANVAR. MDCVI. ÆTAT. LXIX. RELIG. XI

Alessandro Valignano

The Imperial Palace, Peking

A Concert in the Imperial Palace

Studios of the Imperial Palace

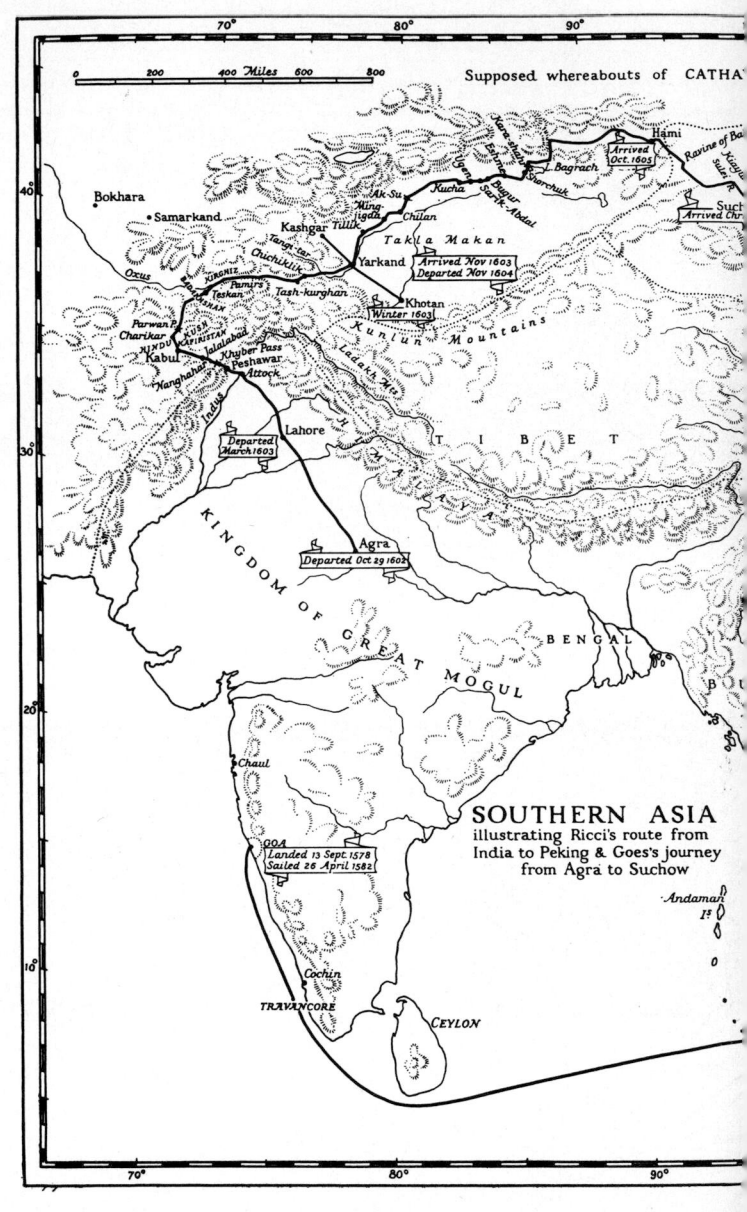

0   200   400 Miles   600   800

40°

Bokhara

• Samarkand

Kashgar Tillik

• Ming-
igda

Ak-Su

Kucha

Chilan

Yangi-tar

Yarkand

Chichiklik

Takla Makan

Hami

Arrived
Oct.1605

Ravine of Ba

Suct.

Arrived Chr.

Arrived Nov 1603
Departed Nov 1604

Oxus

Pamirs
Yeskan

SARIKOL

YANAN

CIRGNIZ

Tash-kurghan

Khotan

Winter 1603

Kunlun Mountains

Parwan P.

Charikar

Kabul

KUSH

HINDU

KAFIRISTAN

Jalalabad

Nanghahar

Khyber Pass

Peshawar

Attock

Ladakh R.

T   I   B   E   T

Indus

Lahore

Departed
March 1603

30°

Agra

Departed Oct 29 1602

K I N G D O M

O F

G R E A T

M O G U L

BENGAL

Bu

20°

• Chaul

SOUTHERN ASIA
illustrating Ricci's route from
India to Peking & Goes's journey
from Agra to Suchow

GOA
Landed 13 Sept. 1578
Sailed 26 April 1582

Andaman
I.

0

18°

Cochin

TRAVANCORE

CEYLON

70°   80°   90°

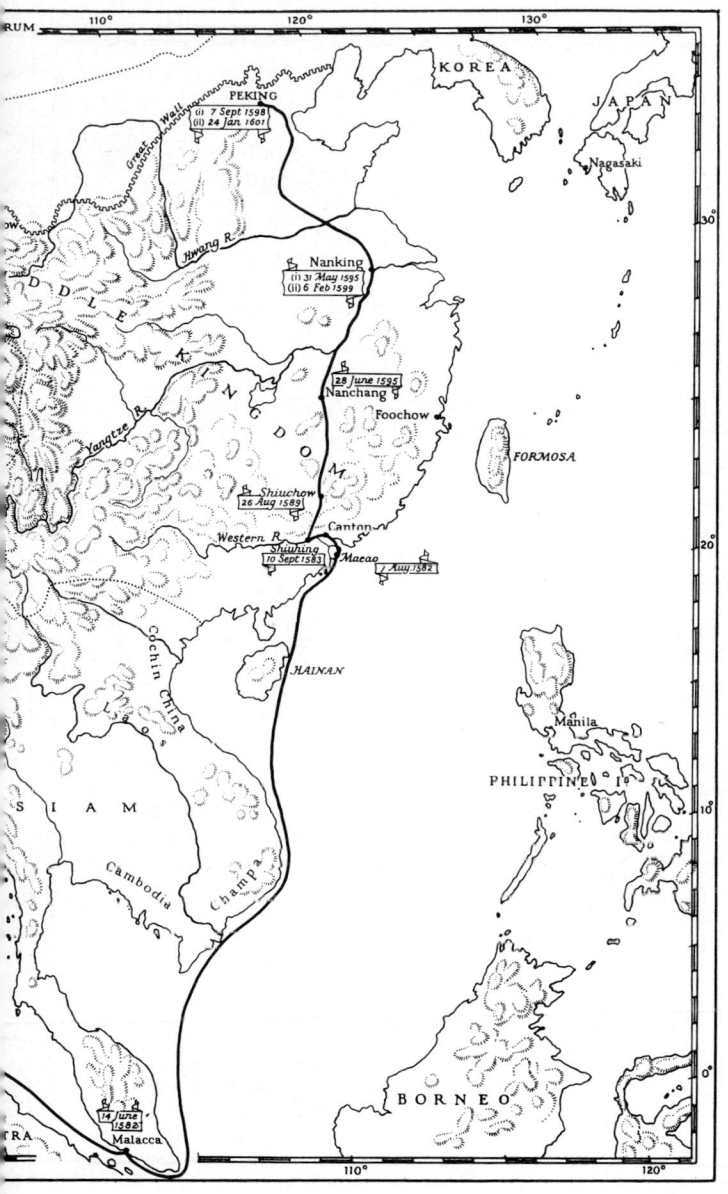

KOREA

JAPAN

Nagasaki

PEKING
(i) 7 Sept 1598
(ii) 24 Jan 1601

Great Wall

Hwang R.

MIDDLE

Nanking
(i) 31 May 1595
(ii) 6 Feb 1599

L·A·N·D·O·M

Yangtze R.

28 June 1595
Nanchang

Foochow

FORMOSA

Shiuchow
26 Aug 1589

Canton
Western R. Shuihing
10 Sept 1583   Macao
7 Aug 1582

HAINAN

Cochin China

Laos

Manila

PHILIPPINES

SIAM

Cambodia

Champa

BORNEO

14 June
1582
Malacca

SUMATRA

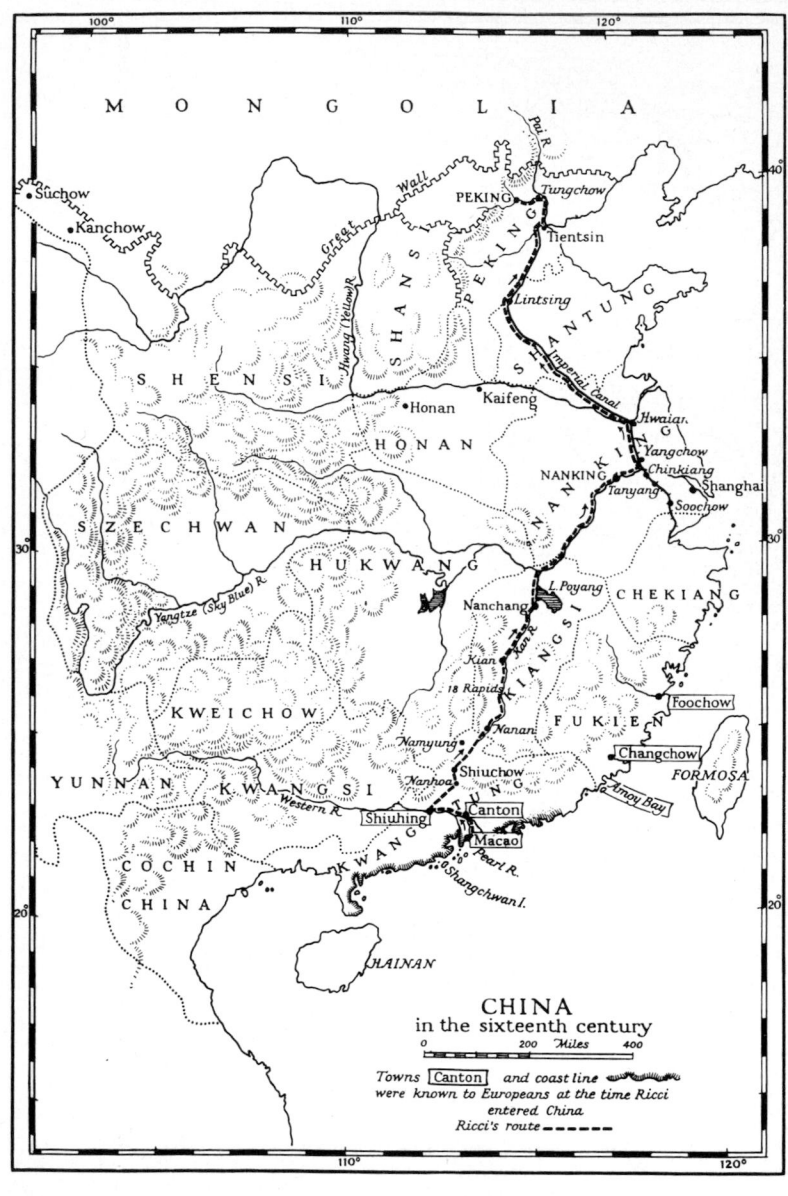

MONGOLIA

Suchow

Kanchow

SHENSI

SHANSI

Great Wall

Peir R.

PEKING

Tungchow

Tientsin

Lintsing

SHANTUNG

Imperial Canal

Hwang (Yellow) R.

Honan

Kaifeng

HONAN

Hwaiai.

NANKING

Yangchow

Chinkiang

Shanghai

Tanyang

Soochow

SZECHWAN

Yangtze (Sky Blue) R.

HUKWANG

L. Poyang

CHEKIANG

Nanchang

Kian

KIANGSI

18 Rapids

Nanan

FUKIEN

Foochow

KWEICHOW

Namyung

Nanhoa

Changchow

FORMOSA

YUNNAN

KWANGSI

Western R.

Shiuchow

NG

Amoy Bay

Shiuhing

Canton

Macao

KWANG

Pearl R.

Shangchwan I.

COCHIN

CHINA

HAINAN

CHINA
in the sixteenth century

0   200 Miles   400

Towns Canton and coast line 〰〰〰
were known to Europeans at the time Ricci
entered China
Ricci's route – – – – –

大明神宗顯皇帝

*Wan Li,
Emperor of China*

*The pious and modest
Empress Hsiao Tun*

孝端顯皇后

Paul Hsü

of the remarkable teaching and fine institutions with which the Imperial Court has endowed all its peoples. I desired to share these advantages and live out my life as one of your Majesty's subjects, hoping in return to be of some small use. With this aim, I said farewell to my country and crossed the oceans. At the end of three years, after a voyage of more than eighty thousand *li*, I finally reached Kwangtung province. First, not understanding the language, I was like a dumb man. I rented a house and studied the written and spoken language, then for fifteen years lived in Shiuhing and Shiuchow. I acquired a good understanding of the doctrine of the ancient philosophers; I read and memorised parts of the Classics and other works; and I understood their meaning a little. Then I crossed the mountains; from Kiangsi I went to Nanking, where I stayed five years. The extreme benevolence which the present glorious dynasty extends to all foreigners has encouraged me to come now even to the imperial palace, bringing gifts from my country, among them a picture of the Lord of Heaven, two pictures of the Mother of the Lord of Heaven, a book of prayers, a cross inlaid with precious stones, two clocks, an atlas and a clavichord. Such are the objects I bring and now respectfully offer to your Majesty. Doubtless they are not very valuable, but coming from the Far West they will appear rare and curious. Like the watercress and warmth of the sun which are all a poor villager can offer, they will testify to the feelings of your Majesty's servant. Since childhood I have aspired to virtue; now I have run more than half my course. Never having married, my only desire is that these gifts may bring your Majesty long life, unalloyed prosperity, the protection of Heaven on the empire and the tranquillity of the people. I humbly beg your Majesty to have compassion on me, since I have come to place myself under your Majesty's law, and deign to accept the European objects I offer. In doing so, your Majesty will increase my gratitude of your Majesty's immense goodness which excludes no one; and your Majesty will give a servant come from afar the means of showing a little of the affection which your Majesty's kindness inspires in him. Formerly, in his own country, your Majesty's servant gradua-

W.M.W.   F

ted : he obtained appointments and rank. He has a sound knowledge of astronomy, geography, geometry and arithmetic. With the help of instruments he observes the stars and he uses the gnomon; his methods are in entire conformity with those formerly practised in your Majesty's kingdom. If your Majesty does not reject an ignorant, incapable man and allows me to exercise my paltry talent, my keenest desire is to employ it in the service of so great a prince. Nevertheless, incapable as I am, I would not dare to promise results. Your Majesty's grateful servant awaits orders : he has written this letter in all humility. Dated the twenty-fourth day of the twelfth moon of the twenty-eighth year of the kingdom of Wan Li."

This document was carefully placed between two yellow tablets and covered with a piece of yellow silk. On January the twenty-seventh the memorial and presents were handed in at the principal gate of the palace, and a musket fired off to let all Peking know that a memorial had been presented to the Son of Heaven.

It might have been a farewell shot burying the whole affair for all Ricci heard during the next few days. He learned that neither gifts nor letter were bound to go further than the Director of the Office for Transmitting Letters, a eunuch who would deal with them as he thought fit. No official receipt arrived. In the palace, a city of ten thousand intriguing eunuchs, how could such paltry objects fail to get lost? Since only eunuchs had news of the palace, he set himself to be pleasant to those who frequented his lodging. He learned that the responsible official had forwarded the gifts, a day later that they had reached the imperial apartments, presently—with a touch of triumph—that they had been offered. When the picture of the Son of God was shown to the Son of Heaven, so the eunuchs related, he cried out in astonishment, " This is a living idol." Ricci treasured the unintentional truth in his words, and believed they boded well.

The next report, however, proved discouraging in itself and as a reflection of the Emperor's character. The Son of Heaven had grown afraid of this living God and had the picture removed from his apartments. The picture of the Virgin he sent to the merciful and prudent Empress Mother. This woman, widowed at an early age, had brought her son up strictly, punishing him when he neglected his studies, waking him herself every morning at an early hour and keeping a firm hold of the boy until the age of seventeen. A fervent Buddhist, she had built many pagodas throughout China and persuaded her son to spend large sums on alms. Strong-minded though she was, she too soon became frightened by the picture's likeness to life, and had it stored in her personal strong-room, at the east side of the Pavilion of the Central Extremity.

Every day, with increasing doubts, Ricci questioned the eunuchs in the hope of hearing the particular piece of news on which he counted. He had to wait more than a week before it arrived. One morning a messenger hurried to the lodgings with an urgent command from the Emperor himself : the large clock had run down and no longer struck the hours. In order to repair it the foreigners were summoned at once to the palace. Ricci and Pantoja were ready and without delay, carried by palanquin and escorted by eunuchs, travelled into the centre of Peking, to the southern of the four entrances to the palace, oriented according to strict geomantic principles. Here they dismounted and entered by one of the side gates, the central of the three, reserved for his Majesty, being always locked. They were in the Forbidden City, standing where no European had ever stood before.

Before them stretched a line of immensely wide courtyards separated by towering gateways and flanked by carved white marble balustrades. At each side, raised on marble terraces, stood red wooden pavilions, many with double, superimposed roofs. Westwards a canal led through gardens rampant with tigers, leopards and bears, to a sequestered lake. The grouping of the buildings, laid out in accordance with the pole star and adjoining constellations, was purposely processional. Man was first rendered insignificant by the vast courtyards, then drawn inwards by a gravity of being to the centre of the terrestrial universe. The walls, roofs and even the parchment windows of the buildings were yellow, colour of earth and of the Emperor who personified earth. All boasted the imperial dragon, a benevolent beast associated with life-giving rain, having a camel's head, a deer's horns, a hare's eyes, a bull's ears, a snake's neck, a carp's scales (to the extremely lucky number of eighty-one), an eagle's five claws, a tiger's paws : a creature evolved imaginatively either from the Yangtze alligator or from some prehistoric saurian. Far off they could glimpse the central apartments, seat of the dragon throne, " of the most powerful of all powers on earth, greater than all who are great under sun and moon."

His sacred person was guarded by four towering walls : within the first privileged courtiers, with the exception of bonzes and women, were allowed to enter by day : the inner two only members of the imperial family, eunuchs and concubines could penetrate. Ricci and Pantoja, looking round in bewilderment at such strangeness and counter-strangeness, were led into a courtyard between the first and second walls, dominated by the Gate of Supreme Harmony. Here, amid a crowd of bystanders who stood gazing and chattering like magpies round a broken egg, the large clock, removed from the inner apartments, had been set up, a new device for taking a more indomitable Troy. A special wooden case had been made at Nanking to protect the face and conceal the weights, four columns surmounted by cornices and a dome, with doors on two sides to regulate the mechanism, carved with foliage, flowers and dragons, varnished and gilded. A special face had also been designed, hours and quarters being designated by Chinese characters, and the hour hand taking the form of an eagle, its beak now hanging lifelessly against the incorrect hour.

The newcomers were introduced to the eunuch of protocol. He asked Ricci why they had given the clock—did they expect some appointment? No, replied Ricci, it was simply a gift of gratitude. The eunuch looked relieved : evidently he feared to be replaced by more knowledgeable foreigners. Ricci soon discovered that the courtier, for all his intelligence, did not know the first thing about clocks; he even had to point out that the dial and chime were for telling the hour, whether by day or night.

"Will you teach us how to regulate it?" Ricci was asked.

These were the words he had been hoping to hear.

" With pleasure," he replied. " But that will require two or three days."

The eunuch seemed surprised and hurried away to report this to the Emperor, who straightway ordered four members of the imperial college of mathematicians to learn how to regulate both clocks and in future to care for them. In three days this and the other clock were to be brought to his apartments.

So excited they could scarcely savour their triumph, Ricci and Pantoja were led to the college of mathematicians, a large pavilion in the same part of the Forbidden City, where they were received with unusual respect. A curious situation had now arisen. A rumour was circulating that Ma T'ang had accepted presents from the foreigners equal to or greater than those given to the Emperor. To silence it, Ma T'ang's agents were spending large sums, bribing hostile eunuchs in the palace and generally currying favour. In order to calm Ricci's supposed wrath, they now insisted on paying the missionaries' expenses at the college.

Here Ricci and Pantoja stayed three days and nights. Pathetically they watched the feverish haste of the eunuch mathematicians, struggling to master the clocks. Every word Ricci said they copied down scrupulously : making a note of all the separate parts, for which Ricci had to find Chinese equivalents, and spending all night trying to memorise them. If they forgot a single detail, the mathematicians said, it would cost them their lives, for the Emperor was atrociously cruel. Time and again for some trifling error he had ordered servants to be beaten to death.

While Ricci hastened to learn what he could about the Emperor and his palace regulations, servants came to ask questions put by the Son of Heaven. " How did people dress in the country of Li Ma-tou? What did they eat? How were their houses constructed? What did they wear? What sort of jewels did they possess? What were their marriage customs?" Already the Emperor's interests were clear. He also asked : how were the funerals of kings conducted? Pantoja was able to give a detailed answer, having recently received news of the death of

Philip II, two and a half years before, and of his magnificent funeral. He replied that in his country kings were buried in a lead coffin, which was placed inside a wooden coffin, then shut up in a stone tomb inside a small, specially constructed church.

The Emperor also asked his eunuchs to discover how much bread and wine they consumed at a meal, for in the palace unleavened bread often replaced the staple rice. To almost every question the missionaries found an answer which clearly implied that they wished to remain in Peking, not in the hope of gifts or an official appointment, but simply to worship the Lord of Heaven. Nothing would please them more than to be assigned a piece of land and a house where they could pass the rest of their lives.

The train of eunuch messengers trotted back and forth, like fallen angels, between outer barbarians and the meeting-place of Heaven and earth. On the evening of the second day the Emperor sent a message asking, " Why haven't the clocks been brought to me?" With trembling fingers the eunuchs hurriedly assembled the parts and carried the timepieces to the imperial apartments. Presently they came back elated. The Emperor was delighted to hear the clocks ticking and striking the hour. As a reward he had promoted the four mathematicians to higher rank, with increased pay. But what they prized most was that every day two of their number were to enter the imperial presence in order to wind the little clock, which the Emperor intended to keep by him day and night.

" Why are you pleased," asked Ricci, " if His Majesty is so unreasonably cruel?"

" Everyone else at court," replied one of the eunuchs, " will be afraid lest we speak ill of them. That could cost them their lives. So they will hold us in respect and give us fine presents."

As the palace apartments proved too low to permit the free hanging of the weights of the large clock, the Emperor later had it erected in his garden, in a small wooden tower, which the missionaries designed, near the Imperial Pavilion of Longevity. The tower had stairs, windows and a verandah, carved, gilded and painted, with a larger bell specially cast.

The Emperor, pleased with his gifts, was anxious to know what their donors looked like, for the eunuchs' reports had not satisfied him. But to see them in person, Ricci was informed, he absolutely refused. During the last sixteen years he had seen no one but his concubines and eunuchs face to face. Formerly he had left the palace, but always with the strictest precautions, as though travelling in enemy country, surrounded by thousands of soldiers, and hidden away in one of many litters—not even members of the court knew which. Fear of assassination and shame at his unsightly body now kept him a prisoner at the heart of his own empire. Indeed, the more the missionaries heard about Wan Li, the more discouraged they became. The extraordinary honours and power he enjoyed in so civilised a country had led them to expect an Augustus; instead he appeared to be a Nero, given to rapacity, anger and insatiable greed. He indulged a passion for rare objects by ordering from the ovens of Ching-te Chen in a single year twenty-seven thousand cups and saucers, six thousand five hundred goblets and seven hundred great vases for goldfish. Laziness had turned him, at the age of thirty-eight, into a bloated monster whose voice could hardly be heard at ten feet. The only man in a city of eunuchs and women, Emperor since the age of nine, he was nevertheless completely dominated by his favourites of the moment and his own lusts. He issued the necessary rescripts but showed no interest in government : he cherished his harem, his porcelain and the cult of himself.

Yet for his people he was not a god but a chosen man, sacrosanct merely because of his relationship with the divine. Through the Emperor Heaven governed earth and earth was attuned to Heaven. Only the Emperor was empowered to offer religious sacrifice, only the Son of Heaven, bearing the destiny of a hundred and ninety million Chinese, was worthy to communicate with Heaven. Twice a year, clad in a silk robe embroidered with dragons, the sun, moon and stars, he mounted the steps which, to the triply sacred and perfect number of nine, preceded a white marble altar lying open to the sky, a round edifice on a square base, its lower circle carved with clouds, the middle with phoenixes, the top with dragons.

There, at dawn, resuming all earthly things in himself, he offered chosen food, bales of silk, a young unblemished bull and pieces of lapis lazuli to the mysterious life-giving Heaven. At the summer and winter solstice, in the capital city, at the point of communication between earth and sky, the Emperor harmonised man with nature in an astrobiological rite, orienting him for another half-year to the dominating stars, to the principles of Yin and Yang.

Since he refused to see the foreigners, the Emperor gave orders that their portraits should be painted. From the college of mathematicians they were escorted to the imperial studios, still inside the palace. Here Ricci and Pantoja stayed several days, while they were both painted full length on rolls of silk. At the end of the sitting they inspected the finished portraits, then looked at each other in silent astonishment. It was impossible to tell which was which : they were unrecognisable, without the smallest likeness. Just as Chinese annalists made unprecedented events conform to past tradition, the account of any one year reading like those of the past two millennia, so the painters, working in a period of artistic decline and slavish imitation of past calligraphic masters, had portrayed two Chinese graduates, distinctive only by their slightly larger eyes and thicker beards. They had drawn barbarians within the orbit of the Flowery Kingdom.

Proudly the painters carried their work to the Emperor and reported his approval : " When His Majesty saw the pictures, he said, ' They are Hoeihoei ' : that is, Saracens of Persia who trade with the Middle Kingdom. But a secretary replied, ' Surely not, Your Majesty, for these foreigners eat pork.' "

Satisfied as to their appearance, the Emperor now posed further questions—difficult to answer orally. " What clothes do your kings wear? Do you have a model of their palaces?" The missionaries were able to provide visible definitions in the form of holy pictures and engravings. One showed angels, living men and the damned kneeling to the name of Jesus, a favourite image of the Order. Among the living stood the Pope, with his triple crown, the kings and queens of Europe and other dignitaries dressed in robes of honour. Ricci considered it a suitable present, implying that the Emperor too should reverence the holy Name. The picture, however, was soon returned, with the complaint that the figures were too small and shadowy. The painters were ordered to make a much larger copy in colour. This they did, eliminating the shadow and perspective, while the missionaries remained a few days longer to suggest and advise.

To provide an idea of a European palace, Ricci sent a servant to his lodgings for a book of engravings of the Escurial and a print of the square, palace and church of St. Mark's, Venice. The painters did not dare present the former, lest the Emperor request an enlargement which, owing to the fineness of detail, would have been quite beyond their powers. When he saw the Venetian print and learned that foreign kings lived in palaces several stories high, the Emperor laughed and said, "That is an exceedingly dangerous practice."

At last the questions came to an end, and the missionaries, with no pretext for remaining, were escorted from the palace. The great southern gate no longer seemed an arch of triumph, for, since there had been no opportunity to speak of religion, they counted their visit a failure. Ricci's first act was to rent a house near one of the palace entrances so that if, as he hoped, a second summons should arrive, they could respond without delay.

Hardly had they transferred their belongings when they received a visit from four more imperial eunuchs. Ricci saw from their dress that they had a much higher rank than the mathematicians : they were in fact imperial musicians—in particular, string instrumentalists—come with orders that the foreigners should teach them how to play the clavichord.

On the following day Ricci and Pantoja again entered the palace, and at the imperial college of music were received with great solemnity. Round the room were ranged chimes of stones, bells and gongs, flutes like twigs on which a bird was perched, brass clappers, horns and trumpets convoluted to resemble beasts, monstrous freaks of musical nature, a kind of organ without bellows, drums of every dimension, wooden tigers with a row of teeth on their backs, gourds and ocarinas.

Ricci recalled a concert in the magnificent Temple of Heaven at Nanking, which had proved interesting rather than pleasurable. The sacred tones had sounded like caterwauling, shattering the geometric order of the great pagoda like the walls of Jericho, for only five notes were employed and not more than fourteen sounds in any composition. With an untempered scale and without semitones no harmony was possible. Yet the classic books defined music as the essence of the harmony between heaven, earth and man; Confucius had loved listening and emphasised its paramount influence for good. When he tactfully mentioned the discrepancy to friends, Ricci was told that the old tradition had been lost almost two millennia before, only the instruments remaining : a parallel to the spheres in the Nanking observatory, but with a different explanation. The usurper Shih Huang-ti, who had built the Great Wall, wishing to pose before posterity as the First Emperor, had destroyed all the classical books by fire. Most philosophical works had been pieced together from memory by scholars, but the music, like its Greek contemporary, had been irretrievably lost.

Ricci and Pantoja were assigned magisterial positions at the north end of the room, facing south. The eunuchs approached from the other end, making four deep prostrations on the way, then knelt before the missionaries, asking them to teach diligently and patiently, and not to grow angry if they were slow learners. To propitiate the clavichord they wanted to pay it the same respect, but Ricci persuaded them that this was unnecessary. Then he and Pantoja began to explain and demonstrate the eight-tone European scale. The eunuchs were astonished at the metal wires struck by tangents, for their custom was to use finger or bow to sound raw silk strings, and still more surprised at the clavichord's sweet tones. Presently the wooden walls, acting as a sounding box, were sending forth madrigals by Animuccia and Nanino which all Italy was singing, across the courtyards and upturned gilded roofs to the Imperial presence.

As the college lay within the third wall, the missionaries came to know more important members of the court and to be regarded as familiar visitors. This advance, however, was threatened from the rear. Ricci had learned that Ma T'ang intended to ask the Emperor, on their behalf, for a large sum of money, of which he would take the lion's share. Having served his purpose, they would then be sent back south, their visit fruitless. Ricci had hoped that by renting a house he would throw off Ma T'ang's men, but in fact a sentry still stood guard and allowed the missionaries to leave only in order to visit the palace.

After the first day at the college of music, Ricci usually let Pantoja go alone, in company with the sentry, while he turned his liberty to good account, paying visits and making what friends he could. None of those to whom he had letters of introduction received him : besides traditional hostility to foreigners and the rivalry which existed between the two court cities, the discovery of the crucifixes, still news at Peking, frightened them. Ricci now realised that his encounter with Ma T'ang had been providential. If he had arrived alone, no one would have dared to present a memorial on a foreigner's behalf. But it was no less clear that he must now escape from the eunuch's clutches.

More than a month passed. The two younger musicians had already learned how to play a madrigal, but they had to wait while the two older men, one of whom was seventy, mastered the instrument. They repeatedly asked for the words of songs, in case his Majesty should ask them to sing. Anxious to profit by even this oblique opportunity, Ricci composed Chinese words to eight madrigals, the theme of each being a moral maxim. All were short and adapted, in imagery and thought, to the Chinese mind. One, *The True Way to Long-evity*, ran, " True longevity is reckoned not by the number of years but according to progress in virtue. If the Lord of Heaven grants me one day more of life, He does so that I may correct yesterday's faults : failure to do this would be a sign of great ingratitude." Another praised indifference to fame and fortune, a third exhorted the mind to sublime thoughts. The eunuchs learned and sang Ricci's songs to the Emperor. At first he was puzzled, but as the weight of tradition in this skill was slight, he soon came to appreciate delicate and tremulous sounds which accorded so well with other Chinese arts. Ricci circulated copies of the songs among his friends, from whom they won acclaim purely as literature. Those who understood his intention congratulated him, saying, " You use musical instruments not only to please the ear but to teach virtuous living."

CHAPTER TEN

The Castle of Barbarians

WESTERN modes seemed on the verge of replacing the old harmony between Heaven and earth, prelude perhaps to a new cosmography and a new religion, for Confucius no less than Plato testified to music's decisive influence on man and his notion of the universe. An old passage in the Classics declared " The *kung* note is a prince; *shang* a minister; *chio* the people; *chih* affairs; and *yü* things. If all five are out of due order, then ruin must follow."

On its highest note, when the Emperor and all Peking were humming madrigals, the new music jarred to a dying fall. One evening towards the end of February a dozen soldiers surrounded the missionaries' house. Their officer sent a message asking leave to enter. Ricci, sensing a trick, refused, whereupon the soldiers seized and bound Brother Sebastian. Realising then that he must come from a high mandarin, Ricci went out and spoke to the officer.

" You are under arrest," he was told.

" On whose authority?"

The officer produced his warrant, signed with the seal of Ts'ai Hsü-t'ai, director of foreign embassies to the Middle Kingdom in the Ministry of Rites. Ricci and his companion were charged with failing to appear at the Ministry. Puzzled, Ricci questioned the officer and learned that Ts'ai had asked Ma T'ang to let his Ministry offer the presents. When Ma T'ang refused, Ts'ai, unable to coerce so powerful a eunuch, was now revenging himself on Ricci.

When Pantoja returned from his music lesson, Ricci explained what had happened and they agreed to submit, as a dangerous but possibly effective way of regaining mandarin patronage. The officer ordered them to be present next day at the Ministry; meanwhile he locked them in the house and set a guard. When Ma T'ang's agent discovered what had happened, he had the locks broken and threatened the guards with arrest.

" You have stolen from the foreigners," he charged. " You have made off with valuables meant for His Majesty. Ma T'ang will make you pay for this."

At the mention of Ma T'ang's name the guards took fright and ran away. The eunuch then said he would transfer them to another house, but Ricci was unwilling to be rescued. If they did not slip out of the eunuch's hands now, the Ministry would perhaps acknowledge defeat and they would lose all hope of remaining in Peking.

" As foreigners," said Ricci, " it would be unwise for us to disobey an official order. I suggest that you accompany us to the Ministry of Rites and explain your grievances there."

To this the eunuch reluctantly agreed.

After an anxious night, the following day Ricci and Pantoja were provided with horses, the usual means of transport in so extensive a city. Like most of their sort, they were geldings— the art of breaking in stallions was unknown, and consequently China had no effective cavalry—poor creatures that plodded at a slow pace. Wearing the customary black veil against dust, which was swept from the unpaved streets by every breath of air, they were escorted towards the Ministry. Though sedans, mules and horses crowded the route, Ricci noticed that circulation was less congested than at Nanking, for the black veils everyone wore prevented recognition, rendering it unnecessary to dismount, bow and converse with every passing acquaintance, a point of etiquette elsewhere in China. The eunuch preceded them, brandishing his master's name, and stalked past the guards into the Ministry.

" His Majesty," he informed Ts'ai, " has placed the whole affair in Ma T'ang's hands. Unless you stop interfering I will send the Emperor a memorial, complaining that your guards have robbed the foreigners' house. You will lose your post."

But the director of foreign embassies was not intimidated. " The laws of the land," he said, " lay down that all foreigners are under my jurisdiction. Moreover, His Majesty's second memorial to Ma T'ang expressly referred Li Ma-tou and his party to me."

At this the eunuch stormed out, threatening to meet words with action, leaving the missionaries, at least momentarily, in the hands of the mandarins.

Presently Ricci, accompanied by Pantoja, was led in to the tribunal and made to kneel down, a humiliation he had not suffered for many years. Ts'ai complained first that Ricci had presented his gifts through the eunuchs, and secondly that he had not reported to the office of foreign embassies. Ricci was prepared and answered without hesitation, " The eunuch Ma T'ang stopped us forcibly on the way to Peking and took charge of the matter, giving us to understand that he was acting legally. As for visiting your office, since the day of our arrival we have been busy in the palace, at His Majesty's command, and our house has been guarded, making official visits impossible. Moreover, no one informed us that I was subject to your department. I have been living in the Middle Kingdom for almost twenty years; I travel widely and have already visited Peking three years ago. Indeed, although a foreigner by birth, I consider myself a citizen of the Middle Kingdom."

This appeared to soothe the director. " You have acted in good faith," he said, " and you evidently feel no more sympathy for the eunuchs than I. I shall present a memorial to the Emperor and arrange for the whole affair to be transferred to my department. Meanwhile, I cannot leave you in charge of the eunuchs. You and your servants must come and live in the Castle of Barbarians, where all foreign embassies are lodged. You will be guests of the Government, and provided with food."

Ricci would have preferred not to limit his freedom, but Ts'ai insisted that only by entering the Castle would he fall, without challenge, under the Ministry's jurisdiction.

He and Pantoja were escorted through the streets, while guards went to fetch the rest of the party and their baggage. The Castle proved to be a large group of buildings, surrounded by high walls and locked gates. The bare rooms, without doors, chairs, benches or beds, more fit for beasts than men, recalled

the palace of the Siamese Ambassadors at Canton. They discovered that no one was allowed out except to visit the
governor of the castle or to pay homage to the Emperor, while
only privileged officials had the right to enter. As barbarian
tribute-bearers they were not guests but prisoners.

The Castle was crowded with uncouth, raucous figures of
every colour and physiognomy, in turbans, marmot toques and
gilt-quilled helmets, a bazaar of Asiatic peoples speaking a
babel of tongues. Ricci met men from Korea, Cochin-China,
Siam, Burma, Formosa, from the Tartar tribes, from Tibet,
Mongolia and the Moslem countries of Turkestan, some of the
embassies, together with servants, numbering over a thousand
men. The Mohammedans interested Ricci most. They came
from far Kashgar and had heard of Italy, Venice, Spain, Portugal and consequently of Christianity. They brought a small
quantity of jade to the Emperor, a stone highly prized in China,
where it was carved by means of abrasive quartz sand. But their
main source of profit was rhubarb, bought cheap in Kansu,
where it grew abundantly, and sold dear in Peking. With
their profits they bought Chinese silk.

Ricci decided to question these merchants about Cathay, a
country which still excited his curiosity. On his first visit to
Peking he had arranged for Brother Sebastian to call on one of
two Mohammedans who had arrived in the capital forty years
previously from Arabia to present the Emperor with a lion, an
animal which the Chinese knew to exist but had seldom seen.
This Arabian had referred to China as Khitai, a name which
Ricci had considered sufficiently similar to Cathay to warrant
amplifying his theory, first suggested by the bridges of Nanking, and to assume that Polo had somehow been writing about
China under the name of Cathay. The Mohammedans in the
Castle now confirmed that they and their countrymen called
the Middle Kingdom Khitai and added that they knew its
capital under the name of Cambaluc. This strengthened Ricci
in his belief, but he refused to jump to conclusions. The
Mohammedans' Chinese was scanty, and their terms might be
general ones, which they would apply to any large kingdom

and city. One day perhaps it would be possible to put the matter to a final proof.

Even more curious than the merchant ambassadors were their presents. Instead of the exotic finery Ricci expected, suitable to the mightiest monarch on earth, many brought in pieces of iron which, with handles of wood cut in the Castle grounds, would be presented as curious swords. What they called cuirasses were pieces of metal tied together with lengths of tow. Others had drooping pack horses—mere skin and bones after the long journey—which would be offered as steeds of Araby.

Gradually Ricci unknotted the explanation. These embassies originated with the vanity of one of the greatest Ming emperors. Wishing to make known the supremacy of China, Yung Lo, some two centuries past, had sent legates all over Asia inviting foreigners to pay homage at Peking, the new capital. The response was immediate and enthusiastic. From every country, small and large, came merchants, under the guise of ambassadors, bent on clandestine trading with a country normally closed to foreigners. In order to justify their large numbers, they explained that to the west of China lay over a hundred and fifty kingdoms all desirous of rendering homage. Their beasts of burden carried valuable merchandise which they sold at Peking; their tribute, a mere pretext, was of no value, yet the Emperor, as befitted so great a lord, was obliged to spend over fifty thousand taels annually on presents for the "ambassadors." Their journey in China, under the strictest surveillance, was paid for by the Government, and they were given free food and lodging. The mandarins knew exactly what was happening, but for several reasons let the farce continue. The trade with foreign countries benefited China; they dared not interfere with a plan which flattered the Emperor's vanity; they feared to offend the merchants, lest they either foment rebellion within or wage war from without; and lastly, they were able to embezzle money intended for the foreigners' expenses.

Ts'ai, the director of foreign embassies, was also Governor of the Castle. Having heard his friends speak highly of Ricci and seeing for himself that the graduate preachers were very different from merchant-ambassadors, he arranged that Ricci and Pantoja should receive preferential treatment : they were assigned rooms normally used by mandarins, with beds, palliasses and silk coverlets, not mouldering and filthy like the rest of the accommodation, but perfectly new. A room was set apart which they used as a chapel for Mass. When he saw that Ricci received visits from high-ranking officials, Ts'ai went a stage further, and invited the Westerners to take meals with him in his private suite, an absolutely unprecedented event, the foreign " ambassadors " being treated like freaks, with utmost scorn. In return, discovering that Ts'ai had passed his doctorate and was interested in mathematics, Ricci gave him spheres, quadrants and a globe of the heavens.

After a few days at the Castle, towards the end of February, Ricci and Pantoja were informed that they had been granted an audience to pay the Emperor homage. Past disappointments crumbled before a neap-tide of hope. If the word " audience " has any meaning, Ricci thought, we will see Wan Li at last, perhaps even be permitted to speak to him. Anxiously and impatiently they awaited the great day, discussing how they could best use the coveted moments of communication.

Rehearsed to perfection in the kowtow and other ritual actions, at five of a dark, frosty morning they and other ambassadors were escorted to the southern gate, wearing clothes of red damask and helmets of silver covered with gilt. All carried ivory tablets some three inches wide and eight inches long, with which to cover their mouths when speaking the words of homage, for their mortal breath must not attain the Emperor. They waited by the triple archway while all Peking slept under the melting stars.

At dawn precisely the five elephants which guarded the southern gate were ridden away like night and the ambassadors ushered through the Gates of Supreme Harmony and Heavenly Purity into the vast courtyard of the Throne Hall of Assured Peace, within the fourth wall, its yellow glazed tiles flushed rose-red. It was a dawn ceremony : their dress had been

designed to mark the fact. Round the courtyard were grouped
pavilions, their decorated beams and brackets painted green,
blue and white. At the north end, approached by three flights
of white marble stairs carved with dragons in high relief, stood
an open-sided arcade landscaped with painted screens, in the
centre of which, between four emblazoned columns, was raised
the dragon throne. Behind ran a balcony with a slatted blind :
here, Ricci had been told, the Emperor might appear, wearing,
to hide his face, a crown from which hung long pendants of
pearls and gems. He too would be holding a tablet fashioned
of precious stones to contain his breath.

As the first rays of light slanted across the low roofs into
the courtyard, the assembly joined their homage to that of the
rising sun. The cosmic rite began. An official called out in a
high voice, " Kneel down," and all present knelt. At another
command, one party rose, moved forward and bowed down to
the empty throne, beating the floor with their heads and calling
out " Ten thousand years," a salutation of long life reserved for
the Emperor alone. To dramatise and protract the homage,
first one group performed it, then another. Grumbling at
having been woken so early, the jade-merchants stumbled
forward and clumsily kowtowed, then the tributary Siamese,
their praise as empty as the throne. Ricci kept his eye on the
balcony but not a shadow passed the slatted screen. Finally it
was his turn. He rose, approached the throne and prostrated
himself. Shielding his mouth with the piece of ivory, he
exclaimed " Ten thousand years." The pavilions caught and
echoed his words, but Wan Li neither appeared nor answered.
Heaven could not acknowledge the things of earth. The hollow
silence which followed was the measure of his humiliation,
kneeling there in the cold dawn. He had stormed Peking,
the forbidden city, the imperial apartments, the dragon throne,
only to confront this void, gaping as a Good Friday taber-
nacle.

As he walked backwards to his place and later down the
immense courtyards to the southern gate, the scene tilted towards lunacy. What was he doing here, under the sign of the
dragon, vested in red damask and gilt helmet? How absurd,

how presumptuous to have dreamed of converting the Emperor! Every event since his arrival in China should have made clear the futility of such an attempt. Always it was he who had given the love, made the overtures and sacrifices—only to be ignored. China simply did not care. Rejection, persecution, bloodshed would have been easier to bear because ultimately fruitful—but empty failure would not fertilise the future. Before this latest blank unrecognising stare he felt desperate, crushed, almost annihilated.

Back in the Castle, however, during the next few days his natural resilience and courage slowly began to reassert themselves. The truths which had triumphed within the Forbidden City were displaced by another, more fundamental : the undertaking on which he had embarked was not merely human. He was beginning, also, to recognise a pattern in his life, that failure preluded success. As the mists of despair dispersed, he set to work revising his plans. The Emperor might be under the control of favourites, but his word still had the force of law. Since he chose to be invisible he must be approached by letter and, apart from eunuchs, the only persons who could submit memorials with any likelihood of success were Ministers. Without delay Ricci went to the Ministry of Rites, where he saw the acting Minister. He was growing accustomed to find deputies in charge, for a mandarin, when he received news of the death of his father or mother, at once returned home to assume mourning for three years, during which time he exercised no official duties.

The acting Minister promised to submit a memorial in Ricci's favour and later sent secretaries to make an inventory of the foreigners' belongings and to question them about their intentions. Ricci replied in writing, going beyond what he had said before, because he realised that if they were classified as foreigners bringing presents, on the completion of their business they would be escorted from the country no less surely than if they still remained in Ma T'ang's hands. He wrote, " We have come to preach the law of the Lord of Heaven in the Middle Kingdom by command of our superiors, and to Peking in order to offer gifts to His Majesty in gratitude for having been allowed to remain so many years in his country. We desire no office, nor a return for our presents : only permission to remain as before in the Middle Kingdom, either in Peking or in some other city that His Majesty may designate."

The acting Minister of Rites sent to ask what doctrine they taught. In reply Ricci offered him a fine breviary and a manuscript of his catechism. The former he returned, the latter he kept for reference. Then the acting Minister submitted an important memorial to the Emperor in these terms : " Li Ma-tou claims to be a man of the Far West, but in the collection of official documents of the Ming Dynasty there is no mention of such a place, therefore it is impossible to know whether he is telling the truth. Since he comes to offer tribute after a twenty years' stay in the Middle Kingdom, the law which prescribes good treatment for whosoever ' comes from far countries, a lover of justice, to offer rare gifts ' is inapplicable. Moreover the gifts he offers, far from being rare, are mere trifles : two pictures of the Lord of Heaven and the Mother of the Lord of Heaven. In his personal baggage he has what he claims are bones of genies, but since genies are incorporeal, how could they have bones? In this connection what the noted writer Han Yü has said of the joints of the Buddha's finger is appropriate : ' It is improper that a dirty and inauspicious piece of refuse should be allowed within the palace precincts.' More serious still, these gifts have been presented to Your Majesty without passing through my Ministry. They were offered by the eunuch Ma T'ang, who must surely be held guilty of interference with the Government. I beg that in accordance with the value of the gifts and according to the usual practice, Li Ma-tou may be given a hat and belt, as well as a number of pieces of silk, with orders to return immediately to his own country. He should not be allowed to remain either in Nanking or in Peking lest, entering into relations with the eunuchs, he stir up rebellion of the people."

The acting Minister of Rites had decided that Ricci's interests must be sacrificed to a graduate victory over the eunuchs, but he had reckoned on the Emperor's neutrality. In fact, the Emperor had been so favourably impressed by the gifts that he was only too willing to listen to his eunuchs' interpretation of events. Learning that Ricci and his party had been shut up in the Castle of Barbarians, he became furious and cried, "Are they robbers to be seized in this way? Let us see what the director of embassies does next!" He put the memorial aside and refused to issue a directive.

As days passed and no rescript came, the acting Minister of Rites and his colleagues grew anxious, for the imperial silence connoted anger and possibly the direst consequences. They believed Ricci had made his eunuch friends in the palace dismiss the memorial in order to avenge himself for being taken to the Castle. This, they were beginning to realise, was a discourtesy to someone who had lived twenty years in China.

Meanwhile his friends, among them high mandarins, continued to visit Ricci in the Castle; others came out of curiosity and asked him to return their visits. Impressed by Ricci's learning and manner, one and all protested that it was shameful for him to be classified and shut up with ignorant " merchant ambassadors." In response to mandarin opinion, the acting Minister of Rites began to treat Ricci more favourably. " Tell your eunuch friends," he said, " to let His Majesty answer my memorial, and I shall obtain all the concessions you wish." Ricci protested that he was not intriguing, but the mandarin could not believe this.

Supposing that the Westerner was holding out for favours, he and Ts'ai, the Governor, began to win Ricci's goodwill. Contrary to regulations, he was allowed to go out of the Castle into any part of Peking. Four guards, under the name of grooms, were detailed to walk behind his horse to prevent escape. These grooms reported to the Governor that Ricci visited such important officials as the Secretary to the Ministry of Civil Appointments, with whom he would stay upwards of three or four hours. Alarmed at this and still receiving no rescript from the palace, the Governor of the Castle and others in his department feared that mandarins no less than eunuchs were being rallied against the Ministry of Rites. In April they decided to trim their sails to the wind. They sent a memorial quite different from the first: it made no mention of the eunuchs; instead of maligning the Europeans, it praised them for having come so courteously in person to present gifts at the imperial court, and proposed that recompense should be paid on a more handsome scale. Ricci was provided with a copy of the text, whereas on the former occasion the Governor had tried —though unsuccessfully—to keep the memorial from him. A week passed and this memorial, too, remained unanswered. All Peking was alarmed at this expression of semi-divine wrath.

One possible explanation Ricci learned from the eunuchs. The Emperor, they said, actually wanted the missionaries to remain in Peking, but did not dare propose it, contrary to all precedent, unless the plan was first put forward by the Ministry of Rites. A break with tradition was the earthly equivalent of a falling star, a disturbance of cosmic order. Ricci urged the Governor to send another memorial, proposing that they remain in the capital, but this he obstinately refused to do. If foreigners were allowed to live wherever they liked in Peking, clearly the Castle of Barbarians and his own office would fall into abeyance.

The college of mathematicians on the other hand, terrified lest the clocks should stop or go irreparably wrong, used all their influence in the opposite direction. The Emperor was passionately attached to the small clock and if by any chance it failed to strike became furious with the eunuchs. When the Empress Mother expressed a desire to see it, the Emperor, afraid she would take his treasure from him, waited for it to run down, then commanded the eunuchs to carry it to her apartments without being rewound. After a few days, when she saw that it did not strike, she returned it, saying " I thought it was a clock which struck by itself."

Three more memorials were sent from the Castle to the imperial presence, each more favourable to the missionaries, but always without the clause asking that they should remain permanently in Peking. Still no word came from the dragon throne. Explanations differed. Pantoja thought the Emperor was unwilling that they should return and spread news of the imperial palace; Ricci accepted the eunuchs' view that he dared not make a new precedent. Whatever the reason, the issue dragged on, undecided, into May, while Ricci urged his friends to secure their release, for missionary work was impossible in the Castle. They had already lost three months of valuable time and acquired the reputation of merchants, almost as offensive to graduates as the title of bonze. Mohammedans in the Castle declared escape hopeless, but they underestimated Ricci's perseverance and charm of manner, which made others play up to his own heroism. Finally he persuaded his most influential friend, a doctor of letters aged forty-seven, Secretary to the Ministry of Civil Appointments, to demand his release. This fearless official, who did not hesitate to accuse the Ministers of War at Peking and Nanking of corruption, bringing about the resignation of both, was already an admirer of Ricci's book on Friendship and had several times visited the Far Westerner on his arrival in Peking.

The Secretary approached the Governor of the Castle and when Ts'ai retorted with the old charges became furious. " Ma T'ang and his mob are murdering travellers by the hundred in open daylight : what could a foreigner do? It is perfectly clear that he abhors the eunuchs and is in complete sympathy with us."

Because Ricci's friend held the higher office and could have the Governor dismissed (in fact, Ts'ai had obtained his appointment through the Secretary's influence), resistance was out of the question. Happily a face-saving solution lay to hand. Ricci was unwell, suffering from confinement and the nervous strain of the last few months. The Governor advised him to send a note to the Ministry, saying that he lay ill and wished to leave the Castle for medical treatment.

At the end of May Ricci received written permission to reside in the city. Ts'ai, determined to exercise authority even outside the Castle walls, laid down that every five days the Castle servants should take provisions of rice, meat, salt, vegetables and wine, together with fuel for cooking, sufficient for five persons, to the missionaries' lodging. Ricci was not displeased with this arrangement, for it would make them less dependent on Macao.

After three months' virtual imprisonment and fruitless attempts to communicate with the Emperor, Ricci and Pantoja walked out of the Castle gates. It was a relief to return to China from this ark of tributary peoples, to wander where they wished, unobserved by vigilant groom-guards. Back at their old lodgings, Ricci's first action, since mandarins and eunuchs baulked each other at every turn, was to appeal directly to the Emperor. With the help of friends he composed a new memorial which the official in charge of transmitting letters, whose friendship he had made a point of winning, promised to deliver. In it Ricci recalled that he had offered clocks and other curios : instead of an appointment or a return of presents he asked for a place to live. This, too, was treated like a prayer from the damned. At first Ricci presumed that according to protocol the letter had been forwarded to the Ministry of Rites, which was so opposed to his remaining. However, he was later informed by eunuchs in touch with the Emperor that he and his party could safely remain in the capital, provided they never spoke of leaving, for that would be considered an insult to the Son of Heaven. With this Ricci had to be content. If he had not been granted official permission to stay, at least his presence was tolerated. Presumably neither Ma T'ang nor officials at the Castle would be able to secure his expulsion. What proved no less important in a country where appearances were paramount, his friends considered he had gained a victory on all fronts. Soon he was receiving calls from the curious and contemptuous, as well as from a few seekers after truth.

Among the first visitors to their lodging was the highest-ranking mandarin of Peking, at that time the only Chancellor of the Empire. Ricci and he exchanged those presents without which no friendship could burgeon, the Chancellor esteeming most an ebony sundial. Ricci was then invited to his home, where they began to discuss Christianity. From experience Ricci had learned to postpone questions of doctrine to a later meeting, for the Chinese were accustomed to retort, " Yes, doubtless that is true, but our beliefs are true also. Religions are many, but reason is one." Instead he excited admiration by enumerating good works practised by Christians : hospitals for the sick and incurable, homes for foundlings and orphans, confraternities for helping the poor, widows, and prisoners; the censorship of books, which prevented the circulation of useless and harmful works; and above all the law forbidding kings, princes, the highest lords and poorest peasants to marry more than one wife, who could never be divorced, even though she never bore a son. When he heard this, the Chancellor turned to other guests. " That in itself is sufficient to prove the Far Westerner's kingdom noble and well governed." But although they praised monogamy, Ricci found it quite another matter to make them practise it. After grave conversations about virtue and the good life, whether at the Chancellor's home or elsewhere, in Peking or in Nanking, the guests departed to that other, seldom-mentioned world which Ricci never entered, to their wives and concubines and softened boys, to Plum Blossom, Orchid, Perfume and Lady of the Vase, to Hibiscus, Chrysanthemum, Moon Lady and Tower of Jade. In-numerable as the flowers whose names they bore, behind every painted screen their high-pitched voices could be heard, raised in song or laughter. Powerful and invisible as the Emperor, they were Ricci's real rivals, undoing with a kiss an evening's arguments. He had summed up the situation in a letter to the General in Rome : " It is exceedingly difficult for a man of authority and self-respect to send one of his wives back to her family, for that implies giving her to another husband. They continually beg us to grant a dispensation in this matter, and indeed we feel pity for them. But in other countries God makes possible a solution to even greater difficulties and we hope that He will do the same in China." Nine years had passed since he had written those words and still no solution had been found.

Soon after their release from the Castle, Ricci received a visit from the four eunuchs of the mathematical college. Some-thing had gone wrong with the Emperor's clock; if they brought it to his lodgings, would he repair it? Ricci agreed, delighted at establishing a new link, however indirect. During the three days it remained in the house his friends crowded in to admire the wonderful object which had pleased the Emperor more than his prettiest blue and white porcelain. When it was repaired and carried back, the Emperor, learning that it had been seen by people outside the palace, trembled with jealousy. " If the clocks stop again," he cried, " summon Li Ma-tou to carry out repairs in the palace." This again was interpreted as a mark of imperial benevolence. Arrangements were made for Ricci and Pantoja to regulate the two clocks four times a year. In fact, the eunuchs allowed them to enter whenever they liked and even to take their friends. Soon Peking, and indeed the whole country, believed the false rumour which Ricci longed to make true—that the graduate preachers often spoke face to face with the Son of Heaven.

During the last six months of 1601 they were invited to more houses than in the whole of Ricci's previous stay in China, often attending two or three banquets in a single evening. It was necessary to accept all dinner invitations, not merely from courtesy but because serious matters such as religion were seldom discussed except in the convivial atmosphere fostered by food and drink. On fast days Ricci, instead of taking a full mid-day meal, was obliged to go hungry until the banquet began at dusk. He knew it was far from being a heroic ordeal, but he had to struggle nonetheless. " If you suffer a little," he exhorted himself, " be patient! It will soon be over."

One of the most intimate of Ricci's new friends was Li Chih-tsao. Born in 1565 of a military family, he took the degree of doctorate at the age of thirty-three, winning eighth place in a list of two hundred and ninety-two. He held an important post in the Ministry of Public Works in Peking, and had come to know Ricci soon after the missionary's arrival. They became close friends, Ricci esteeming the doctor's brilliant intelligence and skill as a geographer, Li the sciences Ricci knew and taught, especially his maps, for he himself as a young man had published an excellent atlas of the world, which showed nothing more than the fifteen provinces of China. At Li's request Ricci prepared a third edition of his map. Over five feet high, in six parts, it was in fact an absolutely new sinusoidal projection which took a year to complete. In the second edition there had been only thirty place-names: in the third there were over a thousand. As well as much astronomical information, he added curious details about each country : " From Labrador to Florida the people are fishermen, wear skins and treat strangers well. Those who live inland, in the mountains, wage perpetual war, eating only snakes, ants, spiders and the like." The balsam and silver of Peru were mentioned, and Ruscelli's legend about Ireland applied to England : " The island has no native snakes or other poisonous reptiles, and when imported such animals became harmless." Li wrote a flattering preface; so did three of Li's friends, all praising the author's virtue and intelligence. The printers pirated it while in the press, so that two impressions were issued, but even so, a few months after publication copies had become unobtainable.

This beautiful and scholarly work was widely acclaimed. Some cities, however, were perturbed. How could Li Ma-tou, being a foreigner, possess such vast knowledge? Ricci was highly amused when, to salve their pride, they concluded that as he had lived some twenty years in China he could not really be considered a foreigner.

Under Ricci's direction, Li learned how to make every kind of sundial and an astrolabe complete with laminae. He translated in an abridged form the works of Clavius called *Gnomonica, Astrolabe* and *Practical Arithmetic*, revealing for the first time in Chinese the method of extracting square and cubic roots from whole numbers and fractions. By translating Clavius's commentary on John Holywood's *Sphere*, he introduced the first Englishman to China. Holywood, born at the end of the twelfth century in Halifax, Yorkshire, studied at Oxford and later settled in Paris. His fame rested entirely on the *Tractatus de Sphaera*, a little work in four chapters treating of the terrestrial globe, of circles great and small, of the rising and setting of the stars, and of the orbits and movements of the planets. It added little to Ptolemy and his Arabic commentators, but enjoyed a great renown during the Middle Ages and, although the discoveries of Copernicus had rendered much of it out of date, remained a standard text-book. Ricci supplemented it by composing a poem in four hundred and twenty verses entitled *Treatise of the Constellations*, giving to each of the twenty-eight Chinese constellations its name, position and degree of luminosity in a form easy to learn by heart. This work too Li translated into Chinese.

The year 1601 convinced Ricci that he had at last won an influential position where his gifts could be used to greatest advantage and which, for the moment, he could not abandon. Yet, as superior of the whole China mission, he must somehow direct and solve the problems of the other houses which had grown up in the wake of his journeys. So far he had governed by letter, but, feeling the need of a more personal report, in the autumn of that year he wrote to Macao, suggesting that one of the Fathers be sent to the three other houses, travel to Peking, then return to discuss any outstanding problems with Valignano when he should next arrive in the enclave. In August 1602 Manoel Dias, a somewhat austere but enterprising Portuguese, travelled to Peking and gave Ricci the full report for which he had asked, an account which stirred the memories of twenty years.

Of the three houses Ricci had founded Shiuchow flourished best, under the direction of a young Sicilian, Nicolò Longobardo, personally selected by the Visitor for his indomitable character and boundless energy. At Nanchang, on the other hand, little progress was made, for the single missionary there had been stricken with consumption. At the southern capital Ricci's friendships had been strengthened, and some fifty new converts were being made every year. In that city an influential Christian mandarin, baptised by Ricci, had recently died. He had asked for Christian burial but most of his family wished to call in the bonzes for the traditional colourful rites, supreme outward proof of filial piety. The missionary in charge had referred the problem to Ricci.

No Chinese ceremony was so elaborate or important. An immensely long cortège would first be formed, led by two men bearing large lanterns recording the family name, age and title of the deceased, followed by sixteen musicians sounding drums and gongs, pipes and trumpets. Next would walk the sons, the eldest, supported in his grief by retainers, carrying in one hand a wooden staff entwined with white paper, in the other, at the end of a bamboo pole, a white streamer called the soul cloth, supposed to summon the errant soul to accompany the body. Then would come the bier, followed by relatives and friends.

At the grave each person would be given a piece of betel nut wrapped in a leaf and a piece of silver in cream-coloured paper. After a masked figure had dispelled evil spirits by striking each corner with a spear, the coffin would be lowered, paper images of servants, elephants, tigers and lions burned and a pot containing rice lowered into the grave as food for the soul. Not until the geomancer had assured himself that it lay straight would the coffin be covered over. When earth had been cast in, the Buddhist bonze in charge would lift a crowing cock high in the air, then bend his body three times to the grave. All the mourners having copied his action, the soul cloth would finally be committed to sacred flames.

The question put to Ricci was : could superstitious elements in these rites be suppressed, while the outward form was adapted to Christianity? Scandal would be caused if a Christian were forbidden to pay his father supreme honours, and the policy of the missionaries had been to tolerate outward forms wherever possible. But in this case Ricci decided that the constituent ceremonies were based on a conception of death alien to the new religion and that, however offensive to Chinese susceptibilities, a complete break must be made. The Nankinese family were ordered to bury the dead man with Christian prayers and the simple ritual of tears.

Dias remained in Peking two months. Ricci was able to take the majority of decisions himself but several requests and difficulties he asked Dias to refer to Valignano. First, if converts were to be made on the scale of Japan—and some of Ricci's European correspondents did not hesitate to criticise what they considered to be his slow progress—more priests were needed, strong men apt at learning a new language. It was asking too much that missionaries, one of them seriously ill, should remain alone for years on end in so alien a country. Valignano, on his arrival in Macao at the beginning of 1603, consolidated Ricci's success, which indeed surpassed his best hopes, by promising to send Dias himself to Nanchang, and to divert other priests destined for Japan to China. A scheme for generous financial help had to be curtailed later in the year when two carracks and a brigantine sailing for Japan in July were captured off Macao by Dutch pirates : symptom of a new and growing threat not only to Portuguese power but to her Catholic mission. The loss to the enclave amounted to 400,000 ducats, and to the Vice-province alone 15,000 ducats, the sum annually invested in trade by the Society.

The second question related to government of the four houses. Ricci, fully occupied at Peking, suggested that Dias, for whose zeal and love of the Chinese he had the highest regard, should succeed him as superior of the mission. Valignano, however, believing that even by letter Ricci could govern more effectively than anyone else in person, declined to relieve his compatriot. Instead, he appointed Dias superior of the three southern houses, subject to Ricci, who in turn was directly answerable to the Vice Provincial of Japan and China. Thirdly, in response to Ricci's request, Valignano gave permission for three more young Chinese, born of Christian parents at Macao, to be received into the Society.

Finally, the Visitor decided a number of very difficult theological questions. At certain times of the year gifts of meat, fruit, pieces of silk—paper, if the family were very poor—and incense were offered before the ancestral tablets which stood in every house. The tablet consisted of a plain, oblong piece of hard wood, split nearly the whole way up and stuck into a small transverse block. On one of the inner surfaces and on the front outer surface were written the name and age of the dead ancestor with other particulars. For the interpretation of these offerings Ricci took his stand on a capital text of the *Doctrine of the Mean*, in which King Wu and the Duke of Chou were said to have " served the dead as they would have served them had they been living, which is the summit of filial piety." In Ricci's opinion, the dead were not believed to eat the offerings, or even to have need of them : the action was simply the outward expression of love and gratitude, instituted for the comfort of the living, not the dead, and to teach sons to honour their parents while alive, seeing that respect was everywhere paid to them even after their death. A careful study of the history of the practices—far older than Buddhism—had convinced Ricci that the veneration paid to parents and the similar honours to Confucius were not idolatrous but purely civil and should be tolerated. Longobardo had recently challenged this opinion, and Ricci now asked for an authoritative ruling.

The issue raised questions of supreme importance. In the savage countries of South America, Indonesia and Africa, Christianity had posed not only as a religion but as a great civilising force. It had spread as a result of physical conquest, and imposed on the people a Western way of life, considered a norm. No distinction was made between the essentials of Christianity and Western trappings, so that everything from the hymns sung in church to the moulding of an altar reredos followed European patterns.

In China, however, as Ricci and Valignano were aware, Christianity was for the first time in history confronted with a civilisation older and at least as great as the Graeco-Roman, with a population far more numerous than that of Europe. Christianity could not conquer here merely by force of arms, numbers or superior intelligence. Abandoning an age-old exclusive provincialism, she must recognise and tolerate all that was best in the older civilisation, and introduce only her essential message : her revelation and theology. If she attempted to impose unessentials—philosophic, literary, artistic or ritual— or to cut Chinese civilisation to Western patterns, she would remain an exotic tied to Occidental methodology and customs which would make her message unacceptable to the Chinese mind. The Church, in fact, in order to show herself truly universal, in order to sail the China sea, must jettison all local and national prejudice, even her age-old habits of mind, and take on a cargo of Eastern wisdom compatible with her message, without deviating one point from her essential course.

Those were the problems raised by Longobardo's challenge. To a Western mind the incense and prostrations before ancestral tablets seemed superstitious—to be condemned as forcibly as Ricci had condemned Buddhist funeral rites—but twenty years' experience of China, poor and rich, together with a profound knowledge of her holy books had taught Ricci, who was always ready to recognise and admire good, whatever its setting, to look beneath the outwardly scandalous performance to the thoughts and motives inspiring the action : in fact, to apply the principles of the New rather than of the Old Testament. He had concluded that the rites to ancestors and Confucious were pious not superstitious ceremonies and could therefore be safely tolerated, though Christians should be encouraged to spend their money to better purpose on alms for the poor.

Valignano discussed the problem with Dias. As early as 1592 the Visitor, faced with a similar dilemma in Japan, had written to Rome suggesting that everything possible should be conceded without countenancing even the suspicion of idolatry or infringing the Faith. The missionaries were dealing with a different mentality and age-old customs : in Israel itself, prepared as it was by centuries of prophecy, the early Christians had turned to good account all that was not hostile. If that had been necessary within the framework of the same civilisation, how much more necessary in a vastly different one.

Eleven years' further experience had confirmed him in his view. After a detailed consideration of the rites question, Valignano informed Ricci that he wholeheartedly approved his present practice.

CHAPTER ELEVEN

Clash with the Buddhists

HELPED by Pantoja, who was able now to speak and write Chinese, Ricci began to reap a harvest among the influential men of Peking. Their first converts included a nobleman, married to the sister of the Emperor's consort, " the pious and modest Empress " Hsiao Tun; two sons of the imperial physician and a nephew of the Minister of Justice. The most brilliant was Li Ying-shih. Five years younger than Ricci, he had commanded a regiment in the Korean war before succeeding his father as " General who owes his rank to meritorious relatives " in the imperial bodyguard. A mathematician, he lived in Peking with his mother, wife and children, and came to know Ricci through his scientific teaching. Primarily an astrologer and an expert in casting horoscopes, Li also knew how to choose the site of a grave or a new house, and the right time to transact business : for which he was esteemed and often consulted at court. To embrace Christianity would mean abandoning his role of cosmic wizard, even—so he imagined—calling his predictions coincidences and himself a charlatan. By explaining that past successes had been obtained through the devil's agency, Ricci showed a sympathy which made conversion possible.

Li was baptised with the name of Paul on the feast of Ricci's own patron saint, 1602. It took him three whole days to destroy the geomantic books in his fine library, most of them manuscript works based on his own calculations and occult formulae collected from all over China. He burned the books publicly, both to proclaim his new creed and to show his former clients that he was no longer a practising astrologer. His mother, wife and two sons were presently converted, together with his old tutor and several servants. He constructed a chapel in his house and had one of his sons, a boy of fourteen, taught the difficult Latin responses so that he could serve Ricci's Mass.

It was Ricci's custom to introduce fasting gradually during Lent and on the vigils of feast-days, but from Macaonese students at the mission house Li learnt and at once scrupulously followed the strict Christian practices. Learning too that a plenary indulgence was granted to anyone making a convert, he determined to achieve this goal. He wanted to travel to Macao to be confirmed by the bishop, but family business soon obliged him to return to his native province of Hukwang. There he baptised several friends *in articulo mortis*, using the formula which Ricci had transliterated from the Latin : Uo-ngo te pa-ti-zo in no-mi-no Pa-te-li-se uo-te Fei-li-i uo-te Se-pei-li-tu-se San-co-ti. Ia-mom : *l* replacing *r*, and *p, t, s, c,* being united to a vowel, since otherwise they were incapable of being pronounced. After the baptisms Paul Li wrote Ricci a triumphant letter—he had gained his plenary pardon at last.

As notable converts increased, it became generally known that the new religion would not tolerate any other creed. The Buddhists, foreseeing the danger should the Emperor, their chief protector, be converted, rallied to the attack. One of Ricci's new opponents was a well-known poet and prose-writer called Huang Hui, who at fourteen had taken the degree of master and now held the high post of Assistant Supervisor of Instruction and Lecturer of the Imperial Academy. He was also tutor to the Emperor's eldest son, who through Huang's influence had recently been proclaimed heir to the throne. His wife had died when he was forty, and Huang had become a Buddhist contemplative, practising fasting and abstinence. Through Ts'ai, Governor of the Castle of Barbarians, he obtained the loan of certain manuscript writings on which Ricci was then engaged. These he perused with a fellow member of the Imperial Academy, writing comments in the margin, Huang in black ink, his friend in red. The notion that God was separate from the human soul seemed particularly ridiculous to Huang, whose sect followed the teaching of Liu Tsung-chou : " Beings are not beings, I am not I; we all form a single substance." When the manuscripts were returned, Ricci, knowing that Huang was planning to give the Emperor a memorial against the missionaries, kept prudent silence. However, he devoted a chapter of his Catechism to monist attacks, without naming their advocates. His chief argument was that if man were of the same substance as God, then the contrary would be true, in which case, given that acts belong to individuals, not to their instruments, sin would be imputable to God.

The Buddhist threat to expel Ricci from China, which at any moment seemed likely to be realised, was presently rendered empty by an unexpected succession of severe reverses. One of the most prominent Buddhists, the bonze who had given Ricci a laudatory poem in Nanking, was on the point of visiting the northern capital, where he had many disciples, when he was accused by an influential censor of preaching a doctrine hostile to Confucius and Mencius. The Emperor, unable to support openly works which so disparaged the national philosophy, ordered the author to be brought to Peking in chains and the wooden blocks of all his books destroyed. In shame and terror, the old man—he was seventy-six—cut his throat with a razor, dying in agony two days later.

The success of this charge prompted the Minister of Rites, a close friend of Ricci, to submit an important memorial against all mandarins and graduates who depreciated Confucianism. He pointed out that students in the examinations (for which his Ministry was responsible) were citing Buddhist works. " Being has become non-being; a famous doctrine has become a chain and discipline a tumour. Bold views are the rage and it is considered brilliant to suppress all distinction between true and false, good and evil. Buddhist sayings about the soul and nature, because of a certain superficial resemblance, are introduced into Confucianism. . . . A man cannot fully master the Classics until his hair has grown white, yet the innovators suggest that to the age-old course should be added other, foreign doctrines : thus they reject the spirit and marrow of our patrimony and abandon the substance of traditional teaching." The Emperor approved the memorial : " Taoism and Buddhism are alien creeds, suitable for hermits who live alone in the woods or on mountain-tops. If any magistrate feels sympathy for them, let him give up his career and join the hermits. These two doctrines can never be ranked with Confucianism, otherwise the empire would be rent by rebellion." This reply was all the more extraordinary since the Emperor, together with his mother, concubines and family, was known to be sympathetic to Buddhism. It was one more proof that he did not dare impose personal beliefs on his people, that his essential role was to preserve the traditional unifying philosophy, counterpart to the order of nature. The Minister of Rites issued a decree forbidding candidates in the examinations to speak of Buddhism unless to refute it. As a result Huang and his fellow Academician retired from public life, and in future no official dared support any but the state philosophy.

The following year, 1603, the Buddhists suffered an even greater blow. Many bonzes were attached to the court, although they could never enter the palace. One in particular, Shen Takuan—whose robe the Emperor's consort, the pious and modest Hsiao Tun, adored as a sacred relic—was influential with the Empress Mother, who gave him alms for temples, idols and the support of thousands of disciples.

Between the Ta Hsueh, or Heavy Snow, and the winter solstice—by Ricci's reckoning, on the morning of December the fourteenth—a printed memorial purporting to be signed by one of the censors was found in the imperial apartments and at the palaces of all the chief mandarins. The pasquinade—an attack on the Emperor and court— claimed that His Majesty had been forced against his will to appoint as heir his first-born son by his official consort, the pious and modest Hsiao Tun, and that later he had secretly changed the succession, giving it to Fu, third son by his favourite concubine. Its sting lay in the fact that one of the Chancellors and the Great Council, to please the Emperor, had projected just such a change.

Determined to find the perpetrator, Wan Li promised a huge reward and high honours to anyone securing his conviction. For fear of spies no one in Peking dared speak of the lampoon, while Ricci as a foreigner was automatically in danger. The bonze Shen, as spiritual adviser to Hsiao Tun, the court physician and many high officials were arrested and tortured. Shen's personal papers, although silent about the lampoon, showed that he had been bribed by friends to obtain appointments. Another bonze was found to be supporting twelve concubines in different provinces. Worst of all was a letter written by Shen to a friend, criticising the Emperor for lack of devotion to Buddhism, and of respect to his mother. The bonze was thrown into prison : the magistrates hated him for his notoriously supercilious attitude to the mandarin class, and had him beaten to death. He used to claim that he cared nothing for his body, but when the blows fell he cried out like any other prisoner and in dying effaced a lifetime's reputation for sanctity.

As for the pasquinade, an educated merchant, who wrote occasional poetry, the style of which was considered similar to that of the offensive document, confessed under torture and was condemned to be cut into 1,600 pieces, without a bone being broken or his head injured, so that he could witness his own disintegration. At the end of the public execution one of the crowd, to gain a large reward promised by the merchant's family, dashed out, severed and seized the dead man's head, then ran away, throwing money over his shoulder in order to delay his pursuers.

With the discrediting of Buddhism, Peking was more in the mood to accept a religion which accepted and brought to perfection the principles of Confucius. Ricci seized the occasion to publish the Catechism on which he had been engaged for the past nine years. He had proceeded warily, knowing that he was casting the mould of Oriental Christianity, selecting Chinese terms which, once in general use, could not easily be replaced. He had circulated the manuscript among his friends, taking their advice about style and noticing the arguments which proved most effective. When a close friend first saw the manuscript, he offered to print it at his own expense. But at that time Valignano's imprimatur had not yet arrived and Ricci replied that he was still polishing it. The friend sent back a message saying " This country is steeped in sin, like a sick man at the point of death. Your book provides the cure. It is a poor answer to say that you want to improve the already clear style. You are like a doctor who attends a very sick patient and writes out a remedy which can save his life, then adds ' Wait a moment while I word the prescription more elegantly.' " In 1603, when the work was completed to Ricci's satisfaction and the imprimatur obtained, the friend paid for the edition, to which he had two years earlier contributed a preface, giving Ricci the title of doctor. This set a precedent and future authors continued to write of " Doctor Li."

Treating not of all the Christian mysteries, which the missionaries explained only to catechumens and converts, but of certain general principles, especially those which could be proved by light of natural reason, *A True Disputation about God* was a work of apologetic in the form of a dialogue between a Chinese and a Western graduate. The existence of God having been proved by four arguments, eleven ancient Chinese texts were cited in which the Supreme Lord, synonym for Heaven, was shown to be a unique, personal, intelligent being. The pantheistic monism maintained by Huang Hui was refuted, Lucifer, who claimed to be like God, being designated the first author of this argument. In a chapter entitled " Refutation of the six ways of the metempsychotic wheel and the prohibition against killing animals, together with a true explanation of fasting " Ricci suggested that Pythagoras was the first man to preach metempsychosis, a doctrine which the Buddhists brought from India, a much less important country than China, as the recent edition of his map had made clear. Since all things were created for man, there could be no law forbidding him to kill his food. Finally, after treating of heaven and hell, human nature, free will and the end of man, the Westerner explained that the Lord of Heaven became man 1,603 years ago. The Chinese graduate was made to answer : " How could people at that time be certain that Jesus was really the Lord of Heaven and not just an outstanding man? His own testimony surely would be insufficient."

The Western graduate replied, " The word ' saint ' has a narrower meaning in the West than in the Middle Kingdom, and even more so when applied to the Lord of Heaven. If the ruler of a country a hundred *li* in circumference rallied his vassals and conquered the Middle Kingdom without committing a single injustice or killing a single innocent person, in the West he would not thereby be called a saint. If an eminent ruler gave up a life of glory to become a poor religious, he would be called no more than ' frugal.' A saint is one who pays diligent honour to the Lord of Heaven, suffers humiliation, says and does extraordinary things beyond man's powers, such as healing incurable diseases without medicine, raising the dead, prophesying. Those whom my humble country terms saints are all men of this kind. . . . The miracles performed by the Lord of Heaven when He was in this world are still more numerous and wonderful than those of saints. They performed miracles through the power of the Lord of Heaven, whereas He used His own power."

After summarising the life of Christ, the Westerner continued : " Four saints wrote down His earthly life and His doctrine in books which circulated in many countries. Then all the people from north, south, east and west embraced His doctrine, observing it from generation to generation. Thenceforward the civilisation of the countries of the Far West made great progress. The annals of the Middle Kingdom recount that the Emperor Ming of the Han dynasty, having heard news of the doctrine, sent ambassadors westwards to ask for its holy books. On the way, mistakenly believing that the Emperor had referred to India, they obtained copies of the Buddhist scriptures and circulated them in the Middle Flowery Kingdom. Your noble country has been misled until now and has heard nothing of the true religion. Surely that is a sad disgrace for learning and the arts?"

This book contained the fruits of Ricci's discussions with such friends as the Ministers of Civil Appointments and of War, with the Censor at Nanking; and with the geographer Li Chih-tsao. Appealing in every case to principles acceptable to most Chinese or to their ancient and authoritative texts, in matter, approach and style a triumph of adaptation, bearing witness to his love and understanding of the Chinese, the book probed beneath all the inessential differences, obvious and subtle, between East and West, to proclaim their unity as men made by the same God. As a climate of thought in which

Christianity would be most likely to flourish, it advocated a return to the purity of ancient religious thought, stripped of the atheist accretions imparted by Chu Hsi. No appeal could have been better attuned to a people in love with the past. The graduates came to view the new doctrine not as an abhorrent novelty but as the crowning of all their noblest traditions, while for Chinese Christians and those drawn to Christianity Ricci's work provided an invaluable summary of apologetic.

The book ran through several editions and was widely read, for mandarins enjoyed works of moral philosophy almost as much as poetry and history. These genres were treated in a highly fastidious and rarefied manner, with never a low note, in striking contrast to the many pornographic novels—this form, like that of the drama, was an importation of the Mongols—which the majority of graduates disdained to open.

In the spring of 1604 one of Nanking's leading Christians, a certain Hsü Kuang-ch'i, came to the northern capital to sit for an examination. Born at Shanghai in 1562, he had become bachelor of arts at the age of nineteen and in 1592 tutor to a family in Shiuchow. Here he became friendly with Cattaneo, who gave him his first religious instruction, which he continued at Nanking under Ricci. In 1601 he had sat his doctorate, passing with honours, seventh on the list. However, the examiners, discovering that they had awarded 301 instead of 300 degrees, decided to rectify their error by deleting one name at random. The unfortunate man was Hsü. In 1603, in the hope of finding Ricci, he had returned to Nanking, where he had been baptised with the name of Paul, usually reserved for the most outstanding converts. Now Ricci, who had the highest respect for his character and intelligence, welcomed Hsü to Peking and wished him success in the doctoral contest, deemed by all China the most important any man could enter. So far no mandarin with the highest degree had accepted Christianity, and it was therefore a matter of great importance to Ricci that Paul Hsü should distinguish himself.

At dawn on the seventh of April, first day of the examination, armed with three brushes, inkpot, ink and paper, Paul approached the immense examination building, surrounded by high walls, characteristic edifice of every provincial capital. At the gate he was stripped and searched, even his inkpot being inspected for cribs. When the candidates, several thousand masters of arts, had assembled, the gates were sealed and a strong guard posted. The examiners, a Chancellor and an Academician, announced the themes for the seven essays to be written that day : three sentences chosen from the Four Books, compulsory for all, and four sentences from each of the other less important works which made up the nine Classics, every candidate specialising in only one of these subsidiary books. The scholars were then led to a central courtyard dominated by a building consisting of four thousand small hutches, each able to hold a man, a desk and a stool. In these the candidates were locked. A light meal had been laid out in the hutches, between which communication was impossible. All day long, in company with the most brilliant men of China, most aged between thirty and forty, but some with white hair, Paul toiled away in his tiny cell, spinning out of himself a cocoon of silken eloquence. Each essay must contain no more and no less than five hundred characters—even here number was king—and would be judged not only for orthodoxy but for style, since the written language stood for national unity. The final versions he wrote in a special book, putting at the end his own name and those of his father, grandfather and great-grandfather, together with his address. At dusk the enclosure was unlocked, the weary candidates stumbled out, to be stripped of their exquisite threads of thought by lean, sharp-eyed officials. They in turn handed the compositions to scribes who copied them in red ink into another book. The anonymous versions in red letters were finally presented to the examiners.

On the second day of the examination, Paul wrote essays on ancient history; on the last day, judgments in three legal cases. The examiners then chose the three hundred best groups of essays, which were compared with the originals to ascertain the successful names. The great day came; lists of the new aristocracy were published and Paul's name was among them. He had attained the coveted rank of doctor of letters—to Ricci's gratification no less than his own. Later a book giving the family and address of successful candidates would be published, together with the most notable compositions. Every year it would be revised in the light of promotions and degradations, for Paul was now linked by a fraternal bond to the other doctors of his year, and by a filial bond to the examiners, whom he would treat with reverential respect until their dying day.

So far the examination had been similar to that for the degree of master of arts. Now followed a distinctive feature. The three hundred successful candidates were marshalled in the palace, where each was obliged to deliver a short extemporaneous discourse on a set theme to decide the final classification on which depended the importance of their appointments.

As a result of this exacting test, Paul was ranked number 121, which meant that he must leave Peking for a provincial post. Ricci was disappointed for his friend's sake and because in the capital so brilliant a convert would have proved an invaluable example. There was only one way to keep him there. Paul, Ricci decided, must sit another series of examinations, open only to doctors, for the Imperial Academy. Members of this college, the most highly esteemed men in China, did not hold official appointments. They composed the Emperor's edicts, wrote official history, laws, statutes; most important in Ricci's eyes, they taught the Emperor's sons. Moreover, as they advanced in age and pomposity, they could earn large fees by writing pieces for special occasions; any thoughtless trifle signed by an Academician was deemed at the very lowest a most elegant, a most extraordinarily well-restrained piece of prose. The old men's platitudes were applauded as the mature fruits of a lifetime, their doddering untruths construed as witty paradox, their effete mimicry hailed as proof of a living tradition.

Only with the greatest reluctance did Paul yield to Ricci. Competition was intense and the examination rigorous : over a period of three years a series of twenty-four papers gave the right to the same number of places. Paul, however, was placed so high in the first five that he could rest assured of success, and in June 1604 he was formally named Bachelor of the Academy. Renting a house close to Ricci's he brought his wife and father, who was over seventy, to live with him. In his new position of authority he became the missionaries' adviser and protector; as Ricci called him, a pillar of the Church. An ardent admirer of the Catechism, he believed that books were the sole means of spreading Christianity and continually pressed Ricci to write new ones, even copying down his sermons and circulating them in manuscript.

But there was little time for writing during 1604, a year when the chief magistrates came to pay triennial homage to the Emperor. About forty thousand crowded Peking, of whom three thousand were punished for some form of misdemeanour. Through Paul and other friends Ricci met the chief mandarins of Nanking, Nanchang and Shiuchow and commended the missionaries to their protection. Seeing Ricci honoured, maintained at public expense and allowed entrance to the palace, most were only too willing to oblige. Those who, either from Buddhist sympathies or xenophobia, remained resentful, dared not harm the missionaries in their province, knowing that Ricci was in a position to report the matter to a Minister and secure their dismissal.

That summer the rivers which gave China her beauty and wealth again proved her ruin. More than once in Shiuhing an April monsoon had heaved the nearby waters over their dykes to flood the mission house. Now the Pai Ho, swollen by very heavy rain, breached the capital walls and made shipwreck of whole streets of houses. Hundreds of people were drowned and even more lost their lives through the accompanying famine. Supplies were cut off and the Emperor distributed food from reserve granaries to the value of 200,000 taels, rice being sold cheaply and the poor given free meals. Infanticide, which every day, even in normal times, accounted for a score of girl babies being strangled and thrown into the canals by parents who hoped they would be reborn to riches, now assumed the proportions of mass murder, while older boys and girls were hawked for the price of a meal.

Still the swirling waters rose and swept away a civilisation which weeks before had seemed beyond challenge. The choice was no longer between the caerulean shade of damask and the mauve, but between high ground and low. Putting aside his purple silk and neat classical allusions, Ricci fought a way through the torrential streets to save stranded survivors and evacuate them to the unflooded mission. The more low-lying single-storeyed houses, like so many skiffs anchored on too short a chain, were one by one engulfed. The blazing sun made the metropolis a mortuary; plague broke out; Peking became a city of the dead and dying. All that summer, while the brown water pounded against improvised dykes, Ricci and his household tended the groaning sick, many of whom had been deserted by their family and friends.

By August the deluge had begun to subside and from the flooded plains emerged a second colleague for the Peking mission, a Portuguese of thirty-five, whom Ricci put in charge of three young Chinese entering on their novitiate. The newcomer's journey from Macao had proved calamitous. First, he had been obliged to bribe the captain of his boat who, half-way, threatened to leave his baggage behind. Later, on the River Pai, the boat had been wrecked by heavy floods, fortunately while most of the passengers were ashore. The most precious possession, an eight-volume Bible, sent expressly for the mission by Cardinal di Santa Severina, and packed in a strong wooden crate, was picked up by sailors from a neighbouring ship, who, believing it to be of value, hid their salvage. The gallant Brother Sebastian had boarded their ship and forced them to open the case. Discovering books written in a foreign language, they were only too willing to hand over for a few coins a work which had cost seventy gold florins.

On the Feast of the Assumption, after Mass, the Bible was solemnly shown to the Christian community. A magnificent edition, published by Christopher Plantin at Antwerp and sponsored by King Phillip II, even in Europe the book excited wonder, where it was known as the " Orbis miraculum." It had been four years in the press, a gestation which, it was hoped, would ensure an almost sybilline age, and the brood limited to some twelve hundred sets, destined for the eyes of kings. Rudolf Acquaviva had offered one to the Great Mogul at Agra; the present set, it was hoped, might penetrate the Forbidden City. The binding like a palace gate opened reluctantly to reveal strong folio pages, an enduring surface on which the well-formed words were arranged not only to impart their sense but choreographically. The Testament was danced out in four sets of costume, Hebrew, Chaldean, Greek and Latin, the New Testament in Greek, Latin and Syriac, every least accent, every hapax legomenon correct, so that the volumes gave an irresistible impression of recorded truth.

Though they could not spell out a word, the Christians were sure so beautiful a work must contain high doctrine. As they turned the gilded pages and the different languages were pointed out to them, it seemed that only Chinese was lacking to bring the work to perfection. " Will you translate it?" they begged Ricci. Looking down bleakly at the eight massive volumes—to compile a few Chinese pages took months of labour, and at that time he could scarcely find leisure to recite his office—Ricci excused himself, saying that he was too occupied, and that, for such a translation, special permission must be given by the Pope. Their absolute trust in his powers could be comical. He had been explaining that the Pope was not a hereditary prince, that a body of holy, learned men of mature age, dedicated from early youth to religion and bound by a vow of chastity, elected their most worthy member to be vicar on earth of the Lord of Heaven. His listeners nodded. They seemed to understand. Then someone exclaimed in all sincerity, " If you return to the Far West, Master Li, you will certainly be elected Pope."

Though the Bible was saved, precious goods worth two hundred taels had foundered, including a consignment of wine for saying Mass, unobtainable in Peking. Ricci asked help from the southern capital; a cask was dispatched but it too was lost on the way, so that for a year they had to ration their supply strictly, using two ablutions of water. The Christian community was specially angry that a picture for their altar had been stolen by the sailors. One of Ricci's friends, a doctor of letters, had the pilot and some of the crew arrested. Under torture, they confessed to having stolen a writing desk, which was recovered but found to contain little besides reliquaries. The friend wanted to prefer charges but, at Ricci's request, he arranged for the sailors' release.

Ricci, overjoyed with the polyglot Bible, hastened to write and thank its donor in Rome. Every summer without fail, four months before the carrack left Macao for India, he harvested the year's memories in a score of letters which were both a testimony of friendship and an antidote to homesickness. Typhoons and Dutch warships rendered communication almost as difficult as with the Emperor; sometimes he had to wait nine years for an answer. More than once he wrote to friends no longer alive, and from a misinformed colleague received a notice of his father's death ten years before the event. But few things gave Ricci such pleasure as those occasional letters from friends, masters and contemporaries, at the Roman College and Coimbra, from his first tutor, Father Bencivegni, and from his family. He read and re-read, seldom without tears in his eyes, the crumpled scraps of paper that had been blown half-way round the world.

In his replies he chose items of news in accordance with the interests of his correspondent, describing to his father the cheapness of pearls and musk which, carried overland from Tibet, commanded exorbitant prices in Italy; the plentiful supplies of rhubarb, which the Chinese used as a dye; and touching upon political and court affairs. Even from the far side of despair he had managed to compose cheerful letters, full of praise for such curiosities as Chinese boats or the disciplined hierarchy of magistrates. The progress of the mission he invariably described as a miracle in which his own efforts were unworthy of remark. Even at the height of success, quite naturally, without a trace of affectation, he continued to designate himself "minimo fratello," "poveretto," "figlio indegno," and besought the help of his friends' prayers. He wrote freely and with high praise of his colleagues, especially the Chinese Brothers, his particular favourites, but of his own state of mind he spoke seldom. " As for me, there's nothing to say except that I am very happy—God be praised—and ready to suffer anything He may wish for the conversion of China through His grace." He enjoyed quoting tags from Horace and Virgil—not without slip—for they brought back his days at the Roman College, which he never tired of recalling. His fondness for statistical truth he indulged in the form of frequent distances, bearings of towns, circumferences of city walls and numbers of baptised. And in every letter, even to colleagues he had not seen for thirty years, he showed the sincere, devoted affection which in Peking was winning him an ever-increasing circle of friends.

At the beginning of the following year, 1605, after a long period of tranquillity, there blew up another of those storms which Ricci believed always marked the voyage of St. Peter's ship. Suspicious of progress without opposition, he found himself welcoming the new attack. It came from the Buddhists, who invoked the age-old custom whereby strangers offering gifts must be rewarded and escorted back to the frontier. As a result of memorials to this effect, court eunuchs hinted that Ricci and his brethren should accept official appointments, thus justifying the money they received. Ricci, however, knowing that this would arouse the envy of the graduates, refused the appointment and proposed to forgo the allowance : an offer which came to nothing. When further hostile memorials were presented, Ricci took bold action : he made known his intention of leaving the capital. As he expected, this silenced the opposition, for it was now well known that the Emperor wanted the graduate preachers to remain at court, though with what motives no one could say for certain. Probably the Emperor found them useful, for they continued to visit the palace regularly to keep the clocks in repair.

Lest he provoke further attacks, Ricci decided that his next publication should be more conciliatory to the Buddhists. The substance of their doctrine was contained in a Sutra called *The Forty-two Paragraphs*, traditionally held to have been compiled by the two Indians who introduced Buddhism in the first century of the Christian era. Ricci now published a book which he had written at Nanking under the title of *Twenty-Five Sentences*. Polemic was avoided, while Stoic arguments were turned to Christian ends : To be happy we must do what lies in our power, that is, what demands work, strength and determination, while remaining indifferent to what we cannot control, such as riches, honours, fame and long life. There can be no disgrace for the man who is content with his lot. When we are falsely accused, let us follow the example of Saint Francis of Assisi and recognise that we have many faults of which others know nothing. Above all we must preserve peace of mind and use things as though they do not belong to us. Man in this world is a guest whom the Lord of Heaven invites to the heavenly banquet.

To this book one of Ricci's friends wrote a preface, claiming. that Yu and Hsia, the two most learned disciples of Confucius, would have found no fault with its arguments. He challenged the reader to compare it with *The Forty-two Paragraphs* and judge which was the more conducive to right living.

Since Chinese books often boasted postfaces as well as prefaces, Paul Hsü the Academician wrote a few concluding words. " Some time ago, on returning from Mount Song in Honan, I saw a painting of the Lord of Heaven which had arrived by sea from Europe. I had already seen a copy of the map published by the Viceroy of Nanking and the Secretary to the Ministry of Public Appointments and knew of the existence of Li Ma-tou. I found him by chance in Nanking and, after a short conversation, realised that he was the most learned man in the whole world. Some time afterwards he arrived in Peking to offer gifts and lived in the Castle of Barbarians. After less than a month he was invited to dinner by the great mandarins. Later his fame spread throughout the Middle Kingdom and the wisest and most famous men went to visit him. . . . Amidst troubles and adversity, during conversation or at dinner, it is impossible to find in a thousand million of his words a single one contrary to the great principles of loyalty to the Emperor and filial piety, not one which does not bring peace of mind and strengthen the moral code. . . . In ancient times, the kiosk where the phoenixes built their nests was considered by the Court a precious object, ensuring peace and stability in the Empire. To-day we have the True Man, learned and great, who brings our moral code to completion and protects our court; is he not a treasure even more precious? Let us praise him to the heights."

CHAPTER TWELVE

Adorers of the Cross

WHILE Peking was still acclaiming the *Twenty-Five Sentences* which appeared in the spring of 1605, Ricci received a visit from a master of arts. He looked about sixty and the name on his visiting-book was Ai T'ien. He had a long face, full lips and an unusually large nose. When, after the customary cere- monies, they were seated, Ai said warmly, "We are members of the same religion, Doctor Li." Ricci did not recognise him but believing that he had come from one of the southern houses, led his visitor into the chapel. For the octave of the feast of St. John the Baptist, there hung a painting of the Virgin with the Christ Child and the Precursor in adoration. Ai immediataely knelt down and paid reverence. "I do not usually venerate pictures," he whispered, "but I must pay reverence to these ancestors of mine." Ricci was puzzled but said nothing. At each side of the chapel was a picture of one of the four evangelists; indicating them, the visitor asked, "Are these the twelve children of the lady above the altar?" Ricci, supposing that he was referring poetically to the twelve apostles, replied Yes, and again his visitor paid homage.

When they returned to Ricci's study, Ai T'ien said, "I have never before seen a painting of Rebecca with Jacob and Esau."

From whom could a Chinese have learned those names? Ricci tried to hide his astonishment. "The painting above the altar?" Ai T'ien nodded. "That shows the Virgin with the Christ Child and John the Baptist." This time it was Ai T'ien who showed surprise. "How did you come to hear of us?" Ricci continued.

"I was reading a book entitled *Strange Forest,* by Chih Yün-chien, the layman from the slope of plum trees. He describes you as having a high brow, deep-set eyes, a rosy complexion and a grey beard. From that I thought you were a Mohammedan, but later he said you did not profess their creed, but adored only the King of Heaven. It was obvious then that we were of the same persuasion."

" What is your sect called?" asked Ricci.

" We are called ' men who cut the sinews of the flesh we eat.' "

Memories of a passage in Genesis came back : " Therefore the children of Israel eat not of the sinew which shrank, which is upon the hollow of the thigh, unto this day." Ricci looked at his visitor's nose. " Are you perhaps a Jew?"

Ai T'ien's face remained impassive. " I have never heard that name," he replied.

Ricci thought a moment, then fetched the first volume of the Plantin Bible. Opening it beside Ai T'ien, he pointed to the Hebrew text, which his visitor studied.

" That is the language of our holy books."

" Then you are a Jew," said Ricci. " Perhaps you call yourself differently : Hebrew? Israelite?"

His visitor smiled in recognition. " It is true that we call ourselves Israelites, but no one else in the Middle Kingdom refers to us by that name."

Ricci learned that Ai was born in Honan province and now lived in Kaifeng, its capital. Eight families of Jews dwelt there with a fine synagogue recently rebuilt after a fire at a cost of ten thousand taels. Here they kept the Pentateuch written on parchment and rolled up in five parts, each kept in a kind of small tent covered with silk, within the sanctuary. The Jews turned towards the West when they prayed and addressed God by several names, including Heaven, Supreme Lord, and Governor of All Things. They ate unleavened bread at Easter and celebrated their liturgical feasts.

Ricci listened with growing astonishment. " How long have your families lived at Kaifeng?" he asked.

" The first synagogue was erected almost five hundred years ago. I think our ancestors travelled from India about that time. Traders they were. But now we have become a very small sect. At Hangchow there is another colony with their synagogue and elsewhere a few scattered families." He lowered his eyes. "Gradually we are dying out."

"It is strange I never heard of you before," said Ricci. "I have studied the dynastic histories and found no mention of your sect."

"There is good reason for that," replied Ai. "We are grouped with the cursed Mohammedans. The people of this country, judging only by appearances, see that both sects abstain from pork. As there are perhaps a million Mohammedans in the Middle Kingdom, and a handful of Israelites, it is we who are given their name."

Ricci began to understand. He had met occasional Chinese Mohammedans: they had entered the country during the Mongol dynasty and lived as Chinese, holding office, but most practised no form of their religion except abstinence from pork.

Now is my chance, thought Ricci, to solve a long-standing problem. Some years ago he had heard that in Shansi province, near the Great Wall, lived a tiny sect called Adorers of the Cross. What he had learned indicated one of the myriad varities of Buddhism—some rare species of flower evolved in a distant mountain valley—but there was, perhaps, a more satisfactory explanation: that this sect comprised descendants of foreign Christians who had once lived in Peking.

If, as Ricci had for many years believed, Marco Polo's Cathay was another name for China, and Cambaluc an older name for Peking, then the Nestorian Christians in Cambaluc attested by Marco Polo, and about which Chinese annals, tradition and contemporary books were suspiciously silent, might have been a foreign community, consisting of occupying troops recruited from Christendom (for the Khan's empire extended to Armenia and Hungary).

The presence of Christians in Cambaluc had been independently recorded by the Franciscan legates dispatched to secure an alliance with the Great Khan. In the thirteenth century John of Plano Carpini, an Italian friar and one of St. Francis's first companions, had made the journey to Cambaluc, the first European to reach the Far East overland. He met with no success and was sent back by the Khan with an insolent letter to the Pope. Several other friars in succeeding years also failed to secure the alliance. Another Franciscan, John of Montecorvino, who travelled by sea, converted some of the Nestorian Christians, who enjoyed favour at the Khan's court, to Catholicism. He was joined in 1313 by three others of his order, who consecrated Montecorvino Archbishop. His successor, John of Marignolli, who arrived with thirty friars, presented the Khan with a magnificent horse from the Pope, but was soon compelled to leave by the first signs of that revolution which heralded the Ming dynasty. Thereafter Franciscan zeal for the East died out. It was no longer possible to travel there by land, and the overthrow of the foreign dynasty had been followed by intense xenophobia. But for over three-quarters of a century the Franciscans had been established, not as missionaries to Cathay but as chaplains to Christians at the cosmopolitan court of Cambaluc. The friars did not learn the language of Cathay; like the majority of their flock they spoke Uigur, the Tartar tongue, in which Mass was celebrated according to the Latin rite.

It was possible that when the Khan's empire collapsed the Christian religion had been identified with foreign conquest and those who professed it expelled by the new Ming dynasty. But Ricci found it inconceivable that they should have left no trace of descendants and, on the assumption that all references to Cambaluc were references to Peking, had long been searching for tell-tale signs—with no more success than the hearsay mention of a curious sect at Shansi.

He now put his important question to the Jew. " Have you heard, anywhere in the Middle Kingdom, of the existence of Christians?" But the word meant nothing to Ai. Not for the first time Ricci was reduced to the rock-bed of visible definition. Producing a crucifix, he explained the elements of Christianity. To Ricci's extreme surprise, the visitor said, " So you are an Adorer of the Cross, Doctor Li! In my own city of Kaifeng there were certain strangers who practised that religion. There were others, I think, in Lintsing and Shansi."

" What do you know about them?"

" Very little," replied the Jew, " except that they recite prayers from our holy books." That might be the psalter, Ricci thought. " But most of them have given up their religion. The Mohammedans hated them because they were brave and war-like, so they roused the mandarins against them. Most became either Mohammedans or Buddhists. Their church at Kaifeng was turned into a pagoda dedicated to the god of war."

" When did the persecution take place?"

" I should say some fifty years ago."

Ricci was puzzled. Were the Adorers of the Cross descendants of Georgians and Armenians in the Mongol armies? Or travellers from the Middle East? Or an even more primitive sect founded by the apostle Bartholomew, who, some claimed, had come to the Far East? " Do you know why they adored the Cross?" asked Ricci.

The Jew spread his hands. " They themselves did not know. They simply retained an old custom—making a cross in the air with their finger over food and drink."

Ricci asked the Jew to write down the names of the Christian families at Kaifeng : they numbered six. He also learned the Chinese name for the sect. Just as Mohammedans were " men who do not eat pork " and Jews " men who do not eat sinews," the descendants of Christians were " men who do not eat animals with a round hoof "—because, while Saracens and Chinese had no scruples about those foods, the Christians evidently abstained from flesh of horse and mule.

Ricci then questioned the Jew about the Old Testament. Ai recited many stories about Abraham, Judith, Mardochai and Esther, using forms of proper names which struck Ricci as strange : Hierosuloim for Jerusalem, Moscia for Messiah. He told Ricci that in Kaifeng many of the Israelites knew Hebrew.

" My brothers are well versed in the language, but I cannot read a word. In fact, when I took my degree I was driven out of the synagogue. You see, it is impossible to practise purifi-cations and refrain from pork while holding an official posi-tion. I was obliged, for my work, to give up those formalities.

But the tie remains. " If I were a doctor of letters," he added regretfully, " I should have the authority to withstand the rabbis and break it altogether."

Ricci was well pleased with this news and later sent Brother Anthony, a young Chinese, to Kaifeng to discover what language and holy pictures the Christians used. He and his companion, a Christian doctor of letters from Honan province, were more warmly welcomed by the Jews than by the supposed Christians. They refused to admit they were related to Adorers of the Cross, either out of fear of persecution or shame at being considered of foreign extraction (although that was clear enough from their faces), since the Chinese considered foreign blood a great dishonour. However, Brother Anthony gathered that their ancestors, Christians of the Greek rite, had come to China five centuries before with the conquering Mongols and, living outside the capital, had not been converted to Catholicism by the Franciscans of the fourteenth century.

Ricci was disappointed that the link had been broken, that the only vestiges of a once flourishing Christian community, numbering tens of thousands, should be a superstitious attitude towards horse-flesh—sign of their European origin—and a gesture before eating. The cross could lose its meaning. Survival was not guaranteed. On the contrary, a minority religion in this alien land would, if cut off for centuries at a time from the main stream, inevitably languish and die. China had assimilated larger bodies by sheer mass—even the Mongol conquerors. At all costs, therefore, the link with Rome must be safeguarded. Xenophobia must be opposed as implacably as Buddhism.

On the same journey Anthony delivered a letter from Ricci to the ruler of the synagogue, saying that in Peking he possessed all the books of the Old Testament, and also the New, which treated of the Messiah's coming into the world. The rabbi replied that that was impossible, for the Messiah would not appear for ten thousand years. However, having heard of Ricci's learning, the community sent a second message : " If you will come and live with us and abstain from pork, we will make you ruler of our synagogue."

At Ricci's request Anthony made copies of the first and last sentences of their Pentateuch. Comparing them with the Plantin Bible, Ricci found that they exactly corresponded, but the Jewish book was written in the ancient fashion, without the marks which indicated vowels.

The visit of T'ien the Jew occurred in June. Later that same summer Ricci made permanent the residence in Peking. During the previous four years they had been living in rented houses, with great inconvenience, without a proper chapel, changing four or five times, never finding one that suited their needs. So many carracks were lost during those years that Macao could not furnish the six hundred taels necessary to purchase a house. Ricci decided to wait no longer. Finding one with forty rooms in the centre of the city at a reasonable price, he spoke to his friends, especially to Paul Hsü; they all agreed to lend the necessary money themselves or obtain loans at low interest. Three days later Ricci bought the house, turning the largest room into a chapel.

At Peking there were now three missionary priests, Ricci, Pantoja and the recently arrived Portuguese, two Chinese ready to begin their novitiate, two candidates for the Society and nine servants. Peking counted over two hundred Christians, China well over a thousand. The numbers were not very great, but all had been chosen carefully and well instructed. Ricci preferred to have a few good converts than thousands of imperfect ones, for at that early stage the bad example of a single individual could undo the work of years. Moreover, the missions were still hampered by shortage of priests, and requests to open houses in other cities had to be refused. The twelve missionaries under Ricci were barely sufficient to look after the four communities and the Chinese novices.

The supply of priests had been kept constant by Valignano, who had recently returned from Japan to Macao. From there he wrote a letter to the General pointing out that for twenty-one years, as Visitor and Provincial, he had been in charge of the countries included in the provinces of India or Japan. Now he felt his strength failing and asked to be allowed to spend his few remaining years in prayer, free from office. While awaiting an answer he devoted his energies to the China mission, and proposed to visit in person all the houses. Ricci was delighted at the news, and Paul Hsü arranged for letters of introduction and a passport granting travel at public expense. Valignano had written to Japan for presents and was awaiting the return of the ship in February or March 1606. He intended to leave at each mission house a thousand taels, the income from which would ensure financial independence from Macao, for relations with the Portuguese enclave still aroused the greatest suspicion. Amidst these arrangements he fell ill of uraemia and after nine days' suffering, during which he spoke repeatedly of China, Valignano died. The date was January the twentieth; his age sixty-six.

When he had disembarked at Goa in 1574, Japan had only twenty European Jesuits and a single indigenous one, while the gates of China remained barred. At his death, Japan boasted a hundred and thirty missionaries, and over a quarter of a million Christians. He had founded two flourishing colleges and started two smaller ones, a novitiate and two seminaries for Japanese, a score of houses and three hundred churches or chapels. For some thirty years he had bestridden Asia from the Indian Ocean to the China Sea like a new colossus. Through typhoon and plague, tropical heat and monsoon, with inadequate supplies of men and money, he had travelled unceasingly, building, strengthening, organising, encouraging. All who knew the Visitor considered him a great man, worthy to rank with Xavier. At the news of their loss, mourning was worn from Mozambique to Nagasaki, from the Mogul's court to Malacca. None felt his death more than Ricci. Valignano had been father not only to the mission, but to himself, since that first day when he had opened the door of the novitiate in Rome and put the questions which had changed his life. For twenty-three years they had worked together, firmly agreed, in an age which viewed such ideas with suspicion, that Christianity must put up her sword and approach the peoples of the East in all humility, that her priests must learn in order to teach, that the Society must open its ranks to Oriental converts. In Ricci's opinion, Valignano's death had orphaned all the missionaries in China.

The future of the mission was still further jeopardised by a second loss. Ricci had sent Brother Francis, one of the two first Chinese Jesuits, to accompany the Visitor on his tour. While staying in the house of a Christian family at Canton he contracted malaria. The city, indeed the whole province, was in turmoil, for some weeks earlier reports that Spaniards had slaughtered 20,000 Chinese in the Philippines had coincided with the building at Macao of extensive Portuguese fortifications against increasingly daring Dutch corsairs. Rumour spread that the Portuguese, Dutch and Japanese were uniting to massacre the Chinese of Macao, invade Kwangtung province, seize the whole country and make one of the Jesuits Emperor. In terror, all the Chinese of the enclave had fled to Canton, where the Haitao, as a defensive measure, ordered houses outside the city walls, several thousand in number, to be pulled down. By February, no foreign attack having been launched, the owners were complaining furiously that the demolition had been unnecessary. A renegade Christian, aware of the mandarins' dilemma, informed them of Brother Francis's presence and accused him of smuggling arquebuses to Macao. It had become essential to find a scapegoat. When his tonsure was discovered, Brother Francis was twice given the bastinado. Already tubercular and greatly weakened by malaria, he collapsed under the blows. He was hurried back towards prison but in the streets of Canton, on a table improvised as a stretcher, he died.

Letters from Longobardo and memorials to the court reported the tragedy to Ricci act by act when it had already been played. His own experience in Shiuhing had shown that, despite all precautions, such incidents were unavoidable: as long as an enclave existed, missionaries would be accused of spying for an imperialist power. He loved Francis—who he had hoped would be one of the first Chinese priests—yet could not regret a death which approached so closely to martyrdom.

Increasingly now he prayed—and asked his friends to pray—
that he might shed his blood as Francis had done. But in fact
enemies had never been fewer, the externals of life never so
smooth. He continued to maintain his prestige, which alone
could protect the three less sheltered houses. Since the key
mandarins in those provinces were continually changing, each
time they visited Peking Ricci had to strengthen friendships or
make them anew. The other strands in his present life were
the instruction of new Christians, sermons on Sundays and
feast-days, his own writing, Chinese lessons to his colleagues
and lessons in philosophy and mathematics to graduates. For
three or four hours every day Paul Hsü worked with him at the
translation of Euclid's first six books, together with other minor
mathematical works. Ricci translated orally while Hsü transcribed. Hsü, who showed a great aptitude for mathematics,
wanted to translate the whole of Euclid, but Ricci explained
that the later books, being beyond most Chinese, would not
further their apostolic work. Only two of Ricci's friends—
Paul Hsü and Li Chih-tsao the geographer—could fully master
Euclid, and the first six books, published in the spring of 1607,
were more admired than understood. Chinese pride was somewhat abased : even the greatest minds in Peking had to admit
that they were unable to grasp a book in their own language.

In the field of astronomy Ricci expected still more useful
results. From Portuguese almanacs he could predict eclipses
more accurately than the college of mathematicians, but he was
not sufficiently skilled to compile a detailed written work,
which alone would convince the Chinese of the value of his
system. In letter after letter to Rome he requested that an
expert astronomer, with books and tables, be sent to Peking, for
he was planning nothing less than the reform of the Chinese
year. The Gregorian calendar, largely the work of his mathematical master, Christopher Clavius, had been adopted in
western Europe in 1582 and promulgated throughout the
Indian province a year later. If Europe had taken the momentous step of changing to a new calendar, might not China also?
Ricci had already adapted the Gregorian system to the lunar
year and translated it into Chinese, so that Christians could

calculate the dates of Sundays and feast-days. But he had not dared to print his manuscript, since that would have been considered a revolutionary act of the first magnitude.

The calendar was the origin and basis of imperial power. Even at the present time acceptance of the Chinese almanac by tributary states was taken as proof of vassalage. The *Book of Rites*, one of the nine vital volumes, made abundantly clear that the Son of Heaven was originally a star-gazer, his purpose to predict the moment when man must play his part in the rites of heaven and earth by sowing fresh grain. Not only did the early Emperors foretell the seasons by the movements of constellations, but they performed a mimetic ritual for bringing the earth through its annual cycle according to a system of metaphor. Every moon was identified with an animal and a host of other objects and qualities which could provide the basis of productive ceremonies and dances. Thus for the first moon it was laid down that its creatures were of the scaly kind, its musical note was *chio*, among the standard pipes it had the T'ai Ts'ou sound, its element was wood, the spleen was the sacrifice to be offered first; its numeral was eight, its taste bitter, its smell rank. During this month the Son of Heaven was obliged to occupy the room to the left of his Green Bright Hall, to ride there in the phoenix carriage, yoked with azure dragons wearing green flags. He was robed in green robes, wore green jade ornaments, ate wheat with mutton, and his vessels were lightly carved in order to aid the springing grain. During other months he ploughed the first sacred furrow and made ritual purifications, changing the colour of his jade at each season.

Nature was beneficial—the fertile soil produced several crops a year—but the rainfall, especially in North China, could be catastrophically variable. Gradually the Emperor came to be identified with the constellation which marked his most important function—the rain-bringing dragon, sign of the fifth month.

China had retained the lunar year, first devised when the needs of earth had made man look to the night sky. She found it difficult to calculate the solar cycle and harmonise it with the lunar appearances, because she held an erroneous view of planetary movement. The chief problem was when and how to insert an intercalary month. At present the insertion was made every three years but at different times in different years, with unsatisfactory results. The year was further complicated by its division into twenty-four fortnightly periods—the joints and breaths—corresponding to the days on which the sun entered each zodiacal sign. The years were dated from the reigning Emperor's accession, and the astronomical character of the present dynasty was still further attested by the ideogram for Ming—composed of the characters signifying sun and moon.

Ricci was convinced that the provision of a more accurate calendar would redound greatly to the credit of Christianity. It might even become possible to replace the lunar by the solar year. That would strike a decisive blow at magical belief; it might shatter the wheel—the twenty-eight constellations of the lunar zodiac—to which China was bound. Feasts of the kitchen god, the god of wealth and a host of other sub-divinities were specified in the Chinese calendar, having been calculated according to the months and certain symbolic numbers. Thus, on the fifth day of the fifth moon presents of mulberries, water chestnuts and cakes were made to ward off disease-bearing spirits, while dragon boats raced on the rivers, survival of a rite to induce celestial dragons to struggle and bring down rain; on the ninth day of the ninth month—the double Yang—the people of Peking, to avoid disaster, would climb such prominent points as the Density of Trees Surrounding the Gate of Chi or the Wall of Pure Metamorphosis. When this cycle of worship and mimesis had been disrupted, China would perhaps consider the acceptance of a supernatural religion less outrageous to nature.

The original link between the Emperor and the peasants whose crops depended on his predictions was retained in other observances, such as the Son of Heaven's practice of marrying not into mandarin stock but into the people, selecting his legal wife and forty-five concubines for their physical excellence, a

rule which also applied to his family. To Ricci's great amuse-
ment, in 1607 printed edicts were distributed in both capitals
and other provinces of high repute urging all parents with sons
of fifteen or sixteen, of good health and physical appearance, to
present the youths to the local mandarins, so that a suitable
husband might be selected for one of Wan Li's daughters.
They were stripped naked and examined minutely to see
whether their bodies were strong and perfectly formed. Since
no graduate or self-respecting father wished his son to suffer
this indignity, the candidates were all plebeian and illiterate. A
choice of two or three hundred was made, and finally narrowed
down to ten. From these Wan Li and his mother, using purely
physical criteria, chose a suitable son-in-law for the Son of
Heaven. The youth was then put in the hands of tutors until
the wedding day. Even after the ceremony he was obliged to
kneel to his wife and had no authority until a son was born to
her. Then he received honorific rank and a good income, but
was allowed no jurisdiction over the people. Nothing must
jeopardise that national unity, whose outward signs were the
mandarin language and the calendar.

From incidents such as this and the fruits of over twenty
years' reading of Chinese history Ricci, in letters to friends in
Europe, found it possible to generalise about a country he had
come to know intimately. The Middle Kingdom was an
agricultural society subservient to the seasons' strict tyranny—
that fact underlay the most striking difference of all between
China and Europe, one at which Ricci never ceased to marvel :
that the most populous and richest nation of the world, with a
well-equipped army of a million men, should have refrained
from aggressive war for many centuries, though she lay close to
petty states capable of being swallowed in a matter of weeks.
As in the recent Korean war, she had occasionally taken up
arms either in self-defence or to fulfil her duties to a tributary
kingdom, but always with extreme reluctance. Her martial
age lay two thousand years in the past; for centuries violence
had been decried; Ming mandarins indulged in nothing more
military than their game of blockade chess, proudly quoting the

proverb: " One stroke of the civilian's pen reduces the military official to abject submission " and Lao Tzu's saw: " The best soldier does not fight."

This tradition was ingrained in rich, brown soil. China was a country with enough of everything—Ricci found only almonds and olives lacking, and these were adequately replaced by sesame oil. Carrying on virtually no foreign trade, she had no need to conquer markets, nor was she tempted by the poor land of neighbouring states. Even if a nearby country had offered voluntary submission, Ricci doubted whether any mandarin would have consented to govern it. Innumerable elegies testified to the Chinese horror of dying away from home, a sentiment which excited surprise at Ricci's own self-imposed exile.

Peace had produced that unity in time as well as in space which made it possible to read and understand the written language of 2,500 years before. It had also produced a remarkable continuity of government, for although each dynasty always issued a penal code of its own, this was generally a more humane version of the preceding collection. To reap riches man had only to subordinate himself to the imperial will and a bountiful heaven. There was no incentive to master nature by means of applied science, nor to perfect military techniques. From the concordant procession of stars the Flowery Kingdom had learned a lesson of peace.

In that same year, 1607, Paul Hsü's father died. Paul escorted the coffin home to repay with three years' mourning the protective care given during three years of helpless infancy. He would sleep apart from his wife on a straw mat beside the coffin, eat neither meat nor seasoned food, use very little wine, take no baths and for some months not even appear in public.

The departure of this friend and colleague, a great blow to Ricci, was partially offset by the arrival of a new missionary. Sabatino De Ursis was an Italian of thirty-two, who had spent his novitiate at the Roman College under the same master as Ricci. He had been in Macao over three years, waiting to go to Japan; but Valignano, shortly before his death, gave orders that he should be sent to China, hoping that his training in mathematics and architecture would prove useful.

Pantoja had never been close to Ricci. He was an efficient administrator—he had a calculating eye which noticed the price of goods—but his Spanish education made him adopt a condescending attitude towards the Chinese, which Ricci more than once had to check. The severer climate did not suit him and a rice diet made him dyspeptic. Ricci continually had to exercise patience, and his warmer nature found no response in the Spaniard. For the candid Southern Italian, however—his birthplace was Lecce—he felt an instinctive sympathy which soon developed into intimate friendship. Not for seven years had he lived with a compatriot, spoken Italian, exchanged memories of the Roman College, which even after a lifetime remained his dearest memory, received news of the General, of friends in the capital and at Coimbra. A deep spiritual life, a love of the Chinese people, unflagging zeal, mathematics : at every level they found common interests. For a long time Ricci had felt the need of such a friend, and now more than ever. It was becoming clear that every fresh triumph forged another manacle chaining him to Peking, a prisoner of the Emperor he had hoped to win. At fifty-four, his face was webbed with lines, his hair and beard prematurely grey. He was beginning to realise that he had undertaken a journey without return.

CHAPTER THIRTEEN

The Quest for Cathay

HIS own days of travel might be ended, but since 1603 Ricci had been accompanying in spirit a member of the Society who had undertaken an unimaginably long journey. He had set out from India to find Cathay and from there proceed to Peking. Since it would decide once and for all the true relations of Cathay and China, Ricci took almost as much interest in the journey as though he himself were making it. He was, moreover, its goal, for the traveller carried letters for the superior of the China mission. Whenever a foreign " embassy " arrived, Ricci anxiously made enquiries at the Castle of Barbarians. Every letter in a strange hand he opened with excitement. Month after month for three years, as he waited in vain for news, he led a dual life of prayer and sympathy for this other Asian explorer. The monstrous tribes, gryphons and ants larger than foxes which still survived on contemporary maps might be fictitious representations of the unknown dangers of central Asia, but those dangers, as he had learned at Goa and the Castle of Barbarians, were none the less formidable in reality. Ricci began to lose hope for the traveller to Peking.

The Provincial in India had informed him of the journey and its chain of causes.

Not long after Ricci's first visit to the northern capital, Acquaviva's successors at the court of the Great Mogul in Agra learned from Mohammedan merchants that Cathay lay northeast of the Mogul's kingdom and—most marvellous of all— was peopled with Christians, having priests, sacraments and churches. Ricci had already written to his brethren in India giving reasons for believing that Cathay and China were one. They found his theory difficult to accept. First, China contained only the faintest vestiges of that Christianity which tradition held to be a distinguishing mark of Cathay, and which the merchants' account confirmed. Secondly, the weight of almost every known authority and many centuries opposed any such identification. Thirdly, court customs in Cathay differed widely from those observed by Ricci. The Visitor in India believed that the name of Cathay, if coterminous with China, might have been extended to the Middle Kingdom. At all events he decided to put the Mohammedan merchants' claim to the test. Having obtained the Pope's support for a mission to Cathay, he wrote to King Philip III for the necessary money. The English still clung to the idea of a north-west passage, and the Dutch were now trying to find a way to Cathay and China, passing north of Norway, through Moscow and Tartary. Hoping to forestall these attempts on Cathaian gold, Philip approved the scheme.

The Visitor decided that, as a preliminary, someone must be sent to discover more certain information about Cathay, to reduce any Christians to Rome and to find out whether a line of communication with China shorter than the sea route could be established. He selected a Portuguese lay brother of the Society called Bento de Goes who spoke fluent Persian and had a thorough knowledge of Mohammedan customs. Goes had been born in the Azores in 1562. As a young man he joined the Army and saw service in India. He led a dissolute life until one day, entering a chapel in Travancore, and praying before a picture of the Virgin, he obtained the grace of total conversion. There and then he vowed to join a religious order and at the age of twenty-two entered the Society. His superiors decided that he should become a lay brother. Angry that he had not been considered suitable for the priesthood, he ran away during his novitiate. Four years later, however, he returned to the Society, and since then had distinguished himself as brave, intelligent and thoroughly reliable.

Goes received his orders at Agra in 1602. His immediate destination was the kingdom of Kashgar; after that he would proceed eastwards through the unmapped regions to the Christian realm, wherever it was; from there to China, Peking and Ricci. Since he would be travelling, at least during the first stages of his journey, among Mohammedans, clearly he must hide the fact that he was a detested Portuguese. He decided to assume the dress and name of an Armenian Christian merchant, exchanging his black soutane for an ankle-length frock and turban, with a scimitar, bow and quiver, and allowing his hair and beard to grow long. He called himself Abdulla, servant of the Lord, with the addition of Isai, meaning the Christian. From the Mogul Akbar, a close friend, he obtained money and letters of recommendation to allied or tributary princes. Jéronimo Xavier, great-nephew of the Apostle of the Indies and Goes's superior, appointed two Greeks as his companions, Leo Grimanus, who spoke fluent Persian, and a merchant called Demetrius. Four Mohammedans newly converted to Christianity would act as servants.

In company with an ambassador from Kashgar who was returning home, Goes set out from Agra on October the twenty-ninth, 1602, and reached Lahore, second capital of the Mogul's kingdom, six weeks later. Here every year a caravan of some five hundred merchants was formed to travel to Kabul. To avert suspicion, Goes shunned the two Jesuit missionaries in Lahore and lodged with a Venetian merchant called Giovanni Battista Galisio. Because they had already proved themselves untrustworthy, he sent back his four servants to Agra and engaged an Armenian Christian named Isaac, who lived in Lahore with his wife and children. Goes also bought camels for the journey and merchandise, mostly lapis lazuli, which would corroborate his disguise and support him on a journey which might last many months. His more precious baggage contained a letter for the people of Cathay, another for Ricci, and a table of movable feasts until the year 1620 : first essential for drawing back an errant body into the orbit of Rome.

In mid-March, season of purple passion-flowers, the caravan set out from Lahore, half a thousand merchants with their servants, camels, horses and baggage carts. Although Kashgar lay almost due north of Lahore, their route ran north-westwards towards the only practicable pass connecting India with the rest of Asia. Strict discipline regimented the days. When it was time to break camp, the captain of the caravan ordered drums to be beaten. At the first roll, everyone packed away tents and equipment in corded bales; at the second, camels and carts were loaded; at the third, the travellers mounted and shambled off. When darkness fell, lest any of the party stray, drummers rode before and behind the column, sounding a way through the night.

Goes spoke Persian to the other merchants and passed without difficulty as a compatriot of his servant Isaac. To observe Lent, he ate only one meal, in the evening: a heap of rice, with onions and flour-cakes baked in ashes. Sometimes a little dried fish was added as a luxury. He had hoped to find time to recite his breviary, but the camel's swaying movement made him too sick to read. He tried nevertheless to pray: he considered his venture into country which no European had traversed an act of obedience, a missionary journey. His destination was Cathay; his task to link a lost people with Rome. Yet he himself stood in danger of becoming lost. He was travelling among militant Mohammedans who might try to force him, at point of argument and scimitar, to apostatise. He was leaving his dearest friends, above all Jerónimo Xavier, to whom he had written before setting out from Lahore: " May Jesus Christ grant me to see your Reverence again in this life; then I shall be able to sing the canticle of Simeon, ' Now lettest thou thy servant depart, O Lord, according to thy word, in peace.' " Alone, he feared to grow tepid, slack, rank—if he survived the physical dangers described by his companions: extremes of heat and cold, gorge and glacier, brigand and wild animal, fever and mountain sickness.

Through sterile, flat plains bordered to the north by a sinuous salt range, the first stage of their route was marked by a line of trees planted by Akbar to commemorate a recent decisive victory over his brother, the Sultan of Kabul. Another monument to this war was their first important stop, Attock on the River Indus, a fortified city built to hold the north-west frontier of the Mogul's kingdom. Through this country the silk route had passed for centuries, from Kashgar to the ports frequented by Alexandrian and Arab sailors, before being destroyed by Mihirakula the Hun. Putting on heavy quilted coats, they climbed steadily up the valley of the Kabul River, between snow-covered peaks, to Peshawar, with its colony of yogis, a garrison town guarding the entrance to the narrow Khyber Pass. Here they rested their animals for twenty days before moving up the defile which entered like a V-shaped wedge into the barrier of mountains, two days' journey due west. Crossing the pass, they descended into the plain of Nanghahar in the fulness of spring : after the arid mountains, fields of rice and cane-sugar, groves of palms and olives, vineyards, peach trees, figs and pomegranates, the blossoming trees alive with monkeys and orioles. In the market towns Goes heard Afghan musicians playing flute and lyre according to modes more familiar than those of Agra, an enticement to continue his journey westwards across the Persian plateaux to Portugal and a green island lying a lifetime away.

In this plain they fell in with a hermit on pilgrimage. Goes spoke with him and learned of a neighbouring country called Kafiristan where Mohammedans were killed on sight. The hermit said the people were famous for their wine and offered Goes some from a goatskin round his neck. To his surprise the traveller found it made from grapes, whereas all the peoples of India drank wine of fermented cane-sugar, despising the other as too weak. For one hopeful moment Goes believed he had stumbled on a Christian sect, until the hermit told him that the Kafirs professed an ancient Iranian religion, one of the few to resist Islam's conquest of central Asia.

As the country grew more steeply mountainous, the caravan was provided with an escort of four hundred soldiers by the chieftain of Jalalabad. While animals and servants followed the valley, troops and merchants crowned the heights, keeping a watch for brigands, whose mode of attack was to roll down rocks on unwary travellers. Despite these precautions, they had to beat off several armed gangs before reaching Kabul, most western point of the journey. A large cosmopolitan town with two fortresses, it stood on high ground, seven thousand feet up, at the foot of bare and rocky mountains, commanding the continental passes through which had swept successive invasions of India by Alexander the Great, Genghis

Khan and, in the previous century, Babur. Here the caravan dispersed, and, since travel alone meant certain death, Goes had to wait until a new company was formed in late summer before resuming his journey. During his stay he had the good fortune to meet a sister of Mohammed Khan, King of Kashgar. The queen was called Hajji Khanum, Lady who has made the pilgrimage to Mecca, whence she was then returning. On the way she had been robbed by brigands and lacked money to complete her journey. Goes sold some of his lapis lazuli, lent her what she needed and in her company set out, after eight months in Kabul, on the next and most difficult stage of the journey. Of his companions two had already lost heart and deserted him, only Isaac remaining faithful.

Crossing the almond and apricot groves of Kohistan the caravan halted at Charikar, a centre of iron-mines. Here Goes fell ill and became embroiled with the local governor, who, refusing to honour King Akbar's letter of exemption, demanded duty on his merchandise. Goes was still feverish when, after three weeks' halt, the caravan resumed its march through hills covered with pistachio bushes and juniper trees into the northern mountain tract of Hindu Kush, the Caucasus of Alexander's historians. From the many dangerous defiles which traversed the range of peaks, some sixteen thousand feet high, they chose the Pass of Parwan, in turn approached by seven minor clefts known as the Haft-bachah, or seven young ones. Through these, now working a vein of quartz along the rock face, now sheltering for days at a time from storms thunderous with avalanche, now worming a path into the very core of the mountains, now zig-zagging up thinly watered gorges, with the whole giant range astraddle their shoulders, they emerged into a world of black and white, compact in the forms of a grotesque primeval geometry. Here they could travel only by night, when the snow had caked and its glitter been thrown to the stars, laying down strips of cloth across the ice to steady their ponies, lurching crassly behind through insidious moraine and the dripping snouts of glaciers. Still they climbed, light-headed and leaden-footed, spun from the twisting path by lariats of mist, seeing in the piled cumulus no end to their journey. And always there rose a further ridge of snow spread-eagled between jagged quoins.

They crossed the pass by night, prancing in triumph above the tumbled stars, and pitched their felt tents beyond the northern escarpment. Next day they began the slow descent through graduated levels of life, pine-clad heights, hog-tracks, coveys of partridges and finally the mud hovels of Badakhshan, a well-watered country of glens and green turf, whose rubies were prized by the princesses of three continents. They found the eastern, more mountainous part of the kingdom in revolt against its ruler, the Khan of Samarkand and Bokhara, who claimed descent from Alexander, and at Teskan a local chieftain halted the caravan lest the insurgents, who were dismounted, gain possession of their four hundred ponies. The captain of the caravan protested and during the ensuing controversy a column of rebels attacked. The chieftain and inhabitants abandoned Teskan, leaving the merchants to their fate. Making a circular rampart of their baggage, they prepared to defend themselves, but the rebels, blond, blue-eyed highlanders like Flemings, soon broke their lines and rounded them up in the empty town. Only a last-minute message threatening retaliation by the Khan's army saved the whole company of merchants from massacre. The rebels contented themselves with plundering their captives' baggage.

Scarcely had they resumed their march when Goes, riding a little apart from the column, was again attacked, this time by four bandits. Outnumbered and outarmed, he had recourse to a trick. Pulling the richly embroidered turban from his head, he flung it behind him; while the brigands stopped to dispute its possession, Goes put spurs to his horse and escaped.

For eight days they trod a precipitous tight-rope path sheer above the upper waters of the Oxus, spurting a way, like the torrent, through tourniquets of rock. In this country of chasms and precipices roamed the Kirghiz, a predatory tribe swarthy and rough-hewn as totems, who twice launched an attack, seized the best beasts of the caravan and again reverted to rock. The merchants escaped their raids only by entering a more complete desolation, winding a trail up the Ak-tash River, past the last clumps of red willows, towards the plateau of the Pamirs, a hundred-mile bulwark, between twelve and fifteen thousand feet high, separating eastern and western Asia. They began to suffer from headaches and bleeding; with galloping pulses went a dragging step; words became a prodigious effort, as though intruders too must conform to the universal quiet. Against mountain-sickness Goes was taught by more experienced companions to eat dried apricots and rub his animals' mouths with garlic. On the last stage, dragging their ponies and yaks, many of which slipped or succumbed, they heaved themselves up by hand and foot over outflung eaves of the plateau known throughout central Asia as the Roof of the World.

They had negotiated the rock-bound coast : this was the sea. To the grey horizon stretched a silent, frozen waste of waves, formed by earth impregnated with salt and covered with loose shale. On slopes bare of snow a trail of skulls, bones and droppings marked their path, while roots and dung served as fuel for fire that yielded a pale, flickering heat. The steppe was unrelieved by any of the fertile valleys which had so far softened their journey. Surrounding peaks, among the highest mountains of the world, seemed mere hills, so high was the plain, and lakes seldom seen and never named were frozen to a depth of two and a half feet. The only living creatures were occasional lynx and sheep grown thin in a vain search for vegetation.

For six weeks they traversed a wilderness of dull continuous grey, a cloud world which even nomad shepherds feared to storm. At Tash-kurghan, a shifting collection of *kirghas,* they halted for two days to rest their beasts, before entering the Chichiklik Pass, a high almost level plateau shut in by mountains and swept by continual ice-storms. Unladen yaks were pulled and driven ahead through the soft snow to beat down a track along which for six days the travellers battled in face of a glacial north wind. Many were swallowed up by drifts; others fell victim to frost-bite and exposure before the survivors emerged on the eastern edge of the Pamirs, whence they could look across to the barren transverse ridges hiding the Turkestan plain and Yarkland, their destination.

The descent proved longer and even more difficult than the climb. They had to cross and recross the Tangi-tar, or narrow gorge, disputing with a swollen torrent the only passage between precipitous rock. On one of these traverses Isaac was swept away by a sudden fall of flood water. He would have been drowned had not Goes rushed ahead and at the next gorge, as though from a wild beast's foaming jaws, wrested the limp bleeding body of his friend. Binding up his wounds and lighting a fire, Goes tried to coax the Armenian back to life. For eight hours Isaac lay unconscious and not until next day could they rejoin the caravan, which had continued the twisting descent. So many animals died on this stage of the journey—the Christians alone lost six—that when they reached the foothills Goes was despatched to Yarkand to send back ponies and provisions.

A descent of thirteen thousand feet had merely changed the form of desolation, from glacial salt to parched desert and the broad wastes of rubble beds, from grey gravel to yellowish-red waves of drift sand. Only after two days' march did water and life surge from the same spring, in an oasis of green fields along carefully irrigated terraces, shaded by white poplars and mulberry trees. As the river widened, mud huts became more highly organised, matching their vivid Khotan carpets with a profusion of flowers; the stare gave way to curt monosyllables, and soon to gentle phrases of welcome.

Yarkand, which Goes reached in November 1603, thirteen months after leaving Agra, was a town of dark sinuous alleys linked to golden bazaars, of low houses with terraced roofs, surmounted by balconies of lattice work, linked to heaven by the shrill minarets of a hundred mosques. To Goes's extreme joy, the people had heard tell of Cathay—it lay several months' journey eastwards; to his despair, caravans were allowed to enter the country only at certain fixed times and the next would not leave for a year. He was condemned to twelve profitless months, a traveller whose halts exceeded his stages.

Renting a house, the islander who had been born within sound of Atlantic breakers now took root, for twelve months, in Central Asia, where water, precious as jade, was kept in large stone basins and used many times over, for bathing, washing and drinking. Its central position between Khotan, the Ladakh range, the Oxus valley and Cathay had made Yarkand a rich trading centre. The bulk of its people were Turki, some fair-complexioned, many with the swollen neck of goitre, nearly all tame and lazy and unfaithful to their wives, enjoying nothing so much as music and song. They farmed in desultory fashion and some hunted on the nearby slopes, setting giant golden eagles to swoop on game. Their only discipline, here at the furthest reach of Islam, was the call to prayer. Five times a day, like iron granules under a magnet, they were called to align themselves south-west towards another minareted town in another desert. Every Friday, after an official had trudged the dusty streets recalling the duties of that day, twelve men armed with thonged whips strode out of the chief mosque and drove the recalcitrant to public prayer.

Goes made no attempt to hide his religion. The people of Yarkand called him an Armenian Roume, for, after thirteen centuries, they still identified men from that region with Roman neighbours of the Parthian Empire. One day he was summoned by the ruler of Kashgar, the Sultan Mohammed, a direct descendant of Genghis Khan, in the presence of his mullahs and theologians. Asked what faith he professed, whether that of Moses, or of David, or of Mohammed, and in what direction he turned his face in prayer, Goes replied that the faith he professed was that of Jesus, whom they called Isai, and that it did not matter to what quarter he turned in prayer, for God was everywhere. His answer caused bewilderment. The theologians began to dispute the matter and although forced to admit the truth of his last statement tried to convert him. They could not understand how an intelligent man could profess any religion but their own. Elsewhere Goes was treated less civilly, several times barely escaping with his life from the scimitars of fanatics determined to make him invoke the name of Mohammed. The mode of his struggle was the same, whether on the Pamirs or at Yarkand : to resist assimilation, by snow, sand or multitudinous Islam.

Among the travellers in the cosmopolitan town was a merchant from Moscow who Goes had sometimes seen make the sign of the cross. One day the Russian came to him gesturing urgently in obvious distress. He led the Portuguese to his house, where his small son lay seriously ill, and signalled that Goes should try to help the boy. Goes thought he wanted a new medicine—but no, it appeared the patient was beyond that—so he laid his breviary on the boy's head, hung a cross round his neck and prayed by his bedside. He heard no more about the matter until three days later the Russian, his son bounding beside, came to the house with smiles and gifts of gratitude.

Another acquaintance was a Tibetan king, captured three years previously and then lying in Yarkand prison. Goes visited him and found that the king's physician spoke Persian. Eagerly Goes questioned him about his religion and learned that their chief Father, whom the physician called Cumgao, wore a mitre on his head and a robe like a chasuble; that the people observed a fast of forty days, taking neither wine nor meat; that they possessed a sacred book called the Kanjur (Goes associated the word with the Latin *evangelium*); that their priests did not marry; that they believed in a day of judgment and in eight hells and three paradises. Goes noted down all these facts with enthusiasm : he thought it possible Tibet practised a variant of Christianity.

More direct evidence of a lost sect was offered by fans, paper, porcelain, and paintings from Cathay which Goes examined in Yarkand. One of the paintings depicted a man wearing a biretta on which was set what appeared to be a crucifix, while another figure stood before him with hands crossed. This Goes believed to be the portrait of a Christian bishop. He also saw painted on porcelain what looked like a Franciscan monk, wearing a long beard and tonsured hair.

At the invitation of the queen whom he had helped at Kabul, Goes visited her palace at Khotan, ten days' journey south-east across the desert, famous throughout Asia for its jade. An inferior variety was mined in blocks from the neighbouring mountains, the best fished from the bed of the Khotan river. The Turkis, believing jade to be crystallised moonlight, noted the stretches where the moon was most brilliantly reflected and dived there during the day. Goes watched the heavy, cold stone being procured and dispatched : vermilion, jet black, green and dusty grey. The queen paid her debt with the most highly prized varieties : white jade with rose-red specks, and green veined with gold.

In the Autumn of 1604 the caravan for Cathay began to take shape. The profitable position of captain was farmed out by the king to the highest bidder, that year it went to a certain Agi Afis for two hundred sacks of musk. Goes paid Agi Afis for the privilege of being numbered among the seventy-two merchants permitted to enter Cathay subject to his authority. He collected eleven horses for himself, Isaac and their merchandise, the remains of their lapis lazuli having been bartered for jade which, they were told, commanded a high price in Cathay.

One night in mid-November provisions were finally packed, water-skins filled to the brim and several hundred beasts enriched against their will with a load of valuable stone. The stars their only map, the caravan filed through the eastern gate of Yarkand into a wilderness bare as the Pamirs. Their route lay across the Takla Makan desert, an elliptic arena surrounded except at the north-east confines by tiers of mountains rising to 18,000 feet. They passed ancient towns choked to death by wind-swept dunes, their only memorial an eroded stump of mulberry jutting like coral from a sea of lapped and furrowed sand. Here only water mattered—and trees, symbol of water—giving a name to the oases where the caravan halted : Tallik, place of willows; Ming-jigda, the thousand white poplars; Chilan, the jujube tree, and a dozen others. At the small town of Ak-Su Goes won the favour of the twelve-year-old Khan with sweets, candied fruit and the performance of a Portuguese *folia* he had not danced for sixteen years : price of exemption from a severe levy. At Kucha, on the other hand, he was fined and chastised for refusing to observe the rites of Ramadan. After a month's halt there, still hugging the mountains, the caravan passed Ugen, Sarik-Abdal, Bugur, Eshme and Shor-chuk : Goes told the names like beads of the Sorrowful Mystery, each with its particular cross : unfaithful servants, nights of frost, ponies that fell lame, sandstorms and un-quenchable thirst. Only at Kara-shahr, which lay beside a lake, did the desert tamarisk and saxaul give way to deep-rooted turf and branches bowed with fruit. Here the captain decided on a long halt, hoping to collect a full complement of merchants and so increase his profit. Goes, impatient at this further delay, was already planning to continue the journey alone when a group of Mohammedans on their way back from Cathay arrived in Kara-shahr. Goes questioned them and was astonished to discover that some had lived at the Castle of Barbarians with the missionaries. They told Goes how the Europeans had pre-sented the Emperor with clocks, a clavichord, paintings and other marvels; were treated respectfully by all the dignitaries of the capital; and—rumour had become accepted fact—that they were often admitted to converse with the Emperor. They described the appearance of the Europeans but could not tell their names. As proof of their story one of the merchants pro-duced a piece of paper covered with Portuguese writing, which he claimed had been written by one of the Westerners. He had rescued the curious rounded script from the sweepings of the room to take back home.

Goes had little doubt that somehow Cathay and China were one, that the great community of Christians was a myth. He had only one desire, to complete a fruitless journey as quickly as possible, to reach Peking and Ricci, and return to India. Despite the opposition of Agi Afis he obtained a pass-port from the local ruler and set off with Isaac and a handful of other merchants who were making for Hami. In mid-October 1605 they arrived at this large and fertile oasis, famed for white-fleshed melons and open-handed hospitality : as Marco Polo had noted, it was customary for a host to leave his house and jasmine-scented wife to any traveller who expressed the wish. Goes remained a month in the town, while its fields of maize and sorghum were being harvested, resting his horses before setting out on the last and most barren stage of the journey.

From red, blue, green and grey stretches of rocky hills, they passed through the Ravine of Baboons into the black grit of the Western Gobi. Here they were obliged to travel silently by night, their way marked by the rotting bodies of merchants who had been killed and stripped by carnivorous Kalmaks. During the day they took turns to climb one of the camel-humped crests of sand in order to keep a watch for assailants, while the rest of the caravan bivouacked and made a scanty meal of parched barley. Along the dry riverbeds and eroded rocky ledges they could find no water to quench their thirst, no fuel to counteract a glacial wind marauding from the north.

Following the route of the conquering Genghis Khan, past cities which had collapsed before the encroaching desert, for three hundred miles Goes and his companions braved a cemetery of sand, thirsty, numb with cold, heavy with sleep. For weeks the world was spun into dust, a lifeless planet where time and again they projected their destination, only to arrive and find it a mirage. One night, however, in the last stages of exhaustion, their patrols found and grasped with a shout a single unmistakable thorn bush. As they approached the River Sulei, slowly living things were created, scrub, reeds and poplars, the first green glimmer of hope, and finally, dividing barbarism from civilisation with a single imperious sweep, following the hills north and south to the horizon, the crenellated line of the Great Wall, which—so the experienced travellers claimed—marked the frontier of Cathay.

At Kiayükwan, Passgate of the Pleasant Valley, the party was halted for twenty-five days while permission was sought to proceed to Suchow. Reaching the town about Christmas 1605 —more than three years after leaving Agra—Goes heard Cambaluc, capital of Cathay, referred to as Peking, and, visiting a pagoda, realised that the Visitor's informants had evidently

confused Christianity and Buddhism because of certain external
resemblances. The dream of Cathay had become the reality of
China.

Suchow and its neighbour Kanchow were garrison towns
which supplied the million men who kept perpetual vigil along
the Great Wall. Half of Suchow was peopled by Chinese, half
by Mohammedans from Kashgar, Persia and other countries
trading through " ambassadors " with China. The merchants,
bankers and warehousemen, together with their wives and
children, formed an enclave similar to Macao. They were
subject to Chinese law, strictly guarded, at night locked in their
own part of the city and, after residing nine years, forbidden to
go home. Goes found that he had gained little by hurrying on
ahead. He was obliged to wait until Agi Afis arrived in
Suchow, with papers signed by the King of Kashgar, authorising the caravan as an embassy come to offer tribute to the
Emperor. These papers would have to be forwarded to
Peking for approval before the caravan could be escorted to the
northern capital.

Goes wrote a letter to the missionaries of Peking, distant a
thousand miles, and entrusted it to Chinese travellers. Because
he did not know how to transliterate the missionaries' names,
nor the exact address in Chinese, the first letter did not arrive.
Receiving no reply, he wrote another on Easter Day 1606 and
entrusted it to a Mohammedan who was visiting the capital
secretly. He wrote : " I am a member of the Society. I was sent
by my superiors to discover Cathay but I now believe that no
such country exists, for I have traversed Asia without finding
it, and this country, which we in Europe call China, is known to
the people of Central Asia as Cathay. I have found no Christians, despite the tales of so many Mohammedans. I beg you,
Fathers, or any other Portuguese or Christians in Peking, to
help me escape from the hands of the infidels. I have suffered
greatly on the journey, am exhausted and wish to return to
India by the sea route. If I wait until the caravan is allowed to
pass to the capital, I shall be here two years, for that is the
customary delay."

In November, eight months after its dispatch, Goes's letter

reached Peking. Ricci was overjoyed. Either because he was unaware of the adopted name Abdulla or because the merchants had arrived in a different caravan, he had learned nothing at the Castle of Barbarians and began to fear for the traveller's safety. His own experience at Tientsin gave Ricci added sympathy for Goes's predicament and impelled him to help at once. He sent a Chinese candidate for admission to the Society, John Fernandes, a prudent, resourceful young man of twenty-five, with orders to bring back Goes and his companions to Peking; and if this proved impossible, to return and consult Ricci. A northern Chinese, a recent convert, would accompany him. In mid-winter the journey would prove formidable; leaving in December they could not hope to reach Suchow before March.

Goes had arrived prosperously, still accompanied by the faithful Isaac, with five servants from Yarkand, two negro servants, the finest jade and merchandise worth three thousand taels, the number of his horses increased to thirteen. But in Suchow he suffered far more than on his travels. Idle and cocksure after the dangerous journey, the Mohammedans began in earnest to persecute the good-natured stranger. He was forced to lend money which was never repaid, and to give extravagant feasts for the members of the caravan. The cost of living was high and as he had little ready silver Goes was obliged to sell his precious jade for half its real value. He then bought four hundred pounds of inferior quality, buried it under the paving stones of his lodging and swore to use it only to reach Peking. With the remaining twelve hundred taels he paid some debts and his current household expenses. The captain continued to borrow more and more money, under threat of leaving Goes behind when the caravan left for Peking. Soon he had become absolutely penniless and in February hunger broke his health. For a month he lay ill. He had received no reply to his letters and supposed them lost. The caravan would not leave for another nine months. How could he survive until then?

Meanwhile Fernandes, also alone—his Christian servant had stolen half the money and fled—was approaching Suchow. At the end of March he arrived in the two-faced city and was directed to Goes's lodging. Entering, he recognised in the emaciated face, worn as the effigy on an old coin, the large eyes and thick beard of a European. He knelt by the bedside and greeted the sick man in Portuguese. A smile softened the wind-whipped face. They joined hands, the Chinese and European lay brothers : the link was made, the journey at an end. Taking Ricci's letters, Goes read them and raised them in his thin fingers to heaven, reciting with tears in his eyes the canticle of Simeon with which he had hoped to greet Father Xavier: " Now lettest thou thy servant depart, O Lord, according to thy word, in peace."

Fernandes discovered that Goes was far too ill to travel to Peking. Having tried without success to find a reliable doctor or medicine, he tended the sick man himself, nourishing him with chicken and trying to rally his spirits. But Goes had been kept alive only by the will to complete a task assigned by his superiors. The force of a lifetime had been spent in conquering Asia : now he lay devastated as the Gobi. His last message was for Ricci. " You should never trust the Mohammedans; as for the journey, it is very long, difficult and dangerous, and I advise no one to undertake it again." He grew steadily weaker and, ten days after Fernandes's arrival, died of exhaustion.

His Mohammedan companions, who had been watching for this, began systematically to rob the house. The most valuable object was a complete diary of his journey, in which Goes had later made a record, in Persian, of his loans. This they tore to pieces, so that the debts could no longer be reclaimed. Isaac and Fernandes, unable to prevent its mutilation, picked up and carefully preserved every scrap they could find. The Mohammedans also wanted to bury Goes according to their religion, so that his property would revert to them. Fernandes forestalled this scheme. Buying a coffin he and Isaac buried outside the town, in Chinese soil, the traveller from the distant Azores, reciting a rosary over his grave.

When the two Christians returned to Suchow, the Mohammedans took captive Isaac and Goes's one surviving negro servant. As the first step in claiming the dead man's hidden jade, they tried to make Isaac invoke the name of Mohammed. When he refused they put him in chains and threatened to kill him. At Fernandes's urgent request, the governor of Suchow held an enquiry at which the merchants claimed Isaac and the negro were Mohammedans whom Goes had captured; and that they had no ties with Fernandes, who had come from Peking to steal them away. When the governor refused to intervene, Fernandes made a three-day journey to present another petition to the viceroy at Kanchow. To save the Armenian's life, Fernandes claimed to be a nephew of both Goes and Isaac, attributing to them his own surname Chung. The viceroy instructed the governor to examine the case again, giving as his opinion that Isaac and Goes's property should be handed over to Fernandes. The merchants however, hoping Fernandes would soon be obliged to leave, bribed the governor with several hundred taels to delay judgment.

The enquiry dragged on for five months. Fernandes and Isaac spent all their money and in order to eat were obliged to sell the clothes off their backs. Isaac meanwhile taught his deliverer sufficient Persian to enable them to converse and to substantiate their supposed relationship. From a chance remark Fernandes evolved a plan. On their next summons to court, he carried with him a piece of pork hidden in his sleeve. When the Mohammedans repeated their old charge that Isaac was one of their number, producing the pork he and Isaac began to eat it voraciously. Throwing up their hands in horror, the thirty merchants spat and anathematised them, then trooped out of court, declaring Isaac had been corrupted. Out of respect for their companions' beliefs, both he and Goes had refrained from eating pork during the three-year journey.

In face of such incontrovertible proof, the governor gave judgment that Isaac, the negro and Goes's property should be handed over to Fernandes. The negro, however, had been so terrified by the merchants that he declared publicly his intention of remaining with them. Selling over half of the four hundred pounds of jade, Fernandes paid Goes's debts and set out for Peking with the remainder of the precious stone.

Fernandes's letters to Peking had been lost on the way, so that Ricci had been without news for ten and a half months when on October 29th, 1607—five years to the day after Goes's departure from Agra—the Armenian and Chinese arrived. At sight of their bowed heads and heavy step, Ricci dismantled his triumphal arches of acclaim and waived all words of welcome. When the story was told, in silence he took from them Goes's trappings, curiously animated now their owner was dead : a gold cross worn on the journey, passports signed by the rulers of Kashgar, Khotan and Kara-shahr, together with letters from Jerónimo Xavier and the Archbishop of Goa. These Ricci kept in the house as relics of a Brother in Christ whom he considered a martyr.

Isaac rested a month in Peking, while Ricci pieced together the diary and learned from the Armenian details of the journey. Ricci then wrote letters to India, pointing out that Goes's journey had proved beyond doubt his theory that Cathay and China were one. As for the " Christians " of Cathay, they were probably " Adorers of the Cross " who had now become almost extinct. Isaac was entrusted with these letters and sent back to Macao, where he received a warm welcome and was given a passage on the carrack for India. In the straits of Singapore the boat was captured by a Dutch privateer. The captain, however, was so impressed by Isaac's account of his journey, that he set him free at Malacca. Several months later he arrived in India, where he was given a pension by the Jesuits. Learning that his wife had died, he preferred not to return home, and ended his days in Chaul.

As a monument to Benedict de Goes, from the scraps of diary and notes taken down from Isaac, Ricci relived those three years and wrote down an account of the journey which in many respects paralleled his own. Goes, in seeking Cathay, had found countries and towns, mountains and deserts marked on no map, Chinese or European. He had stitched the great multi-coloured stuff of central Asia into place between hempen India and silken China, cut open the great melon of which his contemporaries had merely fingered the rind.

Before him, the only Europeans to leave records of a trans-

Asiatic journey were certain Franciscans and Marco Polo, who from the Persian Gulf took a more southerly route through Khotan and Charchan. Polo, in fact, had been precursor both of Goes and of Ricci. For seventeen years he lived in the Middle Kingdom, making two long journeys, along the western mountains and eastern coast. But his vision was bounded by the Khan's court, his account of the country, whose language he never learned, dominated by its array of high numbers, silk and gold.

Goes had given proof that Cathay owed its existence to a confusion. Two words, referring to the same country, had been given substance. In central Asia the term Cathay had prevailed, derived from a tribe called Khitan who had formerly lived in an area south-west of Manchuria and south-east of Mongolia. In the tenth century this people invaded northern China and the name Khitai, written Cathay by Europeans, was applied to China as a whole by Arabs, Persians and Russians. Consequently Marco Polo and the Franciscans, approaching China through Turkestan, knew their destination as Cathay.

The other part of the tangle Ricci had already unravelled. The Chinese themselves were as ignorant of the term Cathay as of China. They called their country Middle Kingdom or by the name of the ruling dynasty. Her neighbours, to the south and east, knew her under the name of the dynasty ruling at the time of their first important encounter. In Japan, China was known as T'ang from a dynasty which ruled from the seventh to the tenth centuries after Christ; in Cochin-China and Siam as Chin, after a principate in north-west China from the eighth to the third centuries before Christ. The Portuguese, who by chance gained their first knowledge of the Middle Kingdom through the Siamese, adopted the name the Siamese used and applied it to the country they reached by the sea route. In its modified form, China, this became general throughout Europe. The difference of name had arisen from a difference of approach. It had fallen to Ricci to discover that neither in fantastic customs nor wealth did the real country fall short of the extravaganza which had excited Europe for centuries, and to begin to justify its title of Christian kingdom.

CHAPTER FOURTEEN

Unless the Grain Die

ONE day at the beginning of 1608 Ricci and Pantoja received an urgent summons to the palace. At the college of mathematicians they found the president and other eunuchs in agitation. The Emperor had sent word that they must make him twelve maps printed on silk in six sections similar to Ricci's third edition. Chinese atlases were fashioned in odd ways—some were carved on wood and could be taken to pieces like a jigsaw puzzle, so that provinces might be studied separately—and it caused Ricci no surprise that the Emperor should ask for his in the form of a folding screen.

Ricci had taken care never to present a map, in case the Emperor, seeing the small extent of his own country, should think the missionaries were depreciating China. A eunuch, however, to whom Ricci had given coloured copies, had recently presented one to the Emperor who, on the contrary, had been delighted with the different kingdoms, each marked with interesting descriptive and ethnological information, and wanted copies for his heir and members of his family.

The eunuch's request for blocks of the third edition put Ricci in a quandary. Li Chih-tsao the geographer, on his return home to Hangchow, had taken one set, which could not be retrieved for at least six months. The printers had had another, but the year before their printing house had collapsed as a result of heavy rains, killing two workmen and destroying the blocks.

To the eunuchs this news was tantamount to a death sentence. They thought Ricci was hiding the truth, and insisted that four of their number should visit the mission residence and inspect the broken blocks. Ricci in pity sent a servant to Paul Li's house for the blocks of a recent fourth edition, in eight sections with an emended text. But the eunuchs did not dare present the Emperor with this when he had specified the other. For three days they remained in terrified perplexity until Ricci, despite his other pressing duties, offered to cut new blocks, like the third edition but better. He proposed to have them ready within a month and to pay for the printing himself. The delighted eunuchs sent the Emperor a memorial to this effect. Ricci finished in time a work which in 1602 had taken a year to complete, being careful to add as many notes as possible favourable to Christianity. Now that all hope of an audience had faded, those oblique marginal comments remained his only means of communication. Later he also printed two hemispheres, one for each side of the dragon throne. Ricci hoped that, seeing these and the map, the Emperor or his family would feel curious about Christianity. At the very least, he believed the sight of so small a China would lessen their arrogance and disdain for strangers.

Also in the first months of 1608 Ricci published a new book which he always referred to as *The Ten Paradoxes*. Its full Chinese title was *Ten Chapters of a Strange Man*. His physiognomy, his extraordinary memory, his mastery of Chinese, his knowledge of polite etiquette, his celibacy, his contempt for honour or public appointments, the rumour that he practised alchemy and his extraordinary doctrine : all these things made Ricci " strange " in Chinese eyes. The phrase in the title had further overtones, for Confucius had said, " The strange man is strange in the eyes of men but like unto Heaven," and fitted in well with the paradoxical nature of the work, cast in the form of ten dialogues, each with a different friend of high rank, including the Minister of Rites and Li Chih-tsao the geographer. The first chapter, dating from 1601, took the form of a conversation about the value of time with the Minister of Civil Appointments ; Ricci, then in his fiftieth year, pointing out that he had irretrievably lost fifty years of his life. The paradox had added force for the Chinese, who were flattered to be considered old : that is, in some sense linked to the glorious, static past. The other chapters were entitled " Man is only a guest in this world," " It is useful to have death constantly in mind," " The constant thought of death is a preparation for the judgment to come," "The man of worth speaks little and would prefer to keep silence," "The true reason for fasting is not that man is forbidden to kill animals," "Nothing is more conducive to a better life than to examine our conscience and discover our faults," "The sanction of good and evil will become evident in the next life," "By foolishly trying to discover the future, a man incurs misfortune" and "The rich miser is more unhappy than the poor beggar." The arguments were drawn from Scripture, Christian saints, Greek philosophers and even Aesop. The book was more admired by the graduates than any of his other works and only a few months after publication was reprinted several times in the provinces. Among the many prefaces for new editions was one by a member of the Academy :

"I have come to know Li Ma-tou. He is a man from the Far West, with a full beard and few words. I know all his writings and am convinced that he is truly an extraordinary man.

"Because they are separated by a distance of a hundred thousand *li* (equal to that between heaven and earth) the Western countries and the Middle Kingdom could not communicate. But now Li Ma-tou has begun to bring them together. After travelling through hundreds of kingdoms and cities, only the Middle Flower has pleased him. Voyaging by sea past places infested with crocodiles, dragons, sirens and countless cannibals, Li Ma-tou remained quietly in his cabin oblivious of dangers. His religion honours virtue, esteems the five social relations and serves heaven; in his words he never contradicts the teaching of Yao, Shun, the Duke of Chou or Confucius."

The pen can convey one's meaning for a thousand miles—so ran the proverb, but in Peking Ricci's lay friends proved a more valuable means towards the hundred or more conversions he made every year. That summer, after an absence of five years, Li Chih-tsao the geographer returned to the capital. For the past three years he had been living in retirement at home, rivals having prevented his appointment to the higher office he deserved. Ricci continually urged him to re-enter public life, knowing what good he could do, for although polygamy prevented his baptism, he was a convinced Christian. Finally the geographer agreed to take up a comparatively minor post, and in August he and Ricci were reunited for a few months. He had converted most of his family and his followers were sympathetic to the new religion. The difficulties which lay in the conversion of one of the geographer's suite, a wealthy courtier also called Li, were typical of countless others in the graduate class.

Besides his legitimate wife Li the courtier was living with the concubine of another man. A possessive woman, when she learned that Li intended to become a Christian and leave her, she became furious, publicly abusing him and Ricci and the religion he taught. If he left her, she threatened to hang herself at his gate, a common enough act of revenge, because the person who caused the suicide was held responsible by law for damages and must reckon with the injured ghost of his victim. Li, who had an exaggerated respect for his good name, was afraid to put her away. Only when Ricci promised to take his part in the law courts and pointed out that even if the woman hanged herself the scandal would redound to his credit and that of Christianity, did he return his mistress to her legal owner, for whom he procured a remunerative appointment. As Ricci had foreseen, the shrew's threat proved empty.

Li the courtier also kept in his house a young girl whom he had been rearing from childhood as a future concubine. At Ricci's insistence Li returned the girl to her father, saying he might marry her to whomever he pleased, that she was still a maiden and that he would reclaim neither the high price he had paid for her nor the cost of her maintenance during many years. This moved Li's legitimate wife to such a point of admiration that she and all her family decided to become Christians. They sent Ricci their wooden and bronze idols, bellies crammed with votive offerings, gold, silver and pearls. The house was already so cluttered with josses that Ricci decided to have the metal ones melted down. When several foundries declined the task, he undertook it himself, using the wooden idols as fuel and obtaining a good supply of metal for globes and astrolabes.

Li had been president of several Buddhist fraternities; one in particular, resentful of his conversion, spread the false rumour that he had embezzled the fraternity funds. Li, already bitterly criticised for ejecting ancestral idols, was completely crushed by this further scandal. On Ricci's advice, however, he agreed to call a meeting and explain exactly what had happened. The members, believing that he was returning in remorse as president, welcomed Li warmly. He made a speech telling them what little fruit he had obtained from so many years' service of idols; that he had decided to become a Christian in order to practise virtue in the years remaining to him. As his friends, they should praise not blame him. They had charged him with embezzlement : in fact he had used his own personal money for the fraternity expenses, but for every tael found missing, he would willingly pay back ten. The Buddhists, moved by Li's frankness, admitted the truth of his statements and agreed he owed them nothing. After he left, the fraternity fell on evil days and began to break up, some of its members even following their president's example.

When all these difficulties had been overcome Li received baptism and the name of Luke. He asked Ricci whether the Christian religion did not possess confraternities similar to the one he had left. Ricci described the association at Rome to which he had belonged as a law student, and Li, with his friends' help, drew up proposed rules for the first Chinese sodality of the Blessed Virgin Mary. Ricci emended them slightly, adding precepts about regular confession, prayers in common and the admission of new members by majority vote. One of its chief ends was to bury the Christian dead solemnly and ceremoniously, the cost being met by a monthly contribution from the sodality's forty members. On certain feasts they provided the chapel with candles, incense and flowers, and on the first Sunday of every month gathered in the president's house (Luke had been unanimously elected to this post) where one of the missionaries gave a sermon and answered questions. Four months later a similar sodality was established at Nanking.

Spiritual direction of the Peking community allowed Ricci

no time for writing new Chinese books, but his previous works grew steadily in popularity. *The Ten Paradoxes,* which some critics were hailing as a masterpiece of Chinese literature, continued to enjoy a particular success : in 1609 it was reprinted for the fifth and sixth times by mandarins in Nanking and Nanchang. Its author had become one of the sights of the capital. His purple-clad figure—full curling beard, long face and nose, even the tall black hat all emphasising his height and suggesting eminence—was pointed out with awe and also with affection, for it was becoming generally known that despite his wisdom Doctor Li was not grave and distant, but had a cheerful word for everyone and made a point of spending more time with humble visitors than with his intimate friends in the Government.

Time and again Ricci became aware—with surprise, so ineffaceable were the years of oppression at Shiuhing and Shiuchow—that he had changed the meaning of the word " foreigner " from " contemptible barbarian " to " stranger worthy of special consideration." For example, taxes on property were payable every year to the Emperor. Although in 1605 Ricci had submitted the deed of his new house in the usual way to be sealed—at a fee of six taels—by a special mandarin, no annual demand for taxes had ever been received and none had been paid. In 1609, however, tax lists were reviewed and Ricci received a summons to explain the arrears. He grew worried lest above what was due he might also have to pay a heavy fine for so long a delay. Discovering that collectors occasionally granted exemption as a personal favour, he wrote to a mandarin friend who knew the tax collector of the central district, asking him to try and obtain exemption " for a foreigner from distant lands." At the mandarin's request, the collector not only cancelled past claims, but also issued a public decree granting the house of the graduate preachers perpetual exemption from taxes. This was not only an indirect official acknowledgement of their right to be living in Peking but, as Ricci liked to phrase it, in a certain sense the beginning of ecclesiastical immunity.

If it relieved him of payment in silver, fame exacted other

more exorbitant dues. His circle of friends and acquaintances, already numbered by thousands, grew still further, while the line clamouring to meet the Far Westerner, to discuss this or that point in religion, mathematics, geography or music, stretched endless as a recurring decimal. In 1609 Ricci perceived with dismay what colleagues had already noticed : that the strain of an apostolate which demanded a multiplication of the self was beginning to weaken his health. Overloaded mind and will rebelled in the form of persistent headaches. His hair and beard were already white; though only fifty-six he felt old and tired out. Even the persecution of early years had been less exacting than the duties of prosperity at Peking. He was carrying out the work of a dozen hard-working men and knew for certain that to continue would be to cut short his life. Of the pioneers Ruggieri had died in 1607, Valignano a year earlier, while Pasio had left China in 1583 for Japan. When he, the sole survivor, was laid on the terrace of night, what record would remain of the early foundations? He himself had listened angrily to garbled accounts of Xavier's mission, the inflated miracles which debased the real, the exaggerations which eclipsed the so much more magnificent truth. He decided to set down in writing the history of the China mission " in order that if God should permit so small a seed to give a good harvest in his holy Catholic Church, the faithful of future generations may give Him thanks and speak of the wonderful things He has done to this distant people. If, however (which God forbid), these first flowers do not yield the promised fruit, at least I shall leave a record of how the Society of Jesus worked and suffered to blaze a trail, how they spent themselves unceasingly to bring the mission to its present hopeful state."

The history, which he entitled *Della entrata della Compagnia di Giesù e Christianità nella Cina*, occupied Ricci during the few spare hours of 1609. He had written a score of short Chinese books, but few gave him as much difficulty as this, because his mother tongue had become alien : before writing letters in Italian, he had for many years been obliged to refresh his memory by reading correspondence received from Rome.

For this reason he chose an extremely simple, unadorned style fitting the straightforward narration of facts. Sometimes he wrote ungrammatically, at other times substituted Portuguese or Spanish words unconsciously or where the Italian escaped him, writing in his beautiful neat script, without crossing out, some fifty lines to each of a hundred and thirty-one folio pages, each headed with the emblem " IHS Maria."

In the first of five books he gathered together what he knew about China, its names and geographical position, its products, its arts and sciences, language, literature and system of examinations, its government, customs and superstitions and finally its religions. By collecting these data he avoided the necessity of interrupting the narrative to follow, provided a summary of the difficulties, direct and indirect, which he and his brethren had faced, and incidentally composed the first complete account of a country known to Europe only through inaccurate travellers' tales.

In the second book he described the first settlement at Shiuhing made by Ruggieri and himself as foreign bonzes, their friendship with Wang P'an, the first map, the adoption of Chinese names, their final expulsion by the Viceroy Liu. For these events of almost thirty years ago he found his own memory served well, and minute details could be checked from memoranda and notes for old letters. The chief events of the third book were the foundation at Shiuchow, the deaths of Almeida and his successor, the adoption of graduate dress, his first unsuccessful journey to Nanking and the residence at Nanchang. Book IV covered the years at Nanking, the fruitless journey to the northern capital, his mathematical school; while Book V was devoted to Peking, his attempts to meet the Emperor, the death of Brother Francis Martinez, Goes's journey and a summary of recent events in the other houses.

As he wrote out the manuscript, he lived again, with heightened intensity now that he was no longer protagonist, the whole course of those twenty-seven years in China, the failures and successes, fears and hopes, doubts and despairs. But personal feelings he allowed little place in the book, which was a history, complete, accurate, sober, recording facts and events, not processes or emotions.

When he completed the bulk of the work, it was as though his life were done. What had been achieved in purely human terms? What had he a right to hope would survive him? The last few years had not in every respect been triumphal. Two missionaries had died : one of tuberculosis at Macao, the other in miasmic Shiuchow. Dias had been appointed rector of the college at Macao, leaving only twelve priests in China. Pasio, although supporting the mission to his utmost, had been unable to continue the supply of men which Valignano's heroic efforts had ensured. To Ricci's extreme disappointment, the often-requested astronomer had not arrived. The stir in Kwangtung province which had cost Brother Francis his life had put a halt to conversions in Shiuchow, and Ricci planned one day to move the missionaries to another town. Similar hostility prevailed at Nanchang. When the priests there had tried to buy a larger house, the bachelors had stirred up a furious attack. For a time they had been forbidden to make converts, and only Ricci's influence with the governor had prevented their expulsion.

On the other hand, Cattaneo, staying with Paul Hsü in Shanghai, had administered over a hundred baptisms, while a novitiate had been opened at Nanchang which counted four young Chinese, bringing to eight the number of Brothers. At the two capital cities both houses flourished. A hundred converts were made every year at Peking, and the Christians of China numbered about 2,500.

In a recent letter Pasio had asked Ricci to ensure the safety of the mission against the time when he could no longer protect it with his immense personal authority. Night and day Ricci gave his mind to this problem. Pasio asked him, in effect, to obtain authorisation to preach Christianity freely in China : his own hope when he had first arrived in Peking. Ricci was reluctant to forward a memorial with this request, believing it might disturb the delicate balance of their present position, and knowing almost for certain that the Emperor could not grant so singular a favour contrary to all tradition. Paul Hsü, with whom he had discussed the problem suggested that Ricci should decline the money he was now receiving and ask, instead, that he and his brethren might be permitted to remain in China as subjects of the Emperor. Ricci opposed this plan because nothing gave them such authority as being supported at the Emperor's expense; and, again, to seek a more favourable settlement might result in their expulsion. He preferred to leave things as they were. Their security, paradoxically, lay in Chinese fear. Knowledge of China and Peking gave the graduate preachers power : as it were, an insight into the mystery at the heart of things. Expelled, they could use that power against the Middle Kingdom either alone or in alliance with the dreaded Japanese or Tartars. It would be less dangerous to allow them to stay. As for his death, which he felt approaching, that would be offset by Wan Li's; he believed the heir to the dragon throne would prove more accessible. Certainly no tradition or law decreed that the Emperor should remain invisible.

As far as he could foresee, two fundamental difficulties would remain. However closely his successors assimilated themselves to Chinese ways, they would always remain suspect because they preached a new doctrine opposed to the established order and had dealings with the outside world, through Macao to Rome. Neither danger could be completely removed, but he believed they could be lessened by emphasising that Christianity was a religion of peace, which encouraged a stable government and, secondly, by buying sufficient property within China to render the mission financially independent. Looking to the distant future, he hoped that the number of Christians in the provinces would grow to such a figure as to render impracticable any repressive measures an alarmed Government might take.

His own experience gave him eight reasons for hope. First, miraculous progress in the face of immense difficulties seemed to show that God favoured the mission's growth. Second, reason being prized above all in China, Christianity, a reasonable religion, appealed at an intellectual as well as a supernatural level. Third, the free circulation of books permitted a vast literary apostolate. Fourth, the Chinese, again in virtue of their intelligence, were open to conviction that Western metaphysics and theology, no less than mathematics and astronomy, were superior to their own. Fifth, he was convinced, not least from a study of their ancient beliefs, that they were essentially a pious people who had evolved a philosophy conforming, at almost every point, to natural reason. Sixth, peace would render Christianity, once established, more or less permanent. Seventh, by adapting themselves to Chinese psychology and etiquette, missionaries would undoubtedly be accepted as learned and holy men. Eighth, the system of Confucius provided an admirable ally against the idolatrous sects.

These conclusions he set down in a final letter to Francis Pasio, colleague at Rome and on the voyages from Lisbon to Macao, now Visitor of the Province of Japan and China, and future strategist of the mission.

Ricci now began to make preparations, in order to avoid burdening his brethren, for the aftermath of death. To transport his coffin from Peking to Macao would be costly and impracticable. He would prefer burial in Peking, to symbolise the mission's permanency, and in January began to look for a piece of frozen ground which could serve as a mission cemetery, even in this final act accommodating himself to Chinese ways. He had almost concluded a bargain for a field outside the city when, inexplicably, negotiations were broken off. Ricci had come to recognise the deaf and dumb language of Providence and when his colleagues questioned him simply answered, " God will give us a better cemetery." He set his correspondence in order and wrote two documents for his successors as superior of the mission and of the Peking house. The former he addressed to Nicholas Longobardo, Superior of the Mission of China : four years earlier he had proposed to the General that the indefatigable Sicilian should succeed to that office. These affairs concluded, he turned to De Ursis, asking him to enumerate all his defects against the general confession he would make in his last hours.

Amid these preparations, in March his friend Li Chih-tsao the geographer, on a short visit to Peking from his provincial post, fell seriously ill. For nine years Ricci had laboured hard for Li's conversion, incurring his colleagues' criticism for devoting so much time to a man who, although convinced intellectually, " refused to give up his concubines for Christ." Ricci saw further and persevered. After Paul Hsü, Li Chih-tsao was the most brilliant Chinese he had met and his conversion could have momentous consequences. Now he persuaded the geographer, on what seemed his deathbed, to retain only his legal wife and baptised him with the name of Leo. The sick man promised, if he recovered, to consecrate the rest of his life to the Lord of Heaven, and meanwhile gave fifty taels to the mission. With this and other contributions Ricci decided to build a church adjoining the house, to replace the small chapel. He and De Ursis drew up plans of a European-style building, some twenty-five feet wide by fifty long, to be erected that spring.

1610 was a year of examinations and homage to the Emperor. In April tens of thousands of magistrates and candidates poured into the northern capital. Twenty visiting-books were left at the house every day; on festival occasions a hundred. Ricci received all comers, whatever their rank, and within four days repaid their calls. Once he mentioned to a friend that the continual visits, with their elaborate ceremonial, proved exhausting to a foreigner.

" In my country," he said, " we are much less formal : if we do not return a call within a few days no one takes offence. But here it is absolutely necessary to visit everyone and to receive every caller."

" Let me give you a piece of advice," his friend replied. " When someone calls and you are feeling tired, simply tell your servant, when he receives the visiting-book, to say that you are not at home. Even Confucius would excuse himself from seeing an unwelcome visitor on the ground that he was sick, although he enjoyed perfect health at the time."

This ruse Ricci was in no position to adopt. Since the days

of Wang P'an the mission had depended for its existence on winning and retaining by every possible mark of courtesy the friendship of influential mandarins.

In Lent visitors would often arrive during the single meal of the day, which Ricci refused to resume after their departure. Everyone of importance wanted to meet the Far Westerner and it was useless for Pantoja or De Ursis to deputise, since they did not have the same reputation. Correspondence, too, poured in from unknown men throughout China approving or disputing arguments in his books. They had to be answered personally in highly stylised phrases. Letters had to be written to Europe, to Nanking, Nanchung, Shiuchow and Macao, Chinese lessons given to De Ursis, sermons delivered every Sunday, confessions heard, spiritual advice given. Li's illness and the erection of the church added to Ricci's labours. And at the heart of each day Mass, his office and private devotions, giving life and value to the other activities, but demanding, also, the first fruits of his strength. Ricci did not flinch before the army of visitors and broadside of letters. He had sought and prayed for martyrdom: this was an unbloody, more refined form of death, a Chinese torture. Like granite by dripping water, his whole being was day after day eroded by the unending succession of visitors.

Under the Dragon Moon, on the evening of May the third, Ricci returned to the mission house after a series of distant calls and went straight to his room. Removing his square black hat, his embroidered slippers and purple silk robe, he lay down on the hard brick-based *kang* and closed his eyes. That night his head throbbed more violently than usual. A never-ending stream of figures greeted him with a polite " Ch'ing ch'ing," smiled an ironical smile and bowed themselves away; inane Chinese words shrieked each other down; gilded idols danced to the clavichord. He tried to find order in the horses' hooves and haggling vendors outside, in the shelves of books, the maps, quadrants and astrolabes which lined the room, in the manuscript and papers neatly stacked on his desk. He struggled as he had done for many hundred nights, but this time the last reinforcements were dispatched in vain. Darkness fell, heightening the action within. Rest, instead of restoring order, made of his whole body pandemonium. He knew then that the branch was broken and would hang creaking helplessly until the wind tore it down at last.

After a sleepless night he received a visit from De Ursis, to whom he confided his foreknowledge. " I don't know which I feel more," he said, " joy at the thought of going to God or sorrow at abandoning you and the mission."

Leo Li, informed of his friend's illness, sent his own doctor, a court physician, to the mission house. He said Ricci's sickness was a trifle which would soon pass, but the medicines he prescribed did not bear out his claim. Two days later Ricci had grown so much weaker that Pantoja called in the six most famous doctors of Peking. Unable to agree on a diagnosis, they left three different prescriptions. Some of the neophytes who crowded the house took the slips of paper and, laying them before the crucifix of the new church, implored God to indicate the best remedy, begging, at the same time, that years might be taken from their lives and added to Ricci's. Finally a prescription was selected and administered.

At the taste of ginseng, his bamboo-walled room became the apothecary's shop at Macerata. Again he was watching his father dispense while the cries of his brothers playing rang through the courtyard; repeating Latin conjugations to Father Bencivegni; riding across the Apennines to Rome. Did that far side of the world still exist? Had he ever been part of it? The twin *torrenti* which tumbled astride Macerata had become the Tiber and Tagus, the Yellow River and the Blue : his life had been a journey by water under the stars. But the thought of dying in Peking no longer caused him regret. He knew now that he had not, after all, undertaken a journey without return and, when the last medicine proved no more efficacious than the first, in the downcast house Ricci alone remained cheerful.

So that he could receive visitors more easily he was moved from his own bedroom to one near the main entrance. Here on Saturday May the eighth he made a general confession to De Ursis, throwing his net wide over a lifetime's faults : grumbling on board the carrack; champing impatience at Goa; despair at

Macao and Shiuhing and Tientsin; pride at Peking; bitterness towards the eunuchs; lack of forbearance with Pantoja; conceit in his predictions about Cathay; and the failure, again and again, to fly out like a flag wide and true before grace. Next morning when Holy Communion was brought into his room, alone, despite his weakness, he rose from the *kang* and knelt down on the floor before the white host. As he recited his last Confiteor he again remembered his failings and wept for shame, moving everyone in the room to tears.

That afternoon he became delirious. For a day and a night he spoke distractedly of his converts, of the new church, of bringing the Chinese and the Emperor to God. On the evening of the tenth he returned to himself and asked for Extreme Unction. He repeated the responses in a clear voice while his eyes, ears, nostrils, lips, the palms of his hands—last marked with consecrated oil at Cochin—were anointed to remit all repented sin. The following day his four brethren—Pantoja, De Ursis and the two Chinese Brothers—asked his farewell blessing. Ricci made the sign of the cross over them and, as the custom was, added private encouragements to virtue. To Brother Emmanuel, whose trials he had come to know in the years at Peking, he said, " Persevere in your vocation. I shall ask Our Lord to let you die in the Society. I know now there is no greater joy than that." Then De Ursis asked whether he realised how desperately they needed him. Ricci explained that his death would benefit the mission and added, " I am leaving you before an open door which leads to great merits, but not without great effort and many dangers." Pantoja asked how they could repay his love for them. " With kindness to Fathers coming from Europe. They have given up the friendly surroundings of a college to come here : you must do more than welcome them : redouble your kindness, to make up for the affection they have left behind."

That afternoon his thoughts again returned to the other hemisphere of his life. He remembered a recent letter referring to the work of Pierre Coton, a Jesuit who had gained the confidence of Henry IV to such an extent as to be appointed confessor to the King and tutor to the Dauphin, exerting the influence which Ricci himself had hoped to wield with the Son of Heaven.

He turned to De Ursis. " I meant to write to Father Coton to congratulate him on the glory he has given to God, and give him news of the mission. That is impossible now : please write for me."

At six in the evening of May the eleventh 1610, turning on his side, Ricci closed his eyes, and the watchers began to recite prayers for the dying. " Unknown to thee be all that shudders in the darkness, and the hiss of flame, and torment and all anguish . . . Receive, O Lord, Thy servant into the place of that Salvation that he must hope for from Thy mercy . . . Deliver, O Lord, the soul of Thy servant, as Thou didst deliver Peter and Paul from their prisons . . . He hath had zeal for God within him, and faithfully hath he worshipped God who made all things." An hour later, as the sun sank behind the western gate of Peking, so calmly that there seemed no transition, Matthew Ricci died.

EPILOGUE

The End of the Mission

AT the request of the community in Peking, Brother Emmanuel, who had learned the elements of Western art in Macao, painted his late superior's portrait in graduate dress. Even in death his face retained its colour and expression, so that the posthumous canvas destined for posterity was truer to life than the stylised sketch on silk which the Emperor possessed.

Leo Li, as the missionary's last spiritual son, provided a simple Chinese coffin of cedar wood three inches thick. Ricci's body was laid in it and the wood sealed with varnish. On May the fourteenth it was carried into the new church, where so great a crowd came to attend the requiem that matting had to be laid on the courtyard for those who could not find place inside. Afterwards the body was taken back to the largest room and laid before a temporary altar, flanked by candles, the walls hung with white linen. Here all the Ministers, members of the Academy and chief mandarins came to pay their final respects, bowing four times before the coffin. The Minister of Rites let it be known that the Emperor, informed of Ricci's death, had shown signs of grief.

Since burial within the walls was forbidden, De Ursis and Pantoja intended to lay their friend in a field in the suburbs. But a Chinese Christian boldly suggested that they could pay Ricci greater honour and strengthen the position of the mission by obtaining a place of burial from the Emperor. It was true that no stranger other than ambassadors and only the greatest Chinese had ever been granted this privilege, but Ricci's life had been exceptional and his gifts were known to have pleased the Son of Heaven. Leo Li and several other high officials promised to support the plan, but without much hope. A petition was drawn up and after some delay, to the general astonishment, approved by the Emperor. The missionaries were to be given land for Ricci's burial as well as a new residence on the outskirts of Peking. After several months' search they found a suitable property half a mile from the city, a large modern brick-built house belonging to a eunuch under sentence of death, which had been turned into a private place of worship called " Pagoda of Good Doctrine." After a further delay and despite the opposition of the Dowager Empress, the villa was secured.

Longobardo arrived to supervise the construction of a cemetery in the garden. At one end a hexagonal brick chapel was built, from either side of which a wall extended forming an enclosure. Here a tomb was dug, an idol from the former pagoda being broken up and crushed to make cement for the brick construction of the vault. Here, on the feast of All Saints 1611 under the Kindly Moon, Ricci was buried, Paul Hsü being one of the four who lowered his friend's coffin into the earth. Above was set a plaque : " To one who loved righteousness and wrote books. To Li Ma-tou the Far Westerner from Huang Chi-shih, governor of Peking." Eastwards in the distance gleamed the yellow roofs of the Forbidden City, but the bustle of the capital was here no more than a vague murmur. Beside the garden soared the rose-red walls of the Pagoda converted into a mission house and chapel. Chinese emblems of mourning, motionless sentinels at each corner of the tomb, stood four tall cypresses.

Shortly before his death Ricci had prophesied that he could best advance the China mission by dying. He foresaw that his body would remain in Peking, part of the Flowery Kingdom, proof that he had come from the ends of the world not to conquer but to give. His Chinese descendants, children born of water and the Holy Spirit, were already numbered by thousands : they would treasure his memory and honour his ideals. His spirit could do more for the mission in heaven than tied to a tired body on earth. But humility had hidden the full truth. After death Ricci's fame as a saint eclipsed his status as Father—De Ursis, Pasio, Cattaneo and Leo Li all spoke of his sanctity. As primitive churches were built on the tombs of holy men and women, so on his bones the church of the Middle Kingdom arose.

Ricci's own methods were treated as guiding principles by his successors. He had been a great pioneer, point of convergence between East and West, the founder, the model. His most daring plan had been the attempt to win the Emperor if not to Christianity at least to an explicitly tolerant attitude. But Ricci had lived when the Ming dynasty was crumbling, the Emperor an inert monster at the mercy of parasites, so that the plan during his own life proved impracticable. It was for his successors to convert the successors of Wan Li.

Three years after Ricci's burial, as a consequence of a serious mistake by the Board of Astronomers in forecasting the eclipse of 1610, the missionaries' friend at court, Leo Li, obtained a decree ordering De Ursis to reform the calendar and to translate European astronomical books. This task he undertook with the assistance of Paul Hsü, who continued to use his high office in the cause of Christianity. The decree was violently opposed by the eunuchs and not until 1630, when Adam Schall von Bell, a German Jesuit skilled in astronomy, arrived at Peking was the work of revision seriously undertaken.

Before it could be completed China suffered an invasion of Tartars from the north-west. Already civil war and the growth of secret societies had indicated Heaven's displeasure with the Ming. Corruption at court had reached a pitch where the chief eunuch allowed himself to be venerated on the same footing as Confucius. Peking fell; the Emperor, a grandson of Wan Li, butchered his harem and hanged himself from a tree in the palace grounds. Some of the Jesuits joined the retreating Ming court, which established itself at Canton. The Empress Dowager was converted and christened Helena, while the heir to the dragon throne was baptised Constantine, a name which revealed the missionaries' expectations. But the tide had turned against the Ming; the new Tartar dynasty proved itself vigorous and efficient; before long the Jesuits' hopes were once again transferred to Peking, where Schall had made a favourable impression on the new court. Soon he was appointed President of the Board of Mathematics and the authority which he gave the mission largely accounted for a rise in the number of Christians, at the time of his death, to a quarter of a million.

At the end of the seventeenth century, France having won the hegemony of continental Europe from Portugal and Spain, French Jesuits began to arrive in China and for the next hundred years played a leading role at court. They were entrusted with the mapping of China; when the Emperor K'ang Hsi fell ill of malaria, they administered a new drug, Jesuit's bark or quinine, recently received from colleagues abroad. Again, two of the French priests proved of great assistance to the Emperor in negotiations with the Russians who, under Peter the Great, were expanding eastwards in quest of sables and gold. Partly as a token of gratitude for arranging a suitable treaty, K'ang Hsi was persuaded in 1692 to take the momentous step of issuing an edict of toleration for the Christian religion. The work which Ricci initiated had been brought to fulfilment.

The missionaries were pioneers not only in bringing Western science to the Orient, but also in revealing China to Europe. Ricci's letters to his friends had been the prototype; now the French began to publish regular *Lettres édifiantes et curieuses*, translations of the classics, books of Chinese history, botany, geography and medicine, while their travels with the Emperor in Tartary confirmed and amplified the discoveries of Bento de Goes.

Nowhere did these publications exert a greater influence than in the arts. As the force of classicism spent itself, Chinese styles moulded the new forms of rococo. But the influence, here as elsewhere, was second-hand and the imitations twice removed from the truth. Pagodas in European parks were not copied directly from Chinese originals but according to verbal specifications in missionary reports. At Worcester, Delft and Sèvres porcelain was produced in imitation of Chinese models yet remained unashamedly European. In drawing-rooms of lacquered furniture and painted screens tea was sipped in china cups "while o'er our cabinets Confucius nods, Mid porcelain elephants and China gods." It scarcely mattered that the lovely pieces bore little relation to their originals. No one but the unreturning missionaries had been to China; no one cared for authenticity. Taste demanded the graceful and fantastic, a world of flowers and funny little figures. Cathay had been superseded by Chinoiserie.

Amid such surroundings, the civilised minds of the day discussed Chinese philosophy and government, praised to the heights by missionaries who enjoyed imperial favour and wished to encourage interest in their work. The imagination of Europe was again captured by furthest Asia. Voltaire could claim without exaggeration that China was better known than some of the provinces of Europe. Confucius was venerated so highly that La Mothe le Vayer could taunt Sinophiles with the mocking invocation "Sancte Confuci, ora pro nobis!" while Leibnitz proposed in all seriousness that Chinese missionaries should be sent to Europe to propound the aim and practice of natural theology. The influence of European thought in China had never been so great as that which China, unknown to any but a handful of missionaries, now exerted on Europe. China appeared the land of tolerance, of virtue without Christianity of philosophical rulers with charming manners, of Deism, of reason triumphant : the very ideal to which Europe must strive to conform. But another group of thinkers also found support for their theories in the Middle Kingdom, where the people believed in human equality and considered it not only their right but their duty to rebel against an immoral and tyrannical dynasty, against a ruler who violated the pattern of universal order. The Bourbons shared the fate of the Ming. When the calm, cultivated voice of Enlightenment had been shouted down by impassioned Progress, enthusiasm for the Orient waned. China, the revolutionaries pointed out, was a static society; for centuries she had made no important advances; her people were enchained by an obsolete morality. The *rêve chinois* faded away.

The unqualified welcome extended to Chinese thought and practices during the eighteenth century was not, however, endorsed by the theologians of Europe. While the missionaries at the court of K'ang Hsi were exerting greater influence than ever before, while the number of Chinese converts reached a total of 300,000, a further aspect of Ricci's programme had aroused bitter controversy.

Ricci had seen that Christianity could never succeed in China as an exotic; it must adapt itself to Oriental ways of thought, graft itself to all that was best in a civilisation older than those within which Christianity had first found expression. All his life he had respected Chinese susceptibilities, believing that to do otherwise was unpardonable egoism. He had used tact and gentleness, realising, with profound sympathy, the difficulties which faced a Chinese confronted with a strange religion. He had laid down that the mysteries of faith must be gradually unfolded, otherwise irreparable shock and damage would be done to Chinese sensibility and natural pride. Afterwards, when grace had worked its miracle, the heights and depths of faith could be revealed. Moreover, after life-long study of Chinese practices he had decided that just as slavery had been tolerated in early Christian centuries until the time should be ripe for its abolition, converts might fulfil their two traditional duties, the veneration of Confucius and the dead members of their family.

As the China mission grew, Franciscans and Dominicans entered the country. Their method of evangelising was direct, uncompromising and took little account of the different psychology of the people to whom it was addressed. The Mendicants walked through the streets holding up crucifixes and, when a crowd gathered, preached in public, very often through interpreters. The Spaniards among them did not hesitate to proclaim that all the long line of Chinese Emperors were burning in hell. When they discovered that converts made by the Jesuits were allowed to honour Confucius and the tablets of the dead, they protested that a tainted form of Christianity had been introduced to China. The Mendicants forbade their converts such concessions and complained to Rome, branding Jesuit methods of adaptation as protective mimicry. Theologians of the Society rallied to the support of their missionaries. For seventy years the controversy raged while Rome, seeing in the problem one of the most difficult and far-reaching that had ever faced the Church, delayed her decision. Both parties accumulated evidence. The Jesuits obtained from K'ang Hsi a written document which they believed would prove decisive. In it the Emperor stated "Honours are paid to Confucius not as a petition for favours, intelligence or high office but as to a Master, because of the magnificent moral teaching which he has left to posterity. As for the ceremony in honour of dead ancestors, it originates in the desire to show filial piety. According to the customs observed by Confucians, this ceremony contains no request for help; it is practised only to show filial respect to the dead. Souls of ancestors are not held to reside in the tablets; these are only symbols which serve to express gratitude and keep the dead in memory, as though they were actually present."

The Jesuits were not scandalised at the phrase "genuflection before the dead," for they had seen sons pay just such respect to their living parents. If food was offered to the dead, that was because the Chinese knew no better way of showing affection and gratitude; as well reprimand Europeans when they laid flowers at a grave because the dead possess no sense of smell. These customs were older far than the Church herself and were part of an inflexible moral system which would never be brought to heel; concessions of less importance had once been granted the less intractable Roman Empire; could the Papacy not afford to be generous? Was not Rome the eternal city, transcending the merely human limitations of thought imposed by race and culture, and therefore bound to embrace both West and East, bound even, because of her physical position, to show special sympathy towards the peoples of Asia?

On their side, the Mendicants maintained that, despite all appeals to authority and tradition, in actual fact such honours, as practised by the majority of Chinese, were tainted with superstition. Confucius, they protested, was venerated not merely as a teacher, but as the highest of the saints, a superhuman being, while most Chinese held that the souls of their ancestors were actually present in the tablets and feasted on the food offered to them.

Nine Cardinals appointed to decide between the conflicting views held their fateful sitting on November 13th, 1704.

All were Italian; they assembled in Rome; the documents they studied were written in Latin; their categories were Aristotelian; none had ever visited the East. Yet the dilemma they faced was the same which Ricci's life had so triumphantly solved; how love the totally other without losing identity? A week later the Cardinals issued their decree, confirmed by Pope Clement XI.

They had chosen to be rigorously inflexible. Their guiding principle had been that integrity must precede charity : the missions must be free not only from formal superstition, but from the very suspicion of such a thing. The veneration of Confucius and dead ancestors was almost without qualification declared superstitious and Christians forbidden to practise such ceremonies. Even the forms of homage paid to Confucius after graduation, as well as any semblance of sacrifices or offerings on the graves of the dead, were prohibited. Ricci's policy of tolerance and adaptation was revoked.

A young Frenchman, Charles de Tournon, who combined religious zeal with overbearing self-assertion and tactlessness, was sent to Peking to enforce the decree. Ignorant of Chinese and distrustful of the Jesuits, he chose as his interpreter a French bishop named Maigrot who had lived twenty years in China, the most outspoken antagonist of Chinese rites. Maigrot was invited by the Emperor, at an interview which took place in the summer of 1706, to discuss those aspects of Confucianism which were held to be incompatible with Christianity. Surprised at Maigrot's faltering Chinese, K'ang Hsi invited the bishop to expound four characters on a scroll which hung behind the dragon throne. Maigrot was able to interpret only one of them correctly. Later he failed to recognise the name Li Ma-tou and confessed that he had never even opened his *Christian Doctrine*, though it was well known to every member of the court. Indeed, several of Ricci's books were now numbered among the greatest works of Chinese literature. At the close of the interview the Emperor, a highly intelligent man with a long record of benevolent rule, expressed astonishment that dunces such as Maigrot and Tournon should claim to decide on the meaning of texts and ceremonies of several thousand years' antiquity. Despite pleas from all sides Tournon refused to admit he had made a mistake in selecting the bishop as his representative. The Emperor, who had already suffered several insults at the hands of Tournon, ordered the legate to return to Canton. On his arrival at Nanking Tournon made public the most important sections of the decree against Chinese rites.

The imperial power was thus directly confronted with the pontifical will, the Son of Heaven with the Holy Father. Christianity appeared to the outraged Tartar no longer a universal religion adaptable to all peoples but a swashbuckling, narrow, prejudiced local cult. He laid down that all missionaries, if they wished to remain in China, must obtain an imperial permit, which would be issued only to those who agreed to abide by the practices of Ricci.

Once the sympathy of the Emperor and high mandarins was lost—as Ricci had foreseen—the authority attaching to Christianity declined. Eleven years after Tournon's visit, the foreign religion was formally prohibited in China and although loyalty to the French Jesuits prevented the execution of this decree during the lifetime of K'ang Hsi, under his successors Christianity suffered oppression. Missionaries nevertheless remained at court, no longer as trusted advisers but as painters, landscape gardeners, fabricators of fountains and mechanical toys, still receiving their annual present of venison, pheasants and frozen fish.

In 1773, after almost two centuries of work in China, during which four hundred and seventy-two of its members, Chinese and European, built up the Church on Ricci's foundations, the Society of Jesus was suppressed. The last remaining bulwark at Peking against outright persecution was broken, the lightning conductor removed. Ebbing religious zeal in France, the French Revolution, the Napoleonic Wars—these, too, had an adverse effect on the mission : the flow of money and priests dwindled; Christianity steadily waned; in a few years the last converts would have died and the final wooden cross been consumed in fire before the statue of Buddha.

The decline was dramatically arrested by the rise of new

forces. Peace in Europe promoted the rapid expansion of mercantile interests in the East. The English, in particular, made substantial profits from the importation of opium to China against tea, silk and porcelain, but their ships and merchants were subjected to the usual cramping conditions and kept at arm's length on the coastal fringe. In 1840 the imperial commissioner of Canton attempted to suppress the opium traffic by seizing and destroying 20,000 cases of the drug. Britain, by Western standards badly treated, declared and won an easy war; treaties were signed between China, on the one hand, and Britain, France and America, opening certain Chinese ports, granting more favourable terms of trade and providing, among other concessions, for the entrance of Christian missionaries. Money and men once more began to flow into China; churches were re-established; many converts made; the old threads, so it seemed, taken up. In 1842 the Jesuits returned, establishing their house in the ancestral village of Paul Hsü. Superficial continuity hid a profound change. The privilege formerly won for Christianity by the virtue and wisdom of its missionaries had now been obtained by superior rifles and long-range guns.

While the West considered China a dodo state which had failed to evolve suitable methods of self-defence, China's first reaction to the invaders was one of resentment and scornful superiority. Much as Rome viewed the Goths and Vandals, she admitted the superiority of the West in the art of killing but viewed its ideals and way of life with contempt. Agriculture, moral philosophy, the mandarin class, hostility to the strange and new—by these she had attained harmony with her surroundings, and she did not intend to jeopardise the delicate balance by trying to improve her material well-being along Western lines. She still believed all change would be change for the worse.

But as the century drew on, China's humiliation became more complete. Adverse terms of trade drained off her silver; the opium traffic debilitated her people; the Western powers exacted one concession after another. In 1895, as had happened three centuries earlier, Korea was invaded by Japan, her power greatly increased by the adoption of Western weapons, and China suffered a crushing defeat. The lesson was inescapable : she must practise the despised modern techniques of Europe and America as the only means to survival. Industrialisation, however, could not be grafted on to the existing régime. Efficiency would entail new social and political institutions, the surrender of privileges and cherished values. Machines, despite their masters' mind, must bring a machine-age.

After several vain attempts the revolution was achieved, the Son of Heaven replaced by a doctor of medicine, graduate of a Western university. The early decades of the twentieth century brought changes more sweeping than any in the past two thousand years. The system of examinations based on Confucianism was abolished; books were written no longer in mandarin but in the Peking dialect; women tripped out of their homes; a modern army was created; the year, significantly, reckoned by the sun instead of the moon. Just as eighteenth-century Europe had enthusiastically accepted many superficial aspects of Chinese thought and life, while remaining ignorant of their spirit, so now China welcomed Western technical achievements—railways, guns, power-houses, machinery—but to Christianity, which fired that civilisation, she remained largely indifferent. Science and democracy became the twin gods : faithful reflection of the contemporary Western attitude. Chinese students at European and American universities found belief in progress, religious agnosticism and a scarcely veiled contempt for Christianity. Returning to their own country, crowded with zealous missionaries, they asked, " Do you propose to convert China and then wait for the Chinese to reconvert the West?" Yen Fu, shortly after the first World War, expressed his people's growing disillusionment with the new experiment. " Western progress," he said, " has culminated in four achievements : to be selfish, to kill others, to feel little integrity and less shame." China, strengthened and modernised, expressed revolt and preference for her traditional way of life in extreme nationalism.

Profiting from the toleration accorded by trade treaties, Christianity meanwhile was making progress, sometimes filling the vacuum, though seldom among the leading intellectuals, as cultural forms were broken up. The Catholic missions in particular received impetus from an important papal decision. In 1939, after the Chinese Government had several times explicitly affirmed the civil character of honours paid to Confucius and the dead, Rome issued a decree tolerating these practices. Ricci, whose reputation had lain under a cloud for two centuries, was finally and completely justified. At a time when the West was branding China's traditional values as backward, inferior and an obstacle to progress, the Church reaffirmed Ricci's belief that Christianity must welcome the best elements in Eastern thought. But Rome's decree had less importance than it would have had in 1704, for mass education and the breaking-up of families by modern methods of communication had weakened Confucianism.

The coming of a Marxist government in 1949, with the election of Mao Tse Tung as President of the Chinese Republic five years later, radically altered the situation of the Catholic Church and other Christian bodies. At university Karl Marx had lost the Christian faith in which he had been brought up and had become a militant atheist. He described religion as mere superstition and a tool whereby the exploiters keep the exploited in subjection; this is widely recognized by scholars today as the aspect of his doctrine least in accord with the facts of history, but the Chinese government not only accepted it but put it into practice. Politics must control religion absolutely as a first step to eliminating it.

The Religious Affairs Bureau of the Government set up the Chinese Catholic Patriotic Association, in effect a national church, and obliged its members to cut all links with Rome. Those who refused to join the Patriotic Association, such as the much respected Bishop Tang of Canton, were thrown into prison. During the Cultural Revolution, Ricci's tomb, which had survived the Boxer Uprising of 1900, was damaged by Red Guards.

In 1976 Mao died, and the notorious Gang of Four were evicted. A new government, desiring rapid economic development and requiring for it the co-operation of the educated classes, allowed religious activity to revive. After twenty-two years in prison for having remained loyal to Rome, Bishop Tang was released. In 1979 a single Catholic church was opened for service in thirteen cities, but these churches were still being run by the Chinese Catholic Patriotic Association.

Article 36 of the new Constitution of the People's Republic of China, which came into force in 1982, has this to say of religion:

> Citizens of the People's Republic of China enjoy freedom of religious belief.
>
> No state organ, public organization or individual may compel citizens to believe in, or not to believe in, any religion; nor may they discriminate against citizens who believe in, or do not believe in, any religion.
>
> The state protects normal religious activities. No one may make use of religion to engage in activities that disrupt public order, impair the health of citizens or interfere with the educational system of the state.
>
> Religious bodies and religious affairs are not subject to any foreign domination.

But the Article is less liberal than it might at first appear. 'Citizens' are those who are loyal to the state; 'normal' religious activities are those decided on by the state, in places decided by the state and under the direction of the state. In practice this means activities directed by the Catholic Patriotic Association. The reference to 'foreign domination' excludes obedience to Rome and links with the Universal Church. Meanwhile government publications have continued to accuse the Pope and the Vatican of interfering in the autonomy of the Chinese people in the conduct of their religious affairs by appointing bishops, praying for Christians suffering in China, and so on.

Christ's words, 'Render unto Caesar the things that are Caesar's, and unto God the things that are God's', make a clear distinction between politics and religion. That distinction the Catholic Church as a teaching body has always upheld, though some of its prelates failed to do so in the bullying centuries of expansion and exploitation.

The tragic irony today is that the Catholic Church, more open to dialogue with the East than at any time in the past, encounters a government which has adopted Marx's blurring of politics and religion, which focuses on failings by the West since the seventeenth century, and which fails to see that Christendom's universal character is the surest guarantee that important moral issues will be lifted clear of national prejudice and, in the framework of a consensus in space and time, judged impartially.

In this seeming impasse the figure of Matteo Ricci has recently assumed importance. In November 1979 the *People's Daily*, organ of the Party Central Committee, published a long article praising Ricci as a pioneer of cultural exchange. Other newspapers referred to Ricci as a good type of foreign visitor, eager to share his technological knowledge and to appreciate what was excellent in China. His damaged tomb was repaired, and although it now stands in a Communist Cadre School of the Peking Municipality, foreign visitors are afforded special permits to visit it.

This appreciation of Ricci by the Chinese authorities is still only partial. They do not mention that Ricci came primarily to bring the Christian religion. But it could well be the beginning of a fruitful dialogue. Ricci, who always made a clear distinction between politics and religion, may yet again become, in Pope John Paul II's phrase, 'a bridge'.

There is also the evidence of the Catholic communities in China. Chinese Catholics living abroad, who in the more relaxed conditions since 1978 have been allowed to visit relatives in China, have discovered a living Church, loyal to Rome. This is especially true of the countryside. There are many villages which are almost entirely Christian, though they may not have a priest. They are not visited by journalists and do not find their way into the Western Press, but they have been described by the eminent China-watcher, Fr Laszlo Ladany, in his *China News Analysis*. During the persecution of recent years, in Fr Ladany's words, 'the majority Chinese bishops, priests and faithful stood firm and were ready t be outcast from society, to suffer prison and labour camps, an even death. The Church in China has passed the supreme test.'

Many Christians – both Catholics and Protestants – believe there are more Christians in China today than in 1949. Some are convinced that there could be as many as five to six million

Catholics. The continued presence of so many practising their religion and remaining loyal to the Holy See must cast serious doubts on the validity of the Marxist view that religion is a tool used by exploiters for oppressing the exploited.

Their perseverance is also a tribute to Ricci, who so remarkably combined spiritual loyalty to a Universal Church with a deep, self-sacrificing love of China. Though the mutual understanding he built up has been shaken and his ideals sometimes betrayed, Ricci's life remains. Defeat now can never be total. At the capital city, part of the brown soil, lies the dust which was his body, given freely, a still unbroken link between the West and furthest Asia.

INDEX